DAILY LIVES OF

Civilians in Wartime Asia

Recent Titles in the
Greenwood Press "Daily Life through History" Series

The Black Death
Joseph P. Byrne

Cooking in America, 1840–1945
Alice L. McLean

Cooking in Ancient Civilizations
Cathy K. Kaufman

Nature and the Environment in Pre-Columbian American Life
Stacy Kowtko

Science and Technology in Medieval European Life
Jeffrey R. Wigelsworth

Daily Lives of Civilians in Wartime Africa: From Slavery Days to the Rwandan Genocide
John Laband, editor

Christians in Ancient Rome
James W. Ermatinger

The Army in Transformation, 1790–1860
James M. McCaffrey

The Korean War
Paul M. Edwards

World War I
Jennifer D. Keene

Daily Lives of Civilians in Wartime Early America: From the Colonial Era to the Civil War
David S. Heidler and Jeanne T. Heidler, editors

Daily Lives of Civilians in Wartime Modern America: From the Indian Wars to the Vietnam War
David S. Heidler and Jeanne T Heidler, editors

DAILY LIVES OF

Civilians in Wartime Asia

From the Taiping Rebellion to the Vietnam War

EDITED BY STEWART LONE

The Greenwood Press "Daily Life Through History" Series

Daily Lives of Civilians during Wartime
David S. Heidler and Jeanne T. Heidler, Series Editors

GREENWOOD PRESS
Westport, Connecticut • London

Library of Congress Cataloging-in-Publication Data

Daily lives of civilians in wartime Asia : from the Taiping Rebellion
to the Vietnam War / edited by Stewart Lone.
    p. cm. — (The Greenwood Press daily life through history
series, ISSN 1080–4749)
  Includes index.
  ISBN–13: 978–0–313–33684–3 (alk. paper)
  ISBN–10: 0–313–33684–9 (alk. paper)
  1. Asia—History—19th century. 2. Asia—History—20th century.
3. Asia—Social conditions—19th century. 4. Asia—Social conditions—
20th century. 5. War—Social aspects—Asia. I. Lone, Stewart.
  DS34.D35   2007
  950.4—dc22   2006030405

British Library Cataloguing in Publication Data is available.

Library of Congress Catalog Card Number: 2006030405
ISBN–10: 0–313–33684–9
ISBN–13: 978–0–313–33684–3
ISSN: 1080–4749

First published in 2007

Greenwood Press, 88 Post Road West, Westport, CT 06881
An imprint of Greenwood Publishing Group, Inc.
www.greenwood.com

Printed in the United States of America

The paper used in this book complies with the
Permanent Paper Standard issued by the National
Information Standards Organization (Z39.48–1984).

10 9 8 7 6 5 4 3 2 1

Copyright Acknowledgment

Every reasonable effort has been made to trace the owners of copyright materials
in this book, but in some instances this has proven impossible. The author and
publisher will be glad to receive information leading to more complete
acknowledgments in subsequent printings of the book and in the meantime
extend their apologies for any omissions.

Contents

Series Foreword   vii

Acknowledgments   xi

Introduction   xiii

Chronology   xix

1. Daily Life in China during the Taiping and
   Nian Rebellions, 1850s–1860s   1
   R. Gary Tiedemann

2. Life in a War of Independence: The Philippine
   Revolution, 1896–1902   29
   Bernardita Reyes Churchill

3. The Wars of Meiji Japan: China (1894–1895)
   and Russia (1904–1905)   65
   Stewart Lone

4. Urban Life in China's Wars, 1937–1949:
   The View from the Teahouse   95
   Di Wang

5. Daily Life of Civilians in Wartime Japan,
   1937–1945   127
   Simon Partner

6. Daily Life in Wartime Indonesia,
    1939–1949   159
    Shigeru Satō

7. Korean Civilians North and South,
    1950–1953   191
    Andrei Lankov

8. Remembering Life in Urban South
    Vietnam, circa 1965–1975   219
    Stewart Lone

Index   247

About the Editor and Contributors   251

Series Foreword

Few scenes are as poignant as that of civilian refugees torn from their homes and put to plodding flight along dusty roads, carrying their possessions in crude bundles and makeshift carts. We have all seen the images. Before photography, paintings and crude drawings told the story, but despite the media, the same sense of the awful emerges from these striking portrayals: The pace of the flight is agonizingly slow; the numbers are sobering and usually arrayed in single file along the edges of byways that stretch to the horizon. The men appear hunched and beaten, the women haggard, the children strangely old, and usually, the wide-eyed look of fear has been replaced by one of bone-grinding weariness. They likely stagger through country redolent with the odor of smoke and death as heavy guns mutter in the distance. It always seems to be raining on these people, or snowing, and it is either brutally cold or oppressively hot. In the past, clattering hooves would send them skittering away from the path of cavalry; more recently, whirring engines of motorized convoys push them from the road. Aside from becoming casualties, civilians who become refugees experience the most devastating impact of war, for they truly become orphans of the storm, lacking the barest necessities of food and clothing, except for what they can carry and, eventually, what they can steal.

The volumes in this series seek to illuminate that extreme example of the civilian experience in wartime and more, for those on distant home fronts also can make remarkable sacrifices, whether through their labors to support the war effort or by enduring the absence of loved ones far from home and in great peril. And war can impinge on indigenous populations in eccentric ways. Stories of a medieval world in which a farmer fearful about his crops could prevail on armies to fight elsewhere are possibly exaggerated, the product of nostalgia for a chivalric code that most likely did not hold much sway during a coarse and vicious time. In any period and at any place, the fundamental reality of war is that organized violence is no less brutal for its being structured by strategy and tactics. The advent of total war might have been signaled by the famous *levee en masse* of the French Revolution, but that development was more a culmination of a trend than an innovation away from more pacific times. In short, all wars have assailed and will assail civilians in one way or another to a greater or lesser degree. The Thirty Years' War displaced populations, just as the American Revolution saw settlements preyed upon, houses razed, and farms pillaged. Modern codes of conduct adopted by both international consent and embraced by the armies of the civilized world have heightened awareness about the sanctity of civilians and have improved vigilance about violations of that sanctity, but in the end, such codes will never guarantee immunity from the rage of battle or the rigors of war.

In this series, accomplished scholars have recruited prescient colleagues to write essays that reveal both the universal civilian experience in wartime and aspects of it made unique by time and place. Readers will discover in these pages the other side of warfare, one that is never placid, even if far removed from the scenes of fighting. As these talented authors show, the shifting expectations of governments markedly transformed the civilian wartime experience from virtual noninvolvement in early modern times to the twentieth century's expectation of sacrifice, exertion, and contribution. Finally, as the Western powers have come full circle by asking virtually no sacrifice from civilians at all, they have stumbled upon the peculiar result that diminishing deprivation during a war can increase civilian dissent against it.

Moreover, the geographical and chronological span of these books is broad and encompassing to reveal the unique perspectives of how war affects people, whether they are separated by hemispheres or centuries, people who are distinct by way of different cultures yet similar because of their common humanity. As readers will see, days on a home front far from battle usually become a surreal routine of the ordinary existing in tandem with the extraordinary, a situation in which hours of waiting and expectation become blurred against the backdrop of normal tasks and everyday events. That situation is a constant, whether for a village in Asia or Africa or in Europe or the Americas.

Consequently, these books confirm that the human condition always produces the similar as well as the singular, a paradox that war tends to amplify.

Every war is much like another, but no war is really the same as any other. All places are much alike, but no place is wholly separable from its matchless identity. The civilian experience in war mirrors these verities. We are certain that readers will find in these books a vivid illumination of those truths.

David S. Heidler and Jeanne T. Heidler, Series Editors

Acknowledgments

In preparing this work, the following scholars were most helpful with assistance, advice, and recommendations: Professor David Marr, Professor Robin Prior, Dr. Mina Roces, and Professor Jonathan Spence. Those who agreed to share their memories of life in Vietnam in the 1960s–1970s deserve a special vote of thanks. In starting those interviews, I am most grateful to Oanh Collins, and in making several other interviews possible, an enormous debt is owed to Liem Duong and his family. Michael Hermann at Greenwood Press and Drs. David and Jeanne Heidler as series editors have been exemplary in bringing this project to fruition. As always, my wife, Yimei, is largely responsible for getting me to the finishing line. Insofar as a collective work can be dedicated by any one of its members, however, this one is dedicated to three individuals, all in military uniform, but all thoughtful, generous, and gentle people: In alphabetical order, they are Christopher Cockerill, Paul Le Duong, and Anita Groves.

S. L.

Introduction

The definition of Asia in this collection of essays ranges from the northeast to the southeast. This is the part of the globe that broadly overlaps what, up to the nineteenth century, has been described by historians as the Chinese World Order. Here the dominant force over much of the past 2,000 years has been China. This influence was primarily cultural and economic. The moral values of China (and in countries such as Japan and Korea, the written language, also) were adopted and assimilated in many parts of the region centuries before the modern age. For those more remote from China's cultural reach, such as the Philippines and Indonesia, both long colonized by European powers (the Philippines takes its name from King Philip of Spain; Indonesia for several centuries was the Dutch East Indies), maritime trade with the Chinese mainland remained of major importance to the local economy. In focusing upon eastern Asia, we are largely excluding those areas in which Indian or Islamic influence was strongest. Thus it may be that another volume is needed to examine the states of south and central Asia.

One of traditional China's values that most directly relates to the topic of this volume is the desire to avoid conflict. At the essence of Chinese Confucianism is an intricate system of social and linguistic rituals designed to give structure to all human relations and minimize the potential for misunderstanding or aggression. Further to this is a social hierarchy in which education, defined as an understanding of moral philosophy, is given the greatest respect. The social status of the soldier, by contrast, is encapsulated in a popular Chinese saying: "One does not use good iron to make nails; one does not use good men to make soldiers." In fact, until the end of the nineteenth century, the soldier in China was generally seen as little more than a bandit. With the exception of Japan, which modified the Chinese system to grant elite status to the samurai military bureaucrats (more bureaucratic than military), this meant that in much of eastern Asia, there was an intrinsic resistance to war and to warriors. As the regional hegemon by virtue of its size, history, and wealth, China established a geopolitical order based on rituals of mutual respect; this respect was demonstrated through gift-giving. Thus smaller states in the region that accepted China's hegemony would send presents to the Chinese emperor. He, being at the top of the hierarchy, was then bound to give even greater gifts to these regional embassies. The success of this system of harmony through ritual and exchange of gifts meant that from about the time that the Qing Dynasty came to power in China in 1644 until the British invasion of China from 1839–1842, there was no major war between two states in north or southeast Asia. There were internal riots and, occasionally, a revolt (often inspired by some form of religious belief), but war did not feature as an aspect of daily life.

This is in contrast to western Europe or, indeed, the United States, in which some level of international or civil war occurred since the late eighteenth century approximately every 30 years or less and therefore was something that civilians had a greater likelihood of experiencing or observing at some point in their lives. Moreover, as one of the pioneers of global history, William McNeill, has suggested, the culture of war and aggressive competition has dominated the thinking of western Europe and the United States. Indeed, one of the more interesting historians of American culture, Richard Slotkin, has coined the term *gunfighter nation* in describing some of its most powerful twentieth-century values.[1] The accepted thinking in the West is that competition and conflict are creative and progressive forces. This belief was accepted even by John Ruskin, one of the leading British critics of the industrial world in the late nineteenth century and a man who advocated a return to the age of handicrafts and a slower, more meditative (and thus, by extension, more peaceful) society. In fact, the great radical philosophers of the industrial age, men like Friedrich Nietzsche, were actually railing against the rise of the middle class and, with it, the victory of comfort and materialism over what they saw as the more primitive but also more dynamic forces of human conflict. As Nietzsche's most famous quote puts it, "what does not kill me, makes me stronger." It is this culture of desiring and seeking challenge or conflict that is often seen in Asia as typical of the West.

From the mid-nineteenth century, the broad starting point for this book, the societies of east Asia were increasingly forced to alter their values and practices. The turning point here is the British government's attack on China in 1839–1842, popularly known as the First Opium War. As a result of China's defeat in this and subsequent wars, and the imposition by the Western powers on Asia of colonial rule or unequal treaties, a new social and cultural order was established. In this, survival as a nation now depended first on creating a nation (principally through mass education for literacy and the development of a new media) and building the socio-economic basis to sustain a mass military. As a consequence, war and the threat of war brought about extraordinary changes in the lives of children (now going to school and being called "schoolchildren"), of women (working in industrial factories where they could earn wages and using their education to branch out into new careers), and of men (now faced with the probability of having to serve in the military). Also, the physical presence and economic power of the military expanded to unprecedented levels. This is obvious if one compares, for example, China or Korea over the past 100 years. The broader point here is that the culture of capitalist development; innovations in military and maritime technology; the rise of the military as an actor in society; the readiness to test body against body, for example, in contact (i.e., combat) sports; and indeed, the importance of physical culture and the determination to mold nature to the needs of man are all values that, it may be argued, have been planted in eastern Asia only in the past century and a half.

And yet war remains one of the most wasteful of human acts. For every bullet or shell that makes an impact on the enemy, many more are expended aimlessly and uselessly. The histories of conflicts are often extreme examples of folly and futility. Indeed, a poignant line from *Shenandoah,* an intelligent film from the 1960s set in the American Civil War, explains that the only real beneficiaries of war are the undertakers. The principal losers, by contrast, are always civilians. This is either because governments and armies commandeer men and resources from civilian society, because battles cause havoc and devastation to the territories in which they are fought, or because civilians pay the bills in terms of taxes or death and disablement. Indeed, it has of late become the common wisdom that casualties in war around the start of the twentieth century were 90 percent military and 10 percent civilian; by the end of the twentieth century, they were 90 percent civilian and 10 percent military. Whatever the accuracy of these figures, the point is clear: War has come home in a very real sense. Therefore any concept of civilian normality in war, that is, the sense of daily life as something defined by routines, has had to adapt to this far greater and more persistent assault of war on civilians.

This is not to suggest that the absolute impact of war on civilian life, even in relative terms, was minor before the twentieth century. This volume starts with the Taiping revolutionary conflict in mid-nineteenth-century China. This lasted 14 years, and estimates of the death toll go as high as 12 million. The concluding chapters deal with the Korean War of the 1950s and the last phase of the Vietnam War, from about 1965 to 1975; in each of these, about three million people lost their lives. Perhaps the greatest change over the past century and a half is simply the speed of destruction on a mass scale. Ever since World War I, it has become increasingly accepted as legitimate by governments and militaries—and by civil societies, also—to use the tactic of bombing urban centers. The reasoning behind this is that it saves the lives of ground troops and forces an enemy quickly to submit. Modern experience, however, including from the Korean and Vietnam wars, suggests that this is an easily contested argument.

Indeed, the chapter by Andrei Lankov quotes a Korean proverb which says that even if the heavens fall, there must still be some holes into which one can escape. What is demonstrated by several of the present authors is that civilian life in modern war often involves going quite literally underground. This was the case in North Korea and South Vietnam during long periods of bombing; it was also the case, of course, in Britain during World War II. Other options, as always in war, include taking flight. The refugee is not a uniquely modern figure, but there have never been so many people who are now, or have been, refugees from war. For them, whether in the earlier Taiping or Filipino revolutionary wars, or later, as in the Korean War, all daily routines are short term as they wait, even for years, to find a new home, work to do, and ways to overcome the stigma of being one of the dislocated.

A further theme that emerges is how deep wars often strike at the very basics of civilian life: food and clothing. One of the major points in the chapter by Shigeru Satō on Indonesia in World War II is the extreme shortage of clothing and, with it, the loss of human dignity, even though there was little direct fighting on the islands. The impact of food shortages appears in several of the chapters: In Japan, during the Pacific War, it was said that there were five colors of rice, mostly from yellow to black, and none of them white; in the Korean War, some evidence suggests that residents of Seoul were turned against the North Korean occupiers in 1950 primarily by their failure to provide food; and in South Vietnam the crisis in food supplies in 1973 may have been decisive in ending public support for the Saigon regime.

An additional theme, however, is the resilience of civilians. Even during periods of intense conflict all around them, there is a remarkable ability of people to find some kind of routine and survive. This may be as simple as visiting a teahouse to pass a few hours drinking, chatting, or reading. For children, one of the most obvious methods to soften the impact of war is to turn it into play. Another technique for survival, whether one is a civilian or a combatant, is humor, and in several of the chapters we have tried to identify some of the forms of satire, and even self-mockery, that helped people overcome the disruptions and instabilities of war.

In considering the daily lives of civilians, one question to ask is, to what extent did the war intrude upon civilian life? In this the war might literally appear right in front of civilians with violence in the street, emerge in a controlled and safe form as news or film, pass almost impressionistically in terms of the movement of soldiers to and from a frontline well out of sight, or work indirectly on life by making food, goods, movement, pleasure, and even speech less accessible and open than in times of peace. The authors hope to provide a range of answers to this question.

The chapters in this volume deliberately employ a variety of approaches. This is in line with the diversity of civilian life. Thus there is the approach that takes a panoramic view of an entire society, the one that focuses on a single city, and the one that uses a central institution of civilian life—the teahouse—as a tool to explore the wider community in war. In general, the authors explain most fully about urban life. This is dictated by the fact that records are usually best kept by the literate and the relatively affluent, and they, in turn, are usually to be found in urban areas. This, of course, as Satō emphasizes at the beginning of his chapter, raises the possibility of many kinds of bias (of class, gender, region, or ethnicity) or simply of ignorance. It is a common request from historians, one repeated here, that the reader accept what follows only conditionally, that is, until further evidence comes to light.

We have added a small number of illustrations to most chapters. The exception is the first chapter, which deals with China in the 1850s–1860s. The reason for this exception is that the age of the photograph was only just beginning at this time. By the 1890s and the topic of the second chapter, the Filipino wars of resistance against the Spanish and Americans, the photograph was established as a part of modern life and had radically altered the way that people saw themselves, saw others, and understood both the present and the immediate past. In fact, the first moving pictures of war date from the late 1890s, and with this, any perception of war among civilians was also fundamentally different from that time. In the 1850s, war was experienced either directly or by hearsay; by the 1890s, one could actually see war, either frozen in a still photograph or moving across a giant cinema screen. It may also be that with this addition of, or competition from, the mechanically reproduced image, writers also began to change the way that they perceived and wrote about war. The authors would therefore ask readers to consider not only what is being said in the following chapters, but also to think about the way in which it is said. This, in part, is a response to the trend in the past four decades that has seen the language of war—at least, as it is used by governments and militaries—take on a life of its own, one seemingly divorced from the realities of civilian life and expression.

NOTE

1. Richard Slotkin, *Gunfighter Nation: The Myth of the Frontier in Twentieth Century America,* New York: Atheneum, 1992. For a brief statement of McNeill's argument, see his essay "European expansion, power and warfare since 1500" in J. A. de Moor and H. L. Wesseling, eds., *Imperialism and War: Essays on Colonial Wars in Asia and Africa,* Leiden: E. J. Brill, 1989.

Chronology

CHINA: THE TAIPING AND NIAN REBELLIONS

1644   Establishment of Qing Dynasty in Beijing

1839–1842 First Opium War: British invasion and instability in southern China

1850   Enthronement of new Qing emperor, Xian Feng (dies 1861); start of Taiping Rebellion, south China, under Hong Xiuquan

1851   Start of Nian Rebellion, north China

1853   Taiping army captures Nanjing, declares it Tianjing, capital of Taiping kingdom

1853–1855 Small Swords Society (Triad group) occupies part of Shanghai

1854   Start of Miao Rebellion, southwest China

1854–1855 Taiping northern and western expeditionary armies defeated

1855–1862 Muslim rebellions in west and southwest China

1856   Taiping and Nian allied force defeats Qing army

1856–1860 Second Opium War (Arrow War): Anglo-French forces occupy Guangzhou (1857), Beijing (1860)

1860   Taiping troops defeated by Anglo-French force at Shanghai

1864   Qing armies retake Nanjing; death of Taiping leader, Hong

1868   Destruction of Nian armies

THE PHILIPPINE WARS OF INDEPENDENCE

1565 Filipinas colonized by Spain, capital from 1571 in the city of Manila

1834 Manila fully opened to foreign trade

1863 Educational Decree gives Filipinos the right to a university education

1868 Guardia Civil set up to suppress rising banditry and rebellion

1872 February—three Filipino secular priests executed publicly in Bagumbayan

1892 July—secret patriotic society, the Katipunan, established in Manila by Andres Bonifacio and Ladislao Diwa

1895 Creation of secret police service, the Cuerpo de Vigilancia y Seguridad, to gather intelligence on life in Manila

1896 August 23—symbolic outbreak of revolution, "The Cry of Pugadlawin"; colonial authorities react with mass arrests, deportations, and executions

1896 September–December—following Katipunan and Spanish military clashes, Bonifacio withdraws his army to Cavite province

1896 December—José Rizal (born 1861), revolutionary and author of *Noli me tangere* and *El filibusterismo,* executed by firing squad on charges of "rebellion, sedition, and formation of illegal societies"

1897 February–May—intense Spanish offensive recovers Cavite

1897 December—truce agreement; Aguinaldo into voluntary exile in Hong Kong

1898 April—start of Spanish-American War; Commodore George Dewey annihilates Spanish navy; May 1—Battle of Manila Bay

1898 May 19—Aguinaldo returns to Philippines; June 12—Filipino revolutionaries declare Philippine independence; Philippine Republic formally inaugurated at Malolos (January 23, 1899)

1898 August–December—Spanish government in the Philippines surrenders to Dewey (August 13); December—Treaty of Paris grants sovereignty over Philippines to United States; President McKinley proclamation on "benevolent assimilation"

1899 February 4—"Black Saturday" and start of Philippine-American War

1899 March—fall of Republican capital at Malolos to U.S. forces

1901 March—Aguinaldo captured; April—Aguinaldo takes oath of allegiance to the United States

1902 July 4—official termination of Philippine-American War

WARS OF MEIJI JAPAN

1853	Arrival off Japan of U.S. fleet
1854	End of Japan's "closed country" policy
1868	Civil war leads to "restoration" of imperial rule; start of Meiji era (to 1912)
1872	Announcement on creation of conscript army
1889	Introduction of constitutional polity
1890	Japan identifies its national security with fate of Korea
1891	Start of Russian construction of Trans-Siberian railway; Japanese fears of Russian expansion
1894	August—Japan instigates war with China over control of Korea; November—Japanese army easily captures Port Arthur (Manchuria)
1895	China sues for peace; April peace treaty; Japan takes island of Taiwan and becomes a colonial power
1897–1898	Germany seizes part of Shandong province, China; other powers demand similar concessions from Beijing; Russia increases its presence in Manchuria
1900	Boxer war, China; Japan fights alongside Western militaries; Russia occupies Manchuria
1902	Announcement of Anglo-Japanese security alliance against Russia
1903	Failed Russo-Japanese talks on compromise over Korea
1904	February—Japan attacks Russian forces in northeast Asia without first declaring war; August—start of Japanese siege of Port Arthur (until January 1905)
1905	March—land battle of Mukden; May—Russian fleet destroyed at Tsushima
1905	September—peace treaty ends war but sparks violent protests in Tokyo (Hibiya riots)

CHINA'S WARS, 1937–1949

1911	Revolution, Qing monarchy collapses; Chinese republic created (January 1912)
1917	Start of warlord conflicts (to 1928)
1919	Political party of Dr. Sun Yatsen renamed Guomindang (Nationalist Party)
1921	Secret formation of Chinese Communist Party

1924	Chiang Kaishek appointed commander-in-chief of Nationalist forces
1926–1928	Guomindang Northern military expedition: Chiang takes control of China
1930–1933	Five Guomindang military campaigns to exterminate Communist groups
1931	Manchurian incident: Japanese military expansion in northeast China
1934–1935	Communist army "Long March": new base at Yan'an
1937	Start of war with Japan; fall of Shanghai in November, Nanjing in December (Nanjing massacre); November—new national capital at Chongqing, Sichuan province
1938	Fall of Guangzhou and Wuhan (both October)
1939–1941	Repeated clashes between Chinese Nationalist and Communist armies
1941	December—Japan attacks Pearl Harbor; entry of United States into World War II; Japan occupies Hong Kong
1942–1943	Chinese forces inflict reverses on Japanese army
1944	First U.S. air raid on Japanese islands sent from Chengdu base
1945	Japanese surrender; resumption of Nationalist–Communist rivalry
1946	Communist forces renamed "People's Liberation Army" (PLA); July—restart of civil war
1947	Major PLA offensives in north and east China; massive inflation undermines civilian life
1948	PLA takes Manchuria
1949	PLA takes Beijing, Nanjing, Shanghai, Chongqing; December—Chiang flees to Taiwan

JAPAN, 1937–1945

1937	July—start of Sino-Japanese War; Japan occupies major Chinese cities north–south, 1937–1938; August—start of National Spiritual Mobilization campaign
1938	April—National Economic Mobilization Law
1938	Fighting with Soviet forces (again in 1939) on Manchuria–Mongolia border
1940	September—Japanese forces enter north Indochina; Japan signs anti-communist Tripartite Alliance with Germany and Italy

1940   Official 2,600th anniversary of founding of Japanese nation

1941   Major educational reforms in Japan

1941   Japan signs treaty of neutrality with Soviet Union; June—Japanese troops enter south Indochina; United States freezes Japanese assets, bans export of oil to Japan

1941   December—attack on Pearl Harbor; United States enters World War II; Japanese armies conquer southeast Asia

1942   June—Japanese navy defeated at battle of Midway

1943   February—Japanese forces in retreat from Guadalcanal

1943   Japanese merchant fleet virtually destroyed

1944   Start of U.S. bombing of Japanese homelands; creation of volunteer kamikaze suicide squads

1945   March 9—one night of B29 bombing of Tokyo causes 120,000 dead and injured

1945   August—use of atomic bombs on Hiroshima and Nagasaki; Soviet Union declares war on Japan; Japan surrenders

INDONESIA'S WARS

1935   Ongoing global economic decline; Dutch colonial authorities start fostering industrialization for economic self-sufficiency

1937   Start of Sino-Japanese War; fall in Sino-Indonesian trade

1939   Formation of *Gabungan Politik Indonesia* (Indonesian Political Federation, GAPI), uniting most nationalist parties

1939   September—start of World War II in Europe; Dutch colonial authorities "compulsory cultivation ordinance" to establish self-sufficiency in food

1940   February—Indonesian nationalists request reforms in colonial parliament, including use of *Indonesia* and *Indonesians* in all official documents

1940   May—Germany conquers the Netherlands; World War II in Europe worsens Indonesian economy, increasing poverty and unemployment

1941   December—Japan bombs Pearl Harbor, declares war against United States and Britain; Dutch government in exile declares war on Japan; December 11—Japan bombs Ambon

1942   January–March—Japanese invasion of Indonesia, including bombing of Ambon, Batavia (Jakarta), and other targets; Dutch use scorched-earth tactics, but surrender (March 9)

1942	April—Japanese navy establishes its Civil Administration in eastern Indonesia.
1942	December 8—Batavia officially renamed Jakarta
1943	April—Japanese system of forced delivery of rice to the government
1943	July—first Allied bombing of Java at Surabaya; Japanese occupation authorities permit use of Indonesian national flag and anthem
1944	April–July—Indonesian peasant rebellions against forced delivery of rice
1944	May–September—Allied bombing of Indonesia, including Surabaya, Ambon, and Jakarta
1945	May—Netherlands liberated; Germany surrenders
1945	August 15—surrender of Japan; August 17—Sukarno declares independence of the Republic of Indonesia; August 23—Dutch forces land at Sabang in Aceh
1946	Initial negotiations between Indonesian and Dutch authorities
1947	July—Dutch launch the first "Police Actions"
1948	December—Dutch launch the second "Police Actions"
1949	April—new talks between Indonesian Republican leaders and Dutch; December—restoration of sovereignty to Indonesian Republic

THE KOREAN WAR

1910	Japan annexes Korea
1945	August—Japan defeated in World War II; Korea regains independence; United States and Union of Soviet Socialist Republics (U.S.S.R.) establish dividing line at 38th parallel
1948	Creation of separate republics, North Korea (D.P.R.K.) and South Korea (R.O.K.)
1949	Victory of Communist Party in China's civil war
1950	June 25—start of Korean civil war; June 27—President Syngman Rhee flees from Seoul; June 28—North Korean forces occupy Seoul; July—R.O.K. provisional capital established at Pusan
1950	September 15—United Nations forces under General MacArthur land at Inchŏn, retake Seoul (September 20–30), occupy Pyongyang (October 19)
1950	November—China enters the war to stop U.N. advance; communist armies retake Pyŏngyang in December

1951	Communist forces occupy Seoul from January until ousted by U.N. forces in March
1951–1953	Military stalemate on the ground; U.S. aerial bombing campaign in North Korea
1953	Armistice halts the fighting in Korea

THE VIETNAM WAR

1950–1954	War against French colonial rule in Vietnam
1954	Geneva agreement temporarily divides Vietnam, north and south
1954	Start of U.S. financial aid to South Vietnamese government
1955	Ngo Dinh Diem proclaims establishment of Republic of Vietnam (South Vietnam)
1957	Start of communist insurgency in South Vietnam
1960	Hanoi creates National Liberation Front for South Vietnam (dubbed "Vietcong" by Saigon government)
1962	United States sets up Military Assistance Command in South Vietnam
1963	May–August—Buddhist anti-Diem protests; military coup and assassination of Diem
1963	15,000 U.S. military advisers in South Vietnam
1964	Tonkin Gulf incident and first U.S. bombing of North Vietnam
1965	First American combat troops to South Vietnam (total 500,000 by end of 1967)
1966	Continued Buddhist protests against Saigon military regime
1968	Tet offensive: North Vietnamese troops and Vietcong attack South Vietnam cities and towns
1969	Ongoing peace negotiations in Paris
1969	March—Secret bombing of Cambodia (Kampuchea) by U.S. forces
1969	June—President Richard Nixon announces the withdrawal of 25,000 U.S. troops (final troops leave March 1973)
1970	April 30—Announcement of combined U.S.–Army of the Republic of Vietnam (ARVN) incursions into Cambodia; May—antiwar protests in Saigon and United States, including Kent State University (May 4)
1971	U.S. forces in Vietnam reduced to 140,000
1972	North Vietnamese offensive into South Vietnam rebuffed

1973   United States and North Vietnam negotiate cease-fire agreements in Paris

1974   South Vietnam President Thieu declares that war has restarted

1975   January–March—communist forces capture major South Vietnamese provinces; April—fall of Saigon

ONE

Daily Life in China during the Taiping and Nian Rebellions, 1850s–1860s

R. Gary Tiedemann

In the wake of the Manchu's capture of Beijing in 1644, the invaders consolidated their control of all of China over the next four decades. For about a century afterward the country experienced peace and prosperity under these foreign rulers of the Qing Dynasty (1644–1912). Successful military campaigns brought vast territories outside China into the realm of the Manchu Empire, namely Mongolia, Tibet, and Eastern Turkestan (now known as Xinjiang). However, toward the end of the eighteenth century, signs of dynastic decline began to appear. Several factors contributed to the growing domestic instability, one of which was the unprecedented population growth during the relatively prosperous years of the eighteenth century. The combination of demographic pressure and partible inheritance, that is, the division of family property among all surviving sons *(fenjia)*, had important long-term implications for social stratification. It brought about an increase in the number of households and, consequently, a reduction in the average size of peasant land holdings. More intensive cultivation of these diminished plots exhausted the soil and contributed to erosion, which, in the longer run, reduced the smallholders' income. Thus an increasing number of peasants who could not meet their subsistence needs from the land they cultivated had to turn to a variety of sideline activities to survive.

Another important consequence of the pressures on the land was the significant migration from the overpopulated provinces of eastern China to the more marginal lands in the frontier zones, including, significantly, the hill country of southwestern China. As these Han Chinese settlers opened up more and more of the hill tracts to agriculture, it brought them into conflict with the ethnic minorities. Among these migrants who had gradually moved onto marginal land in the southwest provinces of Guangdong and Guangxi were the Hakka (*kejia,* or "guest people"), a subethnic Han Chinese group that was to become the key element in the Taiping Rebellion.

A further major factor contributing to social and political instability was the decline of administrative efficiency. During the late imperial period, the vast, centralized polity of China was governed by an overextended civil bureaucracy and thinly deployed military and police forces. At the height of dynastic power the system of governance may have worked reasonably well. However, toward the end of the eighteenth century, administrative decay had certainly set in as part of the long-term process of dynastic decline. Moreover, the Chinese bureaucratic structure had become increasingly susceptible to organized corruption among officeholders, including the misappropriation of funds and supplies and the misuse of official power for private gain in the form of exorbitant taxation, failure to implement tax remissions, embezzlement of public funds, mismanagement of public granaries, neglect of public works—especially those involving flood control—and other administrative abuses. Such corrupt and oppressive behavior by government functionaries and subbureaucratic personnel could and often did precipitate violent popular resistance.

Given the fundamental social, political, and economic changes resulting from demographic pressures, administrative decline, ecological instability, and the incessant struggle against nature, rural society was becoming increasingly restless, fragmented, and fiercely competitive. Over time, the survival strategies employed in response to the various long-term disintegrative pressures fostered the erosion of group loyalties within local systems and weakened traditional mechanisms of social control. Because of the increasing precariousness of human existence and the constant struggle for subsistence, violent conflict appeared from time to time in almost every part of the empire. Depending on particular circumstances, reactions to the harshness of human existence manifested themselves in banditry, piracy, feuding, and tax riots as well as localized uprisings by secret societies and sectarian associations. In the 1840s, the impact of the illegal opium trade and the First Opium War (1839–1842), in which Britain attacked China along its southern coast, exacerbated the deteriorating conditions in the interior. It was this growing insecurity of civilian life that produced the rebellions of the 1850s and 1860s.

WAR AND REBELLIONS IN MID-NINETEENTH-CENTURY CHINA

The Taiping Rebellion was not only the first, but also the largest and most destructive of the massive upheavals in the Manchu Empire at this time. In one way or another, it affected all 18 provinces of "China Proper" (or "Inner China") and ravaged most of the central provinces between 1850 and 1864. This protracted contest with the weakening Qing Dynasty encouraged or coincided with several other, essentially regional uprisings. Thus the Nian Rebellion started on the North China Plain in 1851 and was not subdued until 1868. In Guizhou province Miao minority people and other malcontents started their insurgency in 1854 and kept Qing provincial armies occupied for nearly two decades. A Chinese Muslim revolt erupted in Yunnan province in 1855, followed by another Chinese Muslim rebellion in the provinces of Shaanxi and Gansu in 1862. Two years later, central Asian Muslims rose against the Qing and established an independent Islamic state under Ya'qūb Beg in Eastern Turkestan, far beyond the confines of China Proper. In addition, there were a host of smaller, more localized events, such as the Small Sword Society (or Triad) uprisings in Shanghai (1853–1855) and Xiamen (Amoy) (1853). Other Triad groups, including the Red Turbans, established small "states" in parts of

The Taiping Rebellion, 1850–1864. (David S. Heidler.)

Guangdong and Guangxi. In the early 1860s, small-scale sectarian uprisings occurred in north China. The Second Opium War (or Arrow War), started by British and French forces in 1856 and culminating in the allied occupation of Beijing in 1860, was a further challenge to stability in mid-nineteenth-century China.

Given the widespread and prolonged social unrest, it is reasonable to assume that just about everyone in China was directly or indirectly affected by these military conflicts. However, since it was not only the most devastating episode in nineteenth-century history, but also generated the greatest interest at the time, we shall focus primarily on the impact of the Taiping Rebellion on daily life.

The Taiping Rebellion is intimately connected with the life story of one individual, namely Hong Xiuquan (1814–1864), a failed scholar from a Hakka peasant family in Guangdong. As a result of his casual contact with Protestant Christianity in the city of Guangzhou (known to Westerners as Canton), Hong developed a dynamic new Chinese religion, Taiping Christianity, and proclaimed himself to be the younger brother of Jesus. In the 1840s, Hong began to preach an uncompromising anti-Manchu message and initiated a campaign to destroy Confucian and ancestral shrines. As far as Hong was concerned, "the Manchus were demons fighting against the true God, a God whose purity and presence had existed in China until the forces of Confucian belief swayed the Chinese away from the true path of righteousness."[1] While Hong was able to attract a devoted following among fellow Hakka and certain ethnic minorities in the Thistle Mountain area of the neighboring province of Guangxi, he also provoked the anger of the local elite. Indeed, the Taiping were not only a radical alternative to the Qing Dynasty's adherence to traditional Confucian values, but insisted on wearing their hair long, in deliberate contrast to the queue and shaven forehead imposed on all Han Chinese males by the Manchu conquerors. This was a clear sign of open rebellion and a rejection of the Manchu government.

In the face of growing elite hostility, Hong Xiuquan, in 1850, ordered a general mobilization of his followers, and on January 11, 1851, he declared himself the Heavenly King *(Tianwang)* of the Heavenly Kingdom of Great Peace *(Taiping Tianguo)*. However, a large government army forced the Taiping out of their base by Thistle Mountain. Yet, having occupied the city of Yongan (present-day Mengshan) for a few months, the Taiping then continued their "long march" from resource-poor Guangxi toward the affluent Yangzi valley. Along the way—and especially in Hunan province—the Taiping leadership recognized the importance of rules to prevent abuses by their Heavenly Army and gain the loyalty of the local people. The code of conduct, reminiscent of Mao Zedong's rules for the Chinese Red Army some 80 years later, was spelled out in simple form, as indicated by the following examples:

Let no officer or soldier, male or female, enter into the villages to cook rice or seize food; let no one destroy the dwellings of the people or loot their property; also let no one ransack the apothecaries' or other shops or the offices of the various prefectural and district magistrates.

Let no one set fire to the dwellings of the people, or urinate in the middle of the road or in private houses.

Let no one unjustly put to death the old and the weak who don't have the strength to carry burdens.[2]

Military discipline was essential to further bolster local support, but so was the immediate well-being of ordinary folk. Thus the Taipings ensured that the people were properly compensated for goods required by the troops. At the same time, some of the grain stores, livestock, and other goods seized from the homes of fugitive landlords were shared out among the local villagers. Moreover, the Taipings promised future improvements once they had established their rule over all of China:

After the unification of the rivers and mountains there will be a universal three-year exemption from [land] taxes in cash and grain. The rich should contribute money, the poor should offer up their strength. After the great enterprise is finished all will be rewarded with distinctive and hereditary official positions. Wherever we pass we will concentrate on killing all civil and military officials, and soldiers and militiamen. People will not be harmed and they can certainly pursue their livelihood as usual, and fairly buy and fairly sell. At the same time when a city is taken if all families close their doors we can guarantee an absence of incidents. If you assist the [Manchu] devils in the defense of a city and engage in fighting, you will definitely be completely annihilated.[3]

The egalitarian ambiguity of this passage notwithstanding, the Taiping approach provoked a twofold reaction in Hunan province. The Confucian ruling class regarded the Taipings as rebels against the ruling Manchus, to whom the gentry had pledged allegiance. Furthermore, they rejected heterodox Taiping Christianity for it seriously undermined Confucian culture and thus the traditional fabric of Chinese society. The mass of people, on the other hand, suffering from a spate of natural calamities, found the Taiping program rather more appealing. Consequently, the Heavenly Army gained over 20,000 "new brethren" in Hunan, drawn mainly from among the poor peasants, laborers, bandits, Triads, and other marginals. The Triads, in particular, would subsequently provide important support at critical junctures during the early Taiping years.

Once the Taipings reached the Yangzi at Wuchang, they swiftly moved downriver. In March 1853, they captured the large and strongly fortified city of Nanjing. Renamed Tianjing (Heavenly Capital), it became the seat of the Taiping administration for the next 11 years. During their exodus from Guangxi, the well-trained and ideologically committed Taiping armies had, in their many victorious battles, exposed the weakness of the Qing government forces and captured a number of large cities and smaller towns along the way. At the same time they had devised a millenarian belief system

and a revolutionary program for a radical socioeconomic reorganiza-
tion. Under this system, all money and valuables were pooled in a central "sacred treasury," and instructions against corruption, opium, and
tobacco smoking were to be rigorously enforced. Daily Christian worship
became obligatory. According to the utopian Taiping treatise, *The Land
System of the Heavenly Dynasty,* all land was to be divided according to
family size, with men and women aged 16 years or older receiving equal
shares. Initially, however, men and women were segregated into separate
camps to enforce chastity and safeguard the movement's fighting power.
But no evidence has come to light that the radical land law was ever
implemented. The personnel required to do so were instead employed
to defend Nanjing and other cities against the constant military threat
from Qing loyalist forces. Since Taiping millenarianism posed a serious
challenge to Confucian orthodoxy, the old order was able to gradually
organize effective resistance. In the end the rebels failed to overthrow the
Qing Dynasty but were themselves destroyed in 1864 by the new regional
armies, above all the Xiang Army, recruited primarily in Hunan province
and commanded by the Confucian scholar-bureaucrat Zeng Guofan.

DAILY LIFE IN THE CITY

In times of war, civilian populations usually have to endure great hardship, including the destruction of life and property, when caught up in the
battles. The protracted and exceedingly bitter armed conflict between the
Taipings and Qing loyalists certainly was no exception. It was the cities that
became the principal prizes and scenes of battle, as one side or the other
either tried to defend or capture these traditionally well-fortified urban
centers. But the Taipings attempted to accomplish much more than merely
occupy such places. They sought to radically transform the economic and
political system as well as drastically alter religious and social customs in
conformity with their ideological convictions. Thus in cities they were able
to hold for some time, for example, Wuchang (June 1854–December 1856)
and Anqing (June 1853–September 1861), the new order influenced daily
routines in significant ways. It was, however, in Nanjing—the "second city"
of the Empire—that the most comprehensive changes were observed during
the 11 years of occupation. Since the prolonged presence affected virtually
every aspect of daily life, it is necessary to confine discussion to only some
of the significant features in the context of Taiping conquest, consolidation,
and decline.[4]

The Battle

Even before the battle for Nanjing commenced, many people fled the
city in the midst of panic engendered by a multitude of rumors. Others
stayed behind, in the hope that the city's mighty fortifications would

protect them. Yet the troops stationed in the city to protect its citizens had no experience in combat and were noted for their indiscipline as well as low morale. The hurriedly assembled irregular forces were even less reliable. It is therefore not surprising that the people had little trust in the military prowess of its defenders. Instead, believing the enemy to possess supernatural powers and the ability to cast evil spells, they sought to neutralize the Taipings' supposed magic by frightening away rebel demons with large effigies and by lining up naked women along the city wall. But these measures did not prevent the Taipings breaching the fortifications and entering Nanjing on March 19, 1853. Although the Manchu garrison put up stiff resistance, it was quickly overcome, and its remaining survivors were massacred, including women and children, and their bodies thrown into the river. The Manchu quarter that had once housed 25,000 inhabitants was thoroughly leveled. For a few days afterward the Taiping soldiers were permitted to loot and ransack the houses of the city's fearstricken Chinese inhabitants, thousands of whom committed suicide by hanging, drowning, or burning themselves.[5] Mass suicides after the fall of a city were, however, a recurrent phenomenon in the history of Chinese warfare. Suicides by women fearful of molestation by conquering troops were particularly common.

New Social Practices

Once law and order had been reimposed on the city, the victors set out to establish their vision of society. To the inhabitants of a city steeped in the traditions of Confucianism, the Taipings' appearance and behavior were very different from the social norms and values to which they had hitherto been accustomed. For example, in conformity with their religious principles, the Taipings sought to impose new social customs and new forms of behavior. Certainly the foreign Protestant missionaries were delighted with the rebels' religious outlook and their opposition to slavery, footbinding, prostitution, gambling, and infanticide as well as the prohibition of opium, alcohol, and tobacco. In late 1853 the Reverend Walter Henry Medhurst summed up his appreciation of the new policies:

What a moral revolution! To induce 100,000 Chinamen [in the military], for months and years together, to give up tobacco, opium, lust and covetousness; to deny themselves in lawful gratifications, and what is dearer to a Chinaman's heart than life itself, to consent to live without dollars, and all share and share alike. . . . There may be defective teaching among them, there may be errors of greater of lesser magnitude—but if what is above-detailed be true—or the half of it—it is the wonder of the age.[6]

At least during the early years of the Taiping occupation the new forms of behavior and prohibitions were rigorously enforced, not only among the Taiping military, but also among the ordinary city dwellers.

The Taiping and Women

Perhaps the most unsettling aspect of the Taiping was the more egalitarian role they accorded to women. In this connection it should be noted that the Hakka women of the Taiping movement did not practice footbinding, so ubiquitous among Chinese women elsewhere. In southeastern China, prior to the rebellion, it had enabled Hakka women to participate in the cultivation of fields, and they had become "so skilled at their work that they could even handle a water buffalo with equanimity."[7] Later, during the mobile phase of the Taiping movement, women had formed separate military units and were actively involved in the fighting. A Qing loyalist described them as follows:

Among the [Taiping] bandits there are female soldiers, all of whom are relatives of the Taiping kings. Being of vile minorities such as the Yao and the Zhuang, they grew up in caves and run around with bare feet and turbaned heads. They can scale steep cliffs with ease, and their courage surpasses that of men. On the battlefield, they carry weapons and fight at close quarters. Government troops have been defeated by them in battle.[8]

Now, in 1853, these women appeared among the "civilized" folk of Nanjing. As has already been noted, the Taipings had dissolved the family system and established separate male and female camps when the Heavenly Kingdom of Heavenly Peace was proclaimed. The segregation of the sexes was maintained in Nanjing during the early years of occupation. Consequently, local women were compelled to take up residence in the female halls, and the bindings were forcibly removed from their feet: "Guangxi women made rounds every evening to inspect the feet of women one by one. According to contemporary accounts, they frequently inflicted corporal punishment on women who had not removed their bindings, from the light penalty of flogging to the more severe penalty of cutting off the feet."[9] The Nanjing women were quickly integrated into the female work force and performed a variety of tasks, ranging from assisting in defensive preparations and harvesting crops to digging ditches. Since their feet had been bound prior to the Taipings' arrival, such labor was still arduous and rather painful. Suicide is said to have been particularly prevalent among upper-class women. As Ono points out, however, no information exists to show whether the traditionally much-oppressed daughters-in-law, for instance, regarded the new arrangement as an improvement.

Eventually, the separation of married couples was abolished, and marriages could be entered into on the basis of choice. But later marriages were to take place under state auspices, with the appointment of an official matchmaker. This clearly was an intrusion into what, in the old society, had been a private matter. On the other hand, the costly custom of dowries was no longer part of the proceedings, and the marriage ceremony was paid for out of common funds. Although the Taiping leadership kept a great number of concubines, as far as the common people were concerned, monogamy was considered sacred. A mercenary in Taiping services, Augustus Frederick Lindley, observed in the early 1860s,

I have frequently seen the marriage ceremony performed. . . . When the bridal party are all met together, they proceed to the church (*i.e.* "the Heavenly Hall" . . .), and after many prayers and a severe examination of the bride and bridegroom's theological tenets, the minister joins their right hands together, and when each have accepted the other, pronounces a concluding benediction in the name of the Father, Son, and Holy Spirit.[10]

This was all radically different from traditional marriage arrangements and procedures.

The New Religion

Following their capture of Nanjing, the new masters set out to introduce their Taiping Christianity with characteristic fervor. Within days after the city fell, its great Buddhist and Daoist temples and shrines had been destroyed in a violently iconoclastic campaign. The local people were now obliged to accept the new religion. An enduring method to convert the inhabitants of Nanjing to the new faith was by public exhortation. Joseph Edkins, missionary of the London Missionary Society, described one such occasion in the early 1860s:

Proceeding [to an open space in the city] we found a large concourse of Taipings. A sea of flags and streamers, red, yellow, white and green, floated in the wind over them. There was also an assemblage of horses and sedan chairs. The preacher of the day . . . came in a large yellow chair. Beneath the open sky there was a platform made of square tables, and a table covered with a red and yellow cloth. On this the preacher stood with his pasteboard yellow coronet, and addressed the listening crowd for twenty minutes. . . . He was followed by a more fluent speaker, a high chief, middle-aged, who discussed various moral and political matters. . . . After these addresses, all the listeners, standing on a green sward of the review ground, with a large semicircle of flaunting banners, knelt towards the table where the young chief also knelt. There was silence for a few minutes, as if they were all praying to the Heavenly Father. Then they rose and separated.[11]

All residents were expected to offer up morning and evening prayers and recite the Heavenly Commandments from memory; those who were unable to do so were severely punished. On the Sabbath, people would go to a worship hall, pray to *Shangdi* as the Heavenly Father, and receive further religious instruction. As is recorded in the *Land System of the Heavenly Dynasty*, "in every circle of twenty-five families. . . . Every Sabbath the corporals must lead the men and women to the church, where the males and females are to sit in separate rows. There they will listen to sermons, sing praises, and offer sacrifices to our Heavenly Father, the Supreme Lord and Great God."[12] As the above indicates, the worship was congregational, not individual. Nor was incense used. This was rather different from the established practices in Chinese temples. Indeed, most people found the entire Taiping religion very strange and took part in the services only because they were compelled to do so.

At the same time the Taipings sought to change attitudes toward death. Funerals became much simpler affairs, thereby avoiding the often crippling expense expected in traditional burials. The important Taiping leader during the last years of the Heavenly Kingdom of Great Peace, Hong Ren'gan, dismissed what he regarded to be the hypocritical nature of old funeral practices:

What is more strange is that sons regard their living parents as dispensable, and that after death the parents' corpses are taken as means by which to secure wealth and prominence. While living, the sons do not give their parents meat for food or good clothing to please their hearts, but after death they give them gold, silver, pigs, and sheep, pretending to be filial. Do they believe that they can make up for all their unfilial acts after their parents are dead? Or do they mean that the death of the parents can be considered a means to attain protection and good fortune? These are all absurd ideas.[13]

Under the Taiping regime in Nanjing, the dead were buried without an expensive coffin but were laid to rest in simple cloth wrappings. The Taiping authorities strictly enforced the new burial arrangements. They would break open coffins and destroy funerary objects found therein as well as the soul tablets of the deceased in the ancestral halls. To the conservative people of Nanjing, this was sacrilege that would have dire consequences for the ghosts of the mistreated would surely seek revenge.

The Fall of the Taiping Capital

Although the Taiping attempt to transform human behavior was prompted by sincere motives, it tended to alienate the majority of the people they were trying to save in their struggle between good and evil. The rebels, many of whom were Hakka, thus remained outsiders. The local people felt threatened by their strange appearance, their incomprehensible dialect, their large-footed women, and their uncut hair. More importantly, the Nanjing residents resented the fact that they had been subjected to comprehensive thought reform and that their accustomed way of life had been severely altered: "Passive resistance to the Taiping was endemic, and flight, spying, and defections to the Qing common."[14] Moreover, as the imperial forces intensified their siege of Nanjing in the early 1860s, the city's economic situation deteriorated very rapidly. One important element in Qing strategy was to cut all supply lines before attempting the concerted final assault. In the end, food supplies reaching the Heavenly Capital were cut to a trickle that could only be slipped in by mule from a few places in Jiangsu province. When the city was about to fall to the Qing forces in the early summer of 1864, the remaining population was in a truly pitiful state. Li Xiucheng, the sole remaining Taiping military commander of some ability, wrote of their plight,

In the capital troubles increased daily; poor people, men and women, crowded in front of the [palace] gates, begging for their lives to be saved. There was neither money nor grain in the state treasury, and state affairs were not in my hands. But seeing so many people in tears and crying bitterly, I had no choice but to distribute the grain stored in my own home to save the poor of the city.[15]

Finally, when this supply had been exhausted, Li begged the Taiping leader, Hong, to let the people leave the city, but the Heavenly King issued an edict, saying, "Everyone in the city should eat manna. This will keep them alive." Regardless whether he had biblical precedent in mind (Exodus 16) or was referring to the customary famine food, consisting of certain roots, grasses, or weeds, there simply was not enough to sustain life in the Taiping capital.[16] Consequently, and against Hong Xiuquan's expressed command, Li enabled some of the starving people to leave Nanjing before it was taken by Qing forces. An estimated 130,000 residents are said to have escaped at this time. Thus, on the eve of the final attack, the city's population had been reduced to some 30,000 from an estimated 900,000 in 1852.

Yet for those who stayed behind, worse was to come. After the Taipings had been defeated, it was the turn of the Qing soldiers to go on a rampage, looting everything they could find and indiscriminately killing the remaining inhabitants. Even Zeng Guofan's secretary, Zhao Liewen, alluded in his diary to the Xiang Army's barbarous conduct after the fall of the Heavenly Capital:

Those old Guangdong and Guangxi rebels who were let down over the city wall from all sides were innumerable. Nine-tenths of the corpses lying on the streets were those of the aged. Little children under two and three years old were also slaughtered for fun and their bodies lay prostrate along the roads. Not a single woman under forty was there.[17]

Qing loyalist troops had abducted not only Taiping women, but also local females living in the outskirts of Nanjing. Most of these captives were subsequently taken to Hunan, the home province of the Xiang Army.

The British vice-consul at the newly opened treaty ports of Zhenjiang, Thomas Adkins, visiting Nanjing on the H.M.S. *Slaney* a day or so after its capture by Qing forces, described "the utter desolation of everything within the walls" in terms that were less than flattering to the Taiping:

I think a ride through the streets of Nankin [*sic*], as they are at present, would satisfy the most ardent advocate of the rebel cause of the dreadful hollowness of the system they support. Some eleven years ago the Taipings took Nankin, then one of the finest cities in China. Ever since its capture it has been their head-quarters. In it the chiefs of the movement built their tawdry houses, and from it they dispatched their plundering bands in all directions. Meanwhile the works of civil government and social organization are entirely neglected, and when the city is retaken is found to be a wilderness of empty houses.[18]

Indeed, the old Nanjing itself was dead.

DAILY LIFE IN SHANGHAI

The exodus of local people from Nanjing and its vicinity had, in fact, begun much earlier. While some had managed to leave the city just before or immediately after the Taiping conquest, others were subsequently expelled by the rebels. Thus the commander of the visiting French warship *Cassini,* François de Plas, remarked as early as December 1853,

That town, once so flourishing, inspired in me a feeling of sadness similar to that which one feels in visiting the ruins of Pompeii. The area enclosed within the fortifications is immense, but I doubt if even one-third is inhabited. The ramparts, still in good condition, encircle hills covered with trees where one sees not a single dwelling.[19]

As a consequence of the frequent military campaigns in the Lower Yangzi region after 1853, tens of thousands of uprooted people from Nanjing and the surrounding districts flooded into the large cities of the Jiangnan area that were not yet directly affected by the conflict. Because of its special status, Shanghai became a particularly attractive place of refuge for rich and poor alike. It had been officially opened as a treaty port under the Treaty of Nanjing of 1842, and soon afterward, the first foreign merchants began to arrive and establish themselves outside the old walled city in what became the American, British, and French "settlements," with clearly defined boundaries. Even during the conflict between the Small Sword Society, in control of the walled city between 1853 and 1855, and Qing imperial forces, life in the foreign settlements was peaceful and comparatively safe. Consequently, large numbers of destitute refugees began to crowd into Shanghai, where they frequented the soup kitchens and hoped to find work as coolie laborers or joined the ranks of an ever-growing beggar army.

During this time of frequent armed conflict, wealthy Chinese merchants sought out foreigners in the settlements to protect them from the depredations of rebels and Qing loyalists alike. During the Small Sword uprising as well as in 1860 and 1862, when Taiping forces threatened to attack the walled city of Shanghai, rich Chinese placed their property and possessions—including wives, children, and concubines—into the hands of foreigners for safekeeping. The British merchant and prominent Quaker Thomas Hanbury reported,

Wealthy Chinese are constantly asking me to help them manage their property, to act for them, become trustee and all manner of things . . . actually the other day the title deeds of no fewer than twenty-six landed properties and estates, houses, warehouses, &c. were put into my hands, the value of them all was just over fifty thousand pounds . . . I have no doubt should an attack occur I should have at least 200 men, women and children congregated around me.[20]

One of the wealthiest men who had fled to the settlement begged Hanbury to buy him a large foreign flag for him to stick up on a bamboo pole at his house. He also wanted the Quaker merchant to hire four foreign sailors to mount guard at his country house near Shanghai "to frighten away bad characters." However, the sailors were to be armed with muskets "but provided with no bullets as he fears they may get tipsy and when in that state so common for sailors here be liable to shoot friends as well as foes." Generally speaking, relations between Chinese and foreigners left much to be desired. As Hanbury commented in a letter to his brother on the behavior of British and French troops in the early 1860s,

There have been some horrible scenes in the surrounding country after the late engagements [between foreign troops and the Taiping], English and French soldiers behaving more like wild beasts or fiends than Christians. They become so demoralised that outrages are getting quite common in our settlement, and some are advocating the proclamation of martial law to restrain them.

Likewise, unscrupulous foreigners continued to sell arms and gunpowder to the rebels "and realize enormous profits and the first houses in the place do not consider it beneath them to buy the silk (ridiculously cheap) that they [the Taipings] have stolen from the unfortunate country people."[21] Indeed, Hanbury's friendly intercourse with the Chinese mercantile community was rather unusual. Unlike the many greedy foreigners, he returned all he had been entrusted with to the rightful Chinese owners after the crisis had passed. In gratitude, they showered him with rich presents and favored him above his business rivals.

DAILY LIFE ALONG THE RIVER

As was the case elsewhere in war-torn China, the destruction of life and property along the lower course of the Yangzi River was extensive. Before the outbreak of the mid-nineteenth-century rebellions, this mighty river, with its many tributaries and artificial waterways, had been dominated by a lively traffic of junks and sampans that facilitated trade in Jiangnan, China's most affluent region, and beyond. As has been noted, the Taipings themselves had raced down the Yangzi from Wuchang to Nanjing in their great armada in 1853. However, Taiping control of the Yangzi provinces and the brutal military contest between the rebels and forces loyal to the Qing Dynasty had a most detrimental effect on communication and people's livelihoods along the river. Moreover, after 1853, the annual grain tribute from the food surplus provinces of central China could no longer be shipped along the Yangzi and Grand Canal to the imperial capital, forcing thousands of destitute boatmen and canal workers into the ranks of the unemployed. Suicide and infanticide became rampant. The waterways in the Lower Yangzi valley made drowning a convenient way for poor families to dispose especially of female babies they could not afford to raise. Innumerable corpses floated along the canals and rivers of this hitherto prosperous region.

The depressing state of affairs along the river near Nanjing was also noted by the British army officer Garnet Wolseley in 1861:

On the banks of the river ... numbers of large, straw-built villages are now to be seen, hastily thrown up by the unfortunate refugees, who endeavour to support life by fishing, or by any other local employment they can obtain. In all such places as we had the opportunity of visiting, the distress and misery of the inhabitants were beyond description. Large families were crowded together into low, small, tent-shaped wigwams, constructed of reeds, through the sides of which the cold wind whistled. ... The denizens were clothed in rags of the most loathsome kind, and huddled together for the sake of warmth. The old looked cast down and unable to work from weakness, whilst that eager expression peculiar to starvation, never to be forgotten by those who have once witnessed it, was visible upon the emaciated features of the little children. With most it was a mere question of how many days longer they might drag on their weary lives; whilst even the very moments of many seemed already numbered.[22]

Yet in every prolonged military conflict, there will be some who seek to profit from the destruction and suffering. Since both the Qing loyalists and the Taipings had established blockades along the Yangzi River and other waterways to prevent vital resources reaching the other side, smuggling was rife from the beginning. Convoys of Chinese junks and barges were clandestinely carrying rice, salt, and other commodities through enemy lines with the expectation of being richly rewarded for their efforts. Since many criminal gangs were involved in the smuggling operations, it quickly became quite literally a cutthroat business. Piracy and murder were commonplace on the river.

The prolonged civil war also created new commercial opportunities and profits for foreign merchants, especially the sale of munitions to the imperial as well as Taiping forces. As early as 1853, the sale of ammunition had become such a lucrative trade that it transformed many a merchant into an adventurer. Both the rebels and the Qing used the British colony of Hong Kong to engage soldiers of fortune and to buy Western weapons and vessels. Thus the Qing official Wu Jianzhang engaged 13 Portuguese lorchas and 4 American and British merchant ships. These vessels were armed with guns and were used to patrol the waterways in the vicinity of Shanghai.

Life on the Yangzi River changed even more dramatically after the opening of the riverine treaty ports of Hankou, Jiujiang, and Zhenjiang in 1861. Now foreign-owned steamships, under foreign protection, dominated the trade along the river up to Hankou and generally were not challenged by either Taiping or Qing authorities. The arrival of foreign mercenaries, modern weapons, and steamships were just as much of a challenge to the old way of life as the revolutionary changes imposed by the Taipings.

There was, however, another, more problematic side to the foreign presence on the Yangzi. In addition to a small number of steamships, the foreign merchant houses in Shanghai operated hundreds of Chinese junks on the great river. Many of these vessels were registered in some foreign consulate, commanded by a single foreigner and flying a foreign flag. Thus equipped, they were running the blockades through the whole territory occupied by the Taipings. Some of the blockade-running was also done in well-armed Chinese houseboats, on board which there were at least two or three foreigners. In addition to carrying treasure, opium, and other valuable cargo, these houseboats also convoyed native junks carrying inland produce down the Yangzi to Shanghai. However, this convoying was a risky business since the Qing officials did not necessarily recognize the treaty rights of foreigners passing through their lines into rebel territory. Moreover, Qing and Taiping authorities were in control of particular sections of the river and had, according to William Mesny, one of the British blockade-runners,

established custom-houses at every creek and township along the river levying duty or black-mail on everything passing up or down. . . . It was therefore rather dangerous work to move about in native boats, as places were captured and recaptured in some cases several times a month, and people going with a cargo for the [Qing] Imperialists sometimes found that they had got amongst the rebels who had driven away the Imperialists just before, or *vice versa*.[23]

The British authorities in China, too, complained that both the government officials and the Taipings were detaining junks flying the British flag and holding them to ransom. In May 1862, for example, Qing officials seized several British junks, including the *Heilongjiang* (called *Neptune* in British official sources), and detained members of the Chinese crew. Thereupon its master, William Mesny, alerted the consular authorities, and a gunboat intervened to take possession of five of the Qing war vessels, holding them until the prisoners were released and compensation had been paid for lost or damaged property.

A few months later, in November 1862, William Mesny was captured by allies of the Taipings, namely "Cantonese" Triads, when his convoy of junks was passing Fushan in rebel-held territory near Zhenjiang. While Mesny was held captive for several months, he was finally released in early 1863 as a result of British consular representations and military pressure.[24]

That the Taipings themselves were keen to maintain friendly relations with foreigners was demonstrated on another occasion, when Adkins went to Nanjing to demand compensation for the plundering of British junks. According to the vice-consul, the issue was immediately settled by the Taiping official:

A lot of silver was then brought in and weighed in our presence. In the course of conversation he [the Taiping official] said that the Rebel soldier who had been foremost in plundering the junks had been arrested by his order and would be beheaded. I protested that no such measure was necessary and begged he would release the poor wretch. I had hardly finished speaking when in swaggered a fellow with arms bare to the shoulder and bearing a reeking sword.

Having announced that the decapitation had taken place, the executioner "strode out of the room, the drops of blood dripping from his sword as he moved."[25]

Although it can be argued that both the government officials and Taiping authorities were endeavoring to deny the other side vital resources, it is also clear that many of the foreigners were using their privileged status under the treaties to engage in all manner of nefarious activities. While some junks flew foreign national flags, others used different means to confuse the Chinese authorities. Thus Edward Franklin, commander of the H.M.S. *Banterer,* wrote to his superior in June 1862:

I beg to inform you that a system of British Junks and Lorchas conveying Native Junks, by allowing them to hoist their House Flag, is obtaining in the River. The Junks under convoy are generally laden with Salt, and by means of the House Flag and being closely followed by the convoying Lorcha under British Colors, and flying the same House Flag, escape detention and duties at the Rebel Custom Houses, and I imagine often by the same means, evade the Imperial Custom Houses, who by the House Flag would would [sic] often suppose them British owned.[26]

It was these "foreign scoundrels," sometimes the perpetrators and sometimes the victims of piracy and murder, that infuriated the British vice-consul Thomas Adkins. From his temporary quarters at Silver Island near Zhenjiang as well as during his occasional trips in British naval vessels to Taiping-held Nanjing, Adkins had an excellent opportunity to observe the darker side of life on the river.

Smuggling operations gave certain individuals favorable opportunities for making a great deal of money in a very short time by running cargoes of arms, ammunition, salt, and rice to Nanjing and other places. However, the risks were equally great since the river was infested with daring Chinese and foreign pirates, whose craft were not distinguishable from other Chinese vessels. In his capacity as British consul Adkins investigated several incidents of plunder and murder on the river. In one particularly gruesome case the Cantonese crew of a foreign boat had killed the American master, his Chinese wife, and infant child and run off with a large sum of money. On another occasion, during a visit to Nanjing, Adkins met an American

who related with great glee the dealings he had had with the Rebels, in arms and other things. . . . He said he had made so much money that after one more trip he should sell his boat and return to New York where—he said—"I shall live like a gentleman". This morning, however, a friend of his came to me and produced a waistcoat and a pair of boots all soaked in blood. . . . I have no doubt that the unliked fellow has had his throat cut and that his ill gotten gains have been taken from him.[27]

The presence of foreign adventurers not only made the river a more dangerous place for ordinary people, it also impeded the suppression of the Taiping rebels by the Qing loyalists. Thus Zeng Guofan, trying to implement his strategy of cutting all supply lines to Nanjing, complained in 1863 that foreign smugglers were continuing to ply the Yangzi, bringing food and ammunition to the besieged Taipings. He memorialized the Throne to request the British and French ministers in Beijing to restrict all foreign commerce with Nanjing until after the recovery of the city by imperial forces. Although the diplomats eventually did agree to an embargo, the lawlessness on the Yangzi River subsided only after the Taipings had been defeated.

DAILY LIFE IN RURAL CHINA

Generally speaking, Taiping control was less pervasive in the villages of central China than in the cities. Consequently, the peasant utopia of the Heavenly Kingdom was not established. Yet there were advantages to be had for the peasants during the early years of the rebellion for Taiping taxes were lower than those of the Qing. Furthermore, many of the landlords had fled before the advancing rebels, thereby lessening the burden on the tenants since rents were not collected. At this time, Shi Dakai, one of the prominent leaders of the early Taiping movement, acquired a reputation as an outstanding military commander and administrator during his campaigns in Jiangxi and Anhui. In this connection a Chinese bookseller described the Taiping occupation of his hometown of Fuzhou (Jiangxi) on March 28, 1856:

They afterwards sent recruiting parties through the towns and villages with banners. . . . A volunteer corps of nearly 10,000 was speedily raised, who besides food and clothing received each a hundred cash per diem. Civil officers were appointed in the departmental and district cities. . . . The local gentry were invited to cooperate, and some of them promoted to offices of trust, while many of the scholars were furnished with employment as literary auxiliaries. . . . The latter [Taipings] had gained the good will of the people by reducing the rate of taxation one half, by prohibiting their adherents killing cattle employed in agriculture, and by inflicting summary punishment on such as were guilty of violence. The Imperialists [of the Qing], on the contrary, indulged in the most unbridled licence, killing the cattle of the country people, carrying off their wives and daughters, and extorting contributions from the moneyed gentry.[28]

However, by the time the above account was published, the Taiping movement was about to lose one of its ablest leaders, as a result of the bloody fratricidal strife amongst the leadership at Nanjing in 1856. In late May 1857, Shi Dakai defected with his whole army, said to have numbered 200,000 men. In the following years he led his troops across the provinces of Jiangxi, Hunan, Guangxi, Guizhou, and Sichuan, where he was captured and executed in 1863. Following the leadership crisis of 1856, the Taiping movement abandoned the radical restructuring of rural society as outlined in *The Land System of the Heavenly Dynasty.* Unable to govern the vast countryside directly, the rebels had to rely on the administrative services of local residents. As a consequence, there were certain continuities between local society under the Qing and local society under the Heavenly Kingdom. Nevertheless, even during the late Taiping years, changes occurred in the countryside that tended to benefit the peasantry more than the traditional local elite. Thus when the Taipings brought the affluent districts of eastern Jiangnan under their administration in 1860, the ensuing rent resistance movements weakened the position of landlords. Moreover, the Taipings introduced rent reductions and new tax arrangements in some places that lessened the burden of ordinary rural folk.

While the economic situation may have improved somewhat for the peasantry in some parts of Taiping-occupied Jiangnan, the common people were by no means ready to welcome the rebels. Powerful rumors alleging their rapaciousness and many evil ways had preceded them. As the case of Bao Lisheng's Righteous Army of Dongan shows, simple villagers, too, were deeply concerned about the calamitous changes the rebels might impose on their daily lives, especially with regard to their folk religious beliefs. When the Taipings invaded Shaoxing prefecture in Zhejiang province in 1861, Bao Lisheng, a simple laborer, deplored their uncompromising anti-Buddhist stance. In his call to arms in defense of local interests, Bao stressed the Taipings' cruelty and wanton destructiveness. His cause was aided by the influx into his native village of Baocun of thousands of refugees fleeing ahead of the advancing Heavenly Army. Since Bao had made a name for himself as an accomplished martial arts master, the refugees did not come merely to seek shelter, but they were also convinced of his supernatural powers. Having withstood the attacks by an overwhelming rebel force for several months, Baocun finally fell at the end of July 1862. But as James Cole has pointed out, "the village could never have held out against the Taiping siege for as long as it did had not the Taiping troops themselves believed in Lisheng's supernatural powers."[29]

As the contrasting accounts from Jiangnan indicate, a rather complex situation existed in the Taiping-held countryside. Moreover, as the military situation became ever more desperate in the early 1860s, Taiping military discipline began to break down. In the face of increasing military pressures and dwindling resources, a number of Taiping contingents were sent on long-distance foraging expeditions to secure food, supplies, and recruits for the huge rebel armies. These exactions proved rather harmful to local populations since the military code of conduct of the early Taiping years had by now been abandoned. But at the same time, as the opposing military armies increased in size and their demands grew correspondingly, the rural situation deteriorated alarmingly.

It was, however, in areas directly affected by military conflict where the most destructive changes to daily routines were observed. It is, perhaps, not surprising that Qing government sources generally blamed the Taipings for the increasing hardships among the people. By the early 1860s, most foreign missionaries, too, were blaming the rebels for the "ruinous condition" of the places held by them. As one missionary reported,

One who knows China well, and lately traversed some of the districts they [the Taipings] have occupied for the longest time, describes them to me as a picture of the most lamentable desolation. Whole districts, formerly covered with agriculture, and studded with busy towns and villages, are now deserted, their towns being in ruins, and their fields growing into wilds to be occupied by wolves instead of men. They utterly overlook the importance of rule and protection, coarse and uneducated men are their appointed kings, and their business is that of robbers and murderers.[30]

There is no doubt that during the last phase of the rebellion, desperate Taiping soldiers increasingly used extreme violence to obtain food, captives, or valuables. With regard to the cruelties visited upon the rural dwellers, the British naval officer Lindesay Brine noted that "the imperialists have proved themselves equally to blame, and it would require a delicate balance to show to which side was attached the greater sum of barbarity."[31] Indeed, some Chinese historians have argued that the commander of the loyalist Xiang Army, Zeng Guofan, the chief architect of the Taipings' downfall, pursued a deliberate scorched-earth policy to deny the Taipings vital supplies: "There is evidence that . . . the process of suppression was the most destructive part of the Rebellion."[32] Zeng himself had written, "When the rebels campaign in regions bereft of people, they are like fish in places where there is not water; when they occupy land where there is no [longer any] cultivation, they are like birds on a treeless mountain."[33] As a consequence of the violence and rapacity of the soldiery, a great number of rural inhabitants in western Jiangsu province either died of war, hunger, and epidemics or left for relatively safe places. The commander of the loyalist Huai Army, Li Hongzhang, reported immediately after he had cleared out a rebel force in one region that he "surveyed an area of up to one hundred and several tens of *li* along the way. Villages and towns were destroyed and the cultivated land all lay waste. White skeletons lay on the thorns. There are definitely no residents."[34] It was not until several years after the Taiping Rebellion had been suppressed that the western part of Jiangsu province was resettled by numerous immigrants.

THE NIAN REBELLION

Until now, this chapter has considered the impact of the Taiping Rebellion on people's lives in China's most affluent region, that is, Nanjing and the surrounding area south of the Yangzi River, usually referred to as Jiangnan. The Nian (or Nien) Rebellion in northern China was a rather different affair from the Heavenly Kingdom of Great Peace and affected people's daily lives in different ways. The Taiping were primarily interested in occupying and holding cities; the Nian were and remained a rural phenomenon. Whereas the Taiping were seeking to control people's lives by introducing communitarian social structures and remolding their thoughts and behavior, the Nian had no comprehensive ideological program. They and the rural dwellers at large, living and operating in the highly insecure natural environment on the North China Plain, were primarily concerned with basic survival. Sparse and irregular precipitation impairs soil fertility and reduces crop yields in north China. Yet under this erratic precipitation regime, droughts were even more prevalent and harmful than floods.

How did the local inhabitants respond to the crisis created by natural calamities and famine? More specifically, what is the relationship between disaster-prone environments and collective violence? Elizabeth Perry argues, in her study of mass action violence, that "repeated ravages of floods and drought created a difficult and insecure milieu in which aggressive survival strategies flourished."[35] In such areas, violence was part of the local culture, and people were accustomed to acquiring resources by force, as bandits, as salt smugglers, or in communal feuds.

Between 1853 and 1862, famine occurred almost every year. The peasants, on the verge of starvation, were in despair because of the government's failure to come to their relief. As one old resident of northern Anhui recalled many years later, "During that time, many people died. The corpses were cooked for food. In Mengcheng city, people sold steamed dumplings made of human flesh."[36] In the region north of the Yellow River known as Huaibei, an accumulation of special historical circumstances transformed ordinary civilians into a mass revolutionary force. These circumstances included crippling natural disasters, especially the dramatic change of course of the

Yellow River and its attendant massive dislocations. The problems arising from these disasters were exacerbated by inefficient government and
increased taxes and by the intrusion of the Taiping rebels as well as by the
ambitions of certain bandit chieftains and militia captains. As a first step
in this violent and insecure environment, the Huaibei communities pro-
tected themselves by building earth works *(yuzhai)* around their villages.
These fortified communities provided the Nian with the principal means
to integrate and to consolidate the territories under their control. Subsequently, many small and scattered Nian groups amalgamated into five
large "banners," which provided greater cohesion. Each of the major Nian
banners consisted of numerous smaller banners supported by particular
earth wall communities. Overall leadership over this loose federation of
fortified villages was assumed by Zhang Luoxing, a small landlord and
salt smuggler from northern Anhui. The extent of this Nian nest area can
be gauged from a report by the governor of Anhui province, indicating
that there were at least 2,000 Nian fortresses in the Huaibei area, each with
1,000–3,000 inhabitants.

   However, while the earth walls ensured the Nians' safety, they could
not guard against starvation. Consequently, the rebels periodically went
on plundering expeditions in more distant and still unscathed parts in
Henan, Shandong, and northern Jiangsu for valuable resources, such as
grain, livestock, and human captives. A contemporary account notes that
"usually [the Nian] hoisted flags and massed troops in spring and autumn.
They pillaged near and far areas. Following the wagons heavily loaded
with spoils, [the rebels] feasted and sang on the way home. After the grain
thus collected was consumed, [they] came out again."[37] The Qing authorities may have regarded the Nian as rebels, but impoverished Huaibei
peasants, acting as households, clans, and communities, were primarily
concerned with securing a livelihood in an inhospitable environment by
seizing scarce resources from others. Survival in their home environment
was thus, for most ordinary participants, a more potent motivation than
conscious rebelliousness. A Nian folk song aptly expresses these daily
concerns. It speaks only of famine, flood, starvation, and crippling debt,
and ends with the verse:

> If not for the Nian,
> How could one stand?
> Let's join Old Luo [i.e., Zhang Luoxing] to claim the land.[38]

The young scholar Liu Tang from Henan province, a prisoner in a Nian
village, left the following account of daily life in rebel territory:

Daily meals in the Nien village consisted of lentils or sorghum noodles. Wheat
was never a regular feature of the diet and seldom were there vegetables, with
the exception of an occasional pepper. The land in this particular locale [in northern Anhui] could no longer be farmed and showed few traces of human habitation.

Most households were small, having lost many members to the rampages of bandits and soldiers. The depleted villages then merged, several dozen of them building a common wall in self-defense. Although wild animals were surprisingly abundant, all grain had to be secured from outside. The Nien stole grain on plundering forays, then sold the surplus in their home areas for a very low price. Cash earnings from such a trip were quickly depleted, especially since few banner chiefs could resist frequent trips to market to drink and vie for prestige. In less than a month's time, the money would all be gone and another expedition called together.[39]

During the early years of the rebellion, the Nian succeeded in raiding distant places because of their mastery of cavalry and tactics of elusiveness. Since both horses and men moved as fast as the wind and the rain, the Nian were able not only to launch surprise attacks on targets worth plundering, but also to take evasive action when government forces approached. But as Siang-tseh Chiang has pointed out, "The Nien never fled without purpose. Like mad beasts they kept running until circumstances allowed them to turn back to bite the exhausted hunters."[40] Indeed, employing these tactics in 1865, they managed to trap and destroy a major Qing cavalry force led by the famous Mongolian Prince Senggelinqin, who was killed in the battle.

As has already been noted in connection with the contest between the Taipings and Qing forces, the latter often had a rather more detrimental impact on people's daily lives. The imperial forces sent to suppress the Nian rebels similarly became a major source of rural suffering. Cut off from family ties and required to operate in unfamiliar terrain, the soldiers' behavior was often callous or uncommitted. As one Qing military officer admitted, "Who would have expected that the atrocities of the imperial army would be so much worse than the rebels themselves!" Senggelinqin's cavalry was notoriously corrupt, demanding bribes before they would respond to requests for help. When the people complained of his troops raping and stealing, Senggelinqin is said to have replied, "The soldiers have been away from home for a long time. It's best to make the people move to avoid them."[41]

However, especially after the destruction of the Taiping rebels in 1864, the Qing loyalist armies were in a better position to deal with the Nian problem. This they did in two ways. First, they pursued a policy of "rooting out the nests," i.e., penetrating the fortified communities in the Nian heartland and winning over the people to the imperial cause. In the process the Huaibei peasants revealed their limitations of loyalty to the Nian cause. No longer able to rely on plunder, Huaibei villagers began to experience starvation. In 1863, the people of Mengcheng in northern Anhui were, for example, reduced to eating boiled leather, bark chips, and the pulverized bones of the dead. A pound of human flesh was reported to be selling for a hundred cash. Clearly, for the peasantry, survival was more important than supporting the Nian cause.

At the same time, the Qing commanders employed their troops, who prevented the Nian cavalry from getting back to the nest areas. Unable to return to their home bases after 1865, the remaining rebel forces, in concert with remnant Taipings, began a four-year period as roving bandits in the northern regions. Discipline deteriorated rapidly as the lightning-like cavalry spread its terror to Shandong, Henan, and Shanxi in a bid to obtain resources and evade capture. The devastation resulting from these ever more desperate raids embittered the people in these areas, causing them to transfer their allegiance once more to the reigning dynasty. The Nian movement was further weakened by the absence of an effective centralized command structure. Many subordinate banner leaders went on independent, uncoordinated plundering forays. Individuals and groups frequently changed sides as a result of internal feuding. A good example is the notorious intermittent Nian supporter Miao Peilin, an ambitious and opportunistic militia captain who, by 1859, had gained control over several thousand forts and hundreds of thousands of people in the Huai valley. He subsequently changed sides several times. By the mid-1860s, this loss of Nian unity and the reassertion of Qing power were clear indications that the rebellion was in decline. In 1868, the roving Nian armies were finally destroyed by loyalist forces.

MILITARIZATION OF RURAL SOCIETY

One of the most significant developments in mid-nineteenth-century China was the widespread militarization of the countryside. With the proliferation of rebellious activities throughout much of the empire and the inability of regular imperial government forces to deal with them, ordinary villagers were organized to protect life and property against attacks by other common folk who had joined the insurrectionary forces. When the Taipings invaded Hunan province during their march from Guangxi toward Nanjing, the Qing government authorized the formation of local militia. Since the regular armies proved unable to stop the advancing rebels, some of the Hunan militia units were combined and reorganized into the new regional forces, including Zeng Guofan's Xiang Army. A few years later, Zeng's subordinate Li Hongzhang succeeded in establishing another new force, namely the Huai Army, recruited in the districts lying to the north of the Yangzi, in his home province of Anhui. These regional armies played a decisive role in the eventual defeat of the Taipings and the Nian.

On the North China Plain, the theater of Nian operations, there already existed a culture of violence prior to the rebellions. However, in the face of the Nian's long-distance plundering expeditions, rural militarization proliferated and intensified. Wealthier households outside the Nian areas hired personal vigilantes, and entire villages cooperated in organizing for self-defense. In addition to government-authorized militia, various forms of irregular village and intervillage self-defense were established in many localities. Although ostensibly raised to protect communities from the rebels, the militias were sometimes used to resist a predatory government desperately seeking to increase its revenue. The proliferation of self-defense forces was closely associated with a dramatic rise of tax riots. To complicate matters further, some local militia often engaged in predatory activities themselves, thus blurring the distinction between protectors and predators. But perhaps the most enduring sign of militarization was the construction of earth walls around the thousands of villages in north China. This high degree of militarization remained a characteristic feature in this traditionally insecure region well into the middle of the twentieth century.

CONCLUSION

The two and a half decades after 1850 saw what was probably the greatest wave of popular rebellion in history, and the Taiping Rebellion has been called the greatest civil war. Aside from the Taipings' remarkable attempt to radically change the people's way of life, it was the destruction of life and property that most dramatically affected Chinese society. In addition to the major insurrections considered in this chapter, there were innumerable other revolts in the Qing Empire, mostly involving ethnic minorities or secret societies. Although these insurrections were largely confined to the peripheries of China Proper, the conflicts between Han Chinese and minority peoples, including the Hui (Chinese Muslims), were often rather more bloody affairs, as each side sought to exterminate the other. A total of 50 million people are estimated to have perished from direct or indirect causes of war during the gigantic upheavals that shook the Qing Empire. The experience of death and the much broader phenomenon of fear of death deeply affected the population.

The survivors of the rebellions had to cope with the direct consequences of war. In the cities, public buildings, shops, and many private residences were destroyed, and trade was severely disrupted. In the countryside, mulberry trees, vital to silk production, were cut down, rice terraces were overgrown, and dikes and irrigation ditches were destroyed. As people fled the worst-affected areas, widespread depopulation was the most dramatic result. For decades afterward, people in the most affected parts of the country remained in a nervous and jittery state. Especially in north China, unsettling rumors of impending rebellion could trigger widespread panic among the inhabitants, even during the early decades of the twentieth century. Old village fortifications would be hurriedly repaired. In some areas, peasants sought refuge in long-abandoned hill fortresses. Clearly the memory of those calamitous events of the mid-nineteenth century did not fade easily, even in areas that had not directly experienced the destructiveness of war.

The mid-nineteenth-century rebellions also had an indirect impact on people's lives. For instance, the loss of the Qing state's most important revenue base, namely Jiangnan and the central provinces, to the Taipings meant that additional resources had to be levied more intensively elsewhere. Moreover, the introduction of *lijin* (transit tax on goods) as a new source of revenue hampered trade and made goods more expensive. As far as the Qing Dynasty is concerned, the rebellions changed the relationship between state and society. Amid the devastation of war, local elite activists had assumed responsibility for raising militia forces; setting up charitable organizations, such as burial societies and orphanages; and undertaking relief operations and reconstruction projects. The proliferation of such social organizations beyond government control contributed to the rise of new political forces that later would challenge and eventually topple the imperial dynasty. Indeed, it can be argued that Qing society never fully recovered from the disruptions to daily life caused by the Taiping Rebellion and the other cataclysmic events in China at that time.

NOTES

1. Jonathan D. Spence, *The Search for Modern China,* 2nd ed., New York: W. W. Norton, 1999, p. 173.

2. *Ibid.*, p. 148.

3. *Ibid.*, pp. 170–71.

4. For a comprehensive study of daily life in Nanjing, see the excellent study by John L. Withers II, "The Heavenly Capital: Nanjing under the Taiping, 1853–1864," PhD diss., Yale University, 1983.

5. *Ibid.*, pp. 48–55.

6. Medhurst in the *North-China Herald,* 26 November 1853; reprinted in Prescott Clarke and J. S. Gregory, comps., *Western Reports on the Taiping,* London: Croom Helm, 1982, pp. 89–90.

7. Ono Kazuko, *Chinese Women in a Century of Revolution, 1850–1950,* Stanford, CA: Stanford University Press, 1989, p. 1.

8. *Ibid.*, p. 8.

9. *Ibid.*, p. 11.

10. Augustus F. Lindley, *Ti-Ping Tien-Kwoh: The History of the Ti-Ping Revolution, Including a Narrative of the Author's Personal Adventures,* vol. 1, London: Day, 1866, p. 317.

11. Joseph Edkins, in Jane R. Edkins, *Chinese Scenes and People, with Notices of Christian Missions and Missionary Life in a Series of Letters from Various Parts of China, with Narrative of a Visit to Nanking by Her Husband, The Rev. Joseph Edkins,* London: James Nisbet, 1863, pp. 275–76.

12. Franz Michael, *The Taiping Rebellion,* vol. 2, Seattle: University of Washington Press, 1966, p. 315.

13. Michael, vol. 3, 1971: p. 849.

14. Spence 1999: p. 177.

15. C. A. Curwen, *Taiping Rebel: The Deposition of Li Hsiu-ch'eng,* Cambridge, UK: Cambridge University Press, 1977, p. 150.

16. For Li Xiucheng's account, see Curwen 1977: pp. 145–46, 291, note 92.

17. Zhao Liewen, *Nengjing jushi riji,* 26 July 1864, quoted in Yu-wen Jen [Jian Youwen], *The Taiping Revolutionary Movement,* New Haven, CT: Yale University Press, 1974, p. 531.

18. Thomas Adkins, dispatch dated 29 July 1864, extracts in *The London Gazette,* 30 September 1864.

19. Quoted in Spence 1999: pp. 203–4.

20. Quoted in Maura Muratorio and Grace Kiernan, *Thomas Hanbury and His Garden,* Albenga, Italy: Bacchetta Editore, 1992, p. 55.

21. Quotes in the previous paragraphs from Thomas Hanbury to Daniel Hanbury, letters dated 26 June 1860, 21 November 1860, and 29 May 1862, in Hanbury Papers (privately held).

22. Garnet J. Wolseley, *Narrative of the War with China in 1860 to Which Is Added the Account of a Short Residence with the Taiping Rebels at Nanking and a Voyage from Thence to Hankow,* London: Green, 1862, pp. 350–51.

23. William Mesny, "The Life and Adventures of a British Pioneer," in *Mesny's Chinese Miscellany,* vol. 1, Shanghai, 1895, p. 43.

24. For further details concerning Mesny's adventurous career on the Yangzi River and elsewhere in China, including his Taiping captivity, see Mesny, vols. 1–2, 1895–1896.

25. Thomas Adkins letter to his father, 16 February 1863, Adkins Family Papers, Warwickshire County Record Office, England.

26. Franklin to S. O. Shanghai, H.M.S. *Banterer,* Nanjing, 4 June 1862, Public Record Office, Kew, ADM 125/104, f. 171.

27. Adkins to his father, Zhenjiang, 2 March 1863, in Adkins Papers (privately held). Used with permission of the copyright holder, Mr. Theo Christophers.

28. As reported by the American Presbyterian missionary W.A.P. Martin in the *North-China Herald,* 4 October 1856.

29. James H. Cole, *The People versus the Taipings: Bao Lisheng's "Righteous Army of Dongan,"* Berkeley: Center for Chinese Studies, University of California, 1981, p. 45.

30. Letter dated 29 November 1861, in *The Watchman,* 15 January 1862, p. 21.

31. Lindesay Brine, *The Taeping Rebellion in China,* London: John Murray, 1862, pp. 272–73.

32. Curwen 1977: p. 275, note 18.

33. *Ibid.*

34. Quoted in Yeh-chien Wang, "The Impact of the Taiping Rebellion on Population in Southern Kiangsu," *Papers on China* 19, 1965, p. 128.

35. Elizabeth J. Perry, *Rebels and Revolutionaries in North China, 1845–1945,* Stanford, CA: Stanford University Press, 1980, p. 3.

36. Elizabeth J. Perry, ed., *Chinese Perspectives on the Nien Rebellion,* Armonk, NY: M. E. Sharpe, 1981, p. 41.

37. Quoted in Siang-tse Chiang, *The Nien Rebellion,* Seattle: University of Washington Press, 1954, p. 601.

38. Perry 1980: p. 140.

39. *Ibid.,* p. 136, summarizing Liu Tang's account.

40. Siang-tseh Chiang, *The Nien Rebellion,* Seattle: University of Washington Press, 1954, p. 72.

41. Quoted in Perry 1980: pp. 123, 124.

SELECTED BIBLIOGRAPHY

Bernhardt, Kathryn. "Elite and Peasant during the Taiping Occupation of the Jiangnan, 1860–1864." *Modern China* 13 (1987): 379–410.

>The author examines the complex reality of life in the countryside in the Jiangnan region (i.e., that part of Jiangsu province lying south of the Yangzi River but including the northern districts of Zhejiang province), which had been added to the Taiping realm in 1860.

Chiang, Siang-tseh. *The Nien Rebellion.* Seattle: University of Washington Press, 1954.

>This work contains many useful insights and comments on life in the area controlled or affected by the Nian.

Clarke, Prescott, and J. S. Gregory, comps. *Western Reports on the Taiping.* London: Croom Helm, 1982.

>A comprehensive collection of Western reports and observations on the Taipings, culled from a wide variety of published and unpublished sources.

Curwen, C. A. *Taiping Rebel: The Deposition of Li Hsiu-ch'eng.* Cambridge, UK: Cambridge University Press, 1977.

>The confessions of the Taiping general Li Xiucheng, written in captivity while awaiting execution, describe the Taiping movement in considerable detail. Curwen's copious annotations provide further glimpses of life under the Taipings.

Jen, Yu-wen [Jian Youwen]. *The Taiping Revolutionary Movement.* New Haven, CT: Yale University Press, 1974.

>Jian Youwen was among the first Chinese scholars to take an interest in the Taiping Rebellion. Based on his more voluminous Chinese language publications, the above work is a detailed account of the rise and fall of the Taipings. In particular, it provides helpful information on the major military campaigns and the many individual battles.

Lin-le [Augustus F. Lindley]. *Ti-Ping Tien-Kwoh: The History of the Ti-Ping Revolution, Including a Narrative of the Author's Personal Adventures.* 2 vols. London: Day, 1866. Reprinted in 1970 in one volume.

>The English mercenary Lindley was employed by the Taipings. His observations provide a vivid picture of life in the Heavenly Kingdom of Great Peace.

Michael, Franz. *The Taiping Rebellion.* 3 vols. Seattle: University of Washington Press, 1966–1971.

>This comprehensive collection of Taiping documents, translated into English, affords the reader access to official Taiping writings.

Ono, Kazuko. "Women Who Took to Battle Dress." Chap. 1 in *Chinese Women in a Century of Revolution, 1850–1950.* Stanford, CA: Stanford University Press, 1989.

>Brief though it is, Ono's chapter is the only study of women in the Heavenly Kingdom of Great Peace.

Perry, Elizabeth J. *Rebels and Revolutionaries in North China 1845–1945.* Stanford, CA: Stanford University Press, 1980.

>Perry presents a convincing theoretical framework that explains why collective violence is a persistent feature in certain environments. Chapter 4

deals more specifically with the Nian. It is the most authoritative work on this rebellion.

Spence, Jonathan. *God's Chinese Son: The Taiping Heavenly Kingdom of Hong Xiuquan.* New York: W. W. Norton, 1996.

A well-written history of the Taiping rebellion, with particular emphasis on the peculiar religious ideas of Hong Xiuquan, leader of the movement.

Withers, John L., II. "The Heavenly Capital: Nanjing under the Taiping, 1853–1864." PhD diss., Yale University, 1983.

This unpublished work is especially useful because it focuses solely on life in Nanjing during the Taiping occupation and is largely based on Chinese sources, including translated extracts from the private writings of contemporary Nanjing residents.

TWO

Life in a War of Independence: The Philippine Revolution, 1896–1902

Bernardita Reyes Churchill

Modern anticolonial nationalism in Asia may be said to have emerged first in the Philippines, initially in the call for reforms in the 1880s, later in revolution against Spanish rule in 1896, and finally, in resistance to the U.S. invasion. This was the first nationalist revolution in the region. A revolution, however, takes time to develop. Unlike the usual narrow definition of war, in which there is a moment when battle starts and armies clash, a revolutionary conflict may only gradually become visible, emerging from behind years of sporadic violence and repression, with only the actual declaration of revolution being obvious. The emergence of this first nationalist revolution in Asia was, in a sense, a three-century process, beginning with the first comprehensive and unifying colonialism in Asia. Spanish objectives in this island territory were not primarily trade or plunder, but Christianization and hispanicization. True hispanicization was thwarted by Spaniards in the Philippines, but Spain, through persuasion and coercion, created in most of the Philippines a Catholic society with attendant Hispanic elements. Just as frustrated demands for equality and justice eventually produced the American Revolution from a fractious group of colonies ("no taxation without representation"), so, too, did the Philippine Revolution emerge from frustrated demands for equal access to Spanish rights and privileges.

The long road to becoming Filipinas, a Filipino nation, owes much to Spanish rule. Long before the sixteenth century, the earliest inhabitants of the islands had developed a village, or *barangay*, culture, which

The Philippines. (David S. Heidler.)

spread across the archipelago, enriched by contacts with Chinese traders and sojourners, Muslim Arab merchants, and neighbors in the region.
Spain, with the use of little military force and aided by friar missionaries,
gathered the scattered village communities, organized them into com-
pact towns, or *pueblos*, and gave them to the charge of native town heads.
This process of forced resettlement was called *reducción*, which the native
inhabitants, or *indios*, never completely accepted. In later times, settlements were allowed outside the town center so long as they were *"bajo de
las campanas"*—within hearing distance of the church bells. Larger units
of provinces were established under Spanish governors. In 1565, Filipinas
became the newest kingdom in the Spanish empire, with its capital established in 1571 in the city of Manila, or *Intramuros* (Within the Walls). Here

resided only Spaniards—administrative and ecclesiastical authorities. The former native residents were resettled elsewhere, in what became known as *Bagumbayan*, or "New Town."

The conversion efforts of friar missionaries provided the *indios* with a common religion, with Christianity forming a bond of unity and experience among lowland and coastal Filipinos who came under Spanish rule. This was not the case with the communities in the interior, in the mountains of northern Luzon, and elsewhere in the various islands. It also clearly was not the case with the Muslims (called *Moros*) of Mindanao and Sulu, who resisted Spanish attempts at Christianization and hispanicization.

The lowland and coastal peoples of Luzon and the Visayas, in the main, endured Spanish rule. There were, however, numerous revolts and other forms of everyday resistance marking the entire period. Although Madrid's Laws of the Indies and numerous royal decrees provided for the just and humane treatment of the *indios*, the Spanish colonial administration and the clergy frequently violated these in principle and in practice. Nevertheless, as Christianization and some level of hispanicization took place, there occurred also what may be called a counterprocess of accommodation (including racial), or the filipinization of Spanish culture. This involved a reinterpretation of Spanish institutions to local traditions and values, creating a uniquely Filipino culture.[1]

A major distinction between the Philippines and other Spanish colonies is that with the exception of a very small minority, Filipinos do not speak Spanish. Colonial officials ignored the royal decrees to spread the Spanish tongue, and Christianization was done with the friar missionaries learning the local languages. However, many Spanish words have been incorporated into the Philippine languages, and a great majority of Filipinos use Spanish surnames.

GROWTH OF A REVOLUTIONARY SOCIETY[2]

Spanish rule of over three centuries (from 1565 to 1898) can be characterized in the main as both inept and oppressive, with the islands almost constantly in financial bankruptcy and the *indios* subjected to outright exploitation and abuse by the civil and religious administration. However, there were major social and economic changes from the mid-nineteenth century.

The demise of Spain's local authority began with the loss of its colonies in the Americas. In the Philippines, the end, in 1815, of 250 years of the galleon trade between Manila and Acapulco largely terminated Spanish control of Philippine trade. Non-Spanish entrepreneurs began arriving with capital and technology. In response, an agricultural export economy developed, providing new economic opportunities for many people, especially the *mestizo* (Filipinos of mixed Spanish or Chinese parentage).

From 1834, Manila, and later, other ports, such as Iloilo and Cebu, were fully opened to foreign trade. Foreign merchants were officially allowed to reside in the Philippines, and their presence greatly changed life in the colony. Accordingly, the nineteenth century became a period of economic progress and change. At the same time, however, Spain's loss of her Spanish American colonies and fear of a similar outcome in the Philippines led to the intensification of autocratic rule manifested through greater friar dominance of practically every aspect of Filipino society.

One of the most important of all social changes in the Philippines at the time was the emergence of a new class of progressive provincial elite or gentry. Collectively, they are known as the *principalía*. They were *indios* and Chinese *mestizos* from pueblo families who had prospered from the economic opportunities accompanying the rise of commercial agriculture (in rice, sugar, tobacco, coffee, hemp, or abaca). They were based mainly in the provincial towns in Luzon and the Visayas. From among the *principalía* would come two major groups: the native secular clergy, demanding filipinization of church parishes, and the leaders, first of a reform effort known as the Propaganda Movement, and later of the revolution.

MANILA ON THE EVE OF THE REVOLUTION[3]

Life in Manila, the seat of colonial power, was profoundly changed by the prosperity brought by commercial agriculture and foreign trade. This was also the case, to some extent, in other urban centers, like Iloilo and Cebu. The heart of Spanish Philippines was Intramuros, the Walled City, constructed like a medieval town, encircled by water, and with a moat and drawbridges. Here stood the government offices, churches (seven, including Manila Cathedral), convents, and the principal educational institutions in the colony; these included schools for primary and secondary education for Spanish children and those of Filipino families with means and influence and the Royal and Pontifical University of Santo Tomás. Calle Real was the main street. In the nineteenth century, however, Intramuros was seen as a lifeless city, somber, monastic, and mostly with narrow streets all at right angles to each other. It was home only to Spaniards, residing in large and roomy houses made of stone and wood, roofed with tiles, later with corrugated iron.

Throughout most of the Spanish period, secondary and tertiary education was almost exclusively for Spaniards. It was not until the 1863 Educational Decree that Filipinos had the right to a university education, if they could afford it (previously, some had obtained higher education by entering the priesthood and studying in diocesan seminaries established for the training of secular priests). The decree also provided for a system of compulsory primary education in the villages, replacing the parochial schools that had provided rudimentary education, heavily religious in content, for *indio* children.

Education in the Philippines was under the almost exclusive control of the church. In Intramuros, the Jesuit-run Ateneo Municipal de Manila (1859) was considered the finest school. The largest of the secondary schools was San Juan de Letrán, run by the Dominicans. The University of Santo Tomás offered degrees in law, theology, medicine, and pharmacy. There were also professional schools—an arts school of design and paint-ing, a nautical school, and a school of commerce that also taught French and English. There were several *colegios* for young Spanish girls and an Escuela Municipal de Niñas (1864) for the training of women teachers. The Escuela Normal de Maestros (1863) for schoolmasters was run by the Jesuits.

Outside Intramuros were the suburbs that constituted the Provincia de Manila. These housed the foreign expatriates, affluent Filipinos and *mestizos,* and the masses. The well-to-do lived in big and beautiful houses made of adobe and first-class lumber. The common people's huts were made of light materials—bamboo or wood—and were roofed with thatch. The districts of Tondo, Trozo, San Nicolas, and Sampaloc were the poorest and most densely populated.

Crisscrossing Manila were 35 estuaries covering 21 kilometers (Manila was sometimes called "another Venice"). Native riverboats were the major means of transporting people, goods, and merchandise. However, foreign residents often complained that the estuaries were simply open sewers that posed a menace to public health.

In 1896, the population of the Province of Manila (Intramuros and 28 municipalities) was estimated at 340,000, with the *peninsulares* (Spaniards born in the Iberian Peninsula), *insulares* or *creoles* (Spaniards born in Filipinas), Spanish *mestizos,* and foreigners accounting for 3.1 percent of that number. Intramuros itself had a total population of 16,000, consisting of *peninsulares, insulares,* Spanish *mestizos,* and a few *indio* servants. The leading residents included friars, nuns, government officials, and soldiers.

Outside Intramuros, Manila was changing, with amenities equal to other foreign capitals. After the loss of colonies in the Americas and the open-ing of the Suez Canal in 1869, more Spaniards came to the Philippines, especially those from the military and the friar orders. There also came many other foreigners, including British, Americans, Germans, French, and Chinese, who settled not only in Manila, but also in the provinces. They engaged in trade, with a few marrying Filipino women and setting up families. The prosperity of the mid-nineteenth century led to an unprec-edented surge in population.

This period also saw the arrival of modern communications: a telegraph cable linking Manila to Hong Kong and Singapore, a telephone system in Manila and, eventually, in Iloilo, and overseas mail every two weeks. Elec-tric lighting replaced gas lamps in some parts of Manila, a piped water system provided safer drinking water for residents of the capital, horse drawn and steam tramways in Manila made for more convenient travel, and a railway facilitated movement across central Luzon. Interisland shipping and regular steamship service between Manila and the rest of the archipelago, and between Manila and Europe, also eased and liberalized travel.

The most exciting place in Manila at that time was Binondo, the business district, founded as a Chinese town in 1594. Under the ministry of Dominican friars, it eventually became a community of married Catholic Chinese and their *mestizo* descendants. Calle Escolta was the most prestigious shopping street, with all of the establishments European and American owned. Here one could find the best restaurant—the Restaurant de Paris—at which, after a dinner served in the "European style," one could enjoy the best Manila cigars produced by La Insular or La Flor de la Isabela, reputedly on a par with the Havana.

Binondo was the Fifth Avenue of Manila—an emporium where one could find luxuries from Europe and the Americas, including expensive perfumes and soaps, hats, watches, leather goods, and silverware. Anything and everything could be found here: banks, trading houses, commercial and shipping agents, retail and wholesale stores, warehouses and factories (for cooking oil, chocolates, soaps), theaters and restaurants, and hotels and inns as well as German and British drugstores or Chinese apothecaries. All classes of people came to shop or transact business in Binondo.

Manila had a wide variety of trades and crafts. The Chinese were mainly artisans and merchants who monopolized the wholesale and retail trade

Escolta, business district of Manila.

as well as the industrial life of the colony. Craftsmen among the *indios* and *mestizos* included skilled water colorists, bookbinders, engravers, silversmiths, saddlers, and pharmacists. Women of the poorer classes worked in dressmaking, embroidery, cigar and cigarette making, and midwifery. They were also market vendors selling betel nut, mangoes and other fruits, vegetables, meat, and fish. Men gathered and sold *nipa* palm for roofing material, manufactured bricks and tiles, drove carriages, or were boatmen on the Pasig River. Men, rather than women, worked as domestic servants for wealthy Spaniards and foreigners, who employed them as *mayordomos* (principal servants), cooks, gardeners, coachmen, or houseboys.

There were theaters for all classes of people, presenting musical dramas *(zarzuela)* and metrical romances *(comedia)*, *moro-moro* (plays depicting love and war between Christians and Muslims), and *comedia chinica* for the Chinese. There were also small neighborhood suburban theaters and seasonal open-air theaters, especially during town fiestas and church festivals. However, the most popular sport with Filipinos was cockfighting; this was allowed on Sundays and fiesta days. In the 1880s, the cockpits were convenient venues for news and rumors about the regime and meeting places for secret plots and conspiracies.

In Manila, a special weekly treat during the dry season from January was the concerts performed by native soldiers under the baton of a Spanish conductor. The stage was at the Luneta and attracted audiences of hundreds of people from all classes. Located south of the city walls, Luneta at that time was a carriage road and promenade around an oval of elevated ground. It was one of the best places to view the famous Manila sunset.

Music and dance accompanied almost any occasion in the Philippines. These ranged from grand balls for the Spaniards and in the clubs of the foreign community to an intimate dance of perhaps two couples in the small native huts. Orchestras and bands were indispensable at official functions and festive occasions and later played a major role during the revolution in boosting the spirit of the *revolucionarios.*

LIVING UNDER REPRESSION

From the mid-nineteenth century the situation in the Philippines was increasingly volatile. The new middle class of the *principalía* was discovering a sense of anticolonial nationalism and, to demonstrate a sense of equality with the Spanish, began appropriating the name *Filipino,* a term previously used only for Philippine-born Spaniards.

In response to a growing sense of insecurity, the Guardia Civil (a provincial police corps composed of *indio* guards with Spanish officers) was organized in 1868. This was to suppress the rising banditry and rebellion, but the Guardia were brutal in their methods and only stirred up more resentment of the authorities. Civil protests included Filipino students demanding revision of the outdated university curriculum; Filipino liberals and secular priests calling for political and parish reforms; as well as peasant unrest, often inspired by some messianic or millenarian belief.

The insecurity of the colonial administration was heightened by the small size of its military forces, with a Filipino component of questionable loyalty. Corruption in the government, including among Filipino local officials, was prevalent. Added to this were the occasional rice shortages, cholera outbreaks, and natural disasters. The government's treasury was empty, and there was no continuity in the implementation of policies due to the short-term postings and frequent changes of officials.[4]

The moment at which the civilian population and the colonial government began heading for conflict may be dated to February 17, 1872. On that day, three Filipino secular priests, identified as leaders in the movement for the filipinization of Philippine parishes, were executed publicly by strangulation *(garrote)* in Bagumbayan. This was for their supposed complicity in a mutiny of about 200 Filipino soldiers and workers on January 20 at Fort San Felipe in Cavite, a province south of Manila. Led by corporals and sergeants, they were protesting reduction of their wages and their displacement by Spanish artillerymen and Spanish workers, who were given higher wages. The mutiny was actually no more than local discontent with a reactionary new administration—it was easily suppressed, and those involved were punished severely.

However, the Spanish authorities overreacted. What followed was a reign of terror. Some 120 persons were arrested, among them priests, lawyers, and several traders, all of them *mestizo* and all educated and wealthy. They were subjected to court-martial proceedings that lasted for months and then sentenced to long prison terms or banished to exile. The reign of terror reportedly sent anxious residents of Manila and Cavite fleeing to safe places.

The three secular priests were José Burgos, Jacinto Zamora, and Mariano Gomes. They had been marked as *filibusteros* (subversives) because of their antifriar sentiments and were now accused of being leaders of a conspiracy to establish an independent republic. They were tried in a secret court-martial and sentenced to death within two days of the sentence being announced, unusually fast in the slow-moving Spanish bureaucracy of the time.

The execution of the three priests was witnessed by a crowd estimated at 40,000, some coming to Manila not just from Cavite, but also from other nearby provinces. As early as two days before the execution, they assembled in Bagumbuyan, henceforth to be remembered as "the killing field" for rebels and martyrs. They wore mourning black and fell in absolute silence at the sight of the three priests being led to their deaths. At the moment of the execution of Fr. Burgos, the last of the three priests to be executed, the crowd fell to its knees and in chorus recited the Litany for the Dying. Such a demonstration reportedly unnerved the Spaniards in the crowd, who immediately fled in terror behind the walls of Intramuros.

Spanish action turned a mutiny of limited local significance into a national movement for change. Besides profound sorrow for the victims, there emerged profound hatred for the friars and the regime. This extended to the future leaders, first of reform, and later, of revolution— José Rizal, Marcelo H. del Pilar, Apolinario Mabini, and Emilio Aguinaldo. The acronym from the names of the priests, *Gomburza*, was a password of the secret revolutionary society Katipunan and a battle cry in the Revolution of 1896.[5]

After 1872, there were no more open revolts for two decades, but this was misleading. During these years, peace and order deteriorated. There were constant disturbances, for example, in the Laguna de Bay area in southern Luzon, where bandit gangs operated. Martial law was declared in Cavite and Pampanga due to the depredations of gangs hiding in mountain and forest. Banned religious sects also became stronger among peasant communities in the relatively inaccessible mountainous and forest areas. They would later participate in the revolution.[6]

The Spanish regime embarked on weeding out "dangerous" elements. Persons identified as *filibusteros* were denounced by the friars, and outspoken reformists were ordered into exile; they were sent to remote areas in the archipelago (this was referred to as "enforced change of domicile" in Palawan, Sulu, and Mindanao) and even to far-off Spanish territories outside the Philippines, such as the Marianas, Spanish America, and Africa. Filipino life would come even more under the pervasive domination of the friars, now seen as the most potent instrument of state power.

THE CAMPAIGN FOR REFORMS: THE PROPAGANDA MOVEMENT[7]

In the 1880s and 1890s, a campaign for reforms was conducted by Filipino *ilustrados*. They were active mainly in Europe—Spain, France, England, Germany, and Switzerland—but also in the Philippines and, to a lesser extent, in Singapore, Hong Kong, and Japan. These men had first sought education in Manila after university education was opened to Filipinos in 1863, and then in Europe, where the political climate was not as oppressive as at home. They worked with sympathetic Spanish liberals, including Freemasons, who also welcomed them to their secret society. The aim of this movement was to propagandize the dismal conditions of autocratic rule in the Philippines, especially the anomalous friar domination. The propagandists hoped that they could work, through peaceful means, for changes in the social, political, and economic life of the Filipinos.

The mouthpiece of the propagandists was the fortnightly *La Solidaridad*, which published articles exposing the conditions in the Philippines. The *Sol*, as it was known, circulated freely in Europe. However, in the Philippines, no publication could be released or circulated without the approval of a censorship commission. Thus copies of the *Sol* had to be smuggled into Manila from Hong Kong by passengers and crew of incoming ships. Those identified with the publication or caught in possession of the newspaper and other antigovernment or antifriar materials faced possible deportation. Under these circumstances, the *Sol* was limited mainly to the few reformers who secretly supported the expatriate movement in Spain with funds collected among fellow sympathizers in Manila. Even had more copies been smuggled in, because the articles were in Spanish, few could have read them. Despite progress in public instruction after 1863, only a tiny number of men and women in the Philippines could speak and read Spanish.

Civilians in the capital nevertheless could, if they looked and listened in the right places, see an anticolonial movement in development. In Manila, there was an underground press that distributed *libritos* (booklets) among the people, some written in Tagalog, mostly antifriar in content. These materials were printed to resemble the friar booklets and so could be distributed in public without the knowledge of the authorities.

At the level of the official media, however, daily life seemed relatively undisturbed. The authorities ensured that many news stories were kept out of print. Manila had five dailies—in the mornings, *El Diario de Manila* and *La Oceania Española,* and in the evenings, *El Comercio, La Voz Española,* and *La Correspondencia de Manila*—plus a biweekly *La Opinion.* There were also provincial newspapers, for instance, in Cebu and Iloilo. Newspapers from Spain were generally not sold in Manila; those that did appear came through private subscription, and many of those considered "dangerously liberal" were proscribed.

The country's national hero, José Rizal (1861–1896), was a major force in this propaganda movement. A man of culture, he was a gifted poet, satirist, novelist, historian, scientist, journalist, linguist, and political activist. Rizal's condemnation of the evils in colonial Philippine society is best documented in his novels—*Noli Me Tangere* and *El Filibusterismo.* In these he exposed the corruption and brutality of the Spanish regime and the immorality, wealth, and avarice of the Spanish friars. But even though Rizal would go from advocating reform in the *Noli* to revolution in the *Fili,* the novels were more than an attack on the Spanish establishment in the Philippines. They were also a call for the spiritual and moral renewal of the Filipino people, which he felt was badly needed among his countrymen.

Indeed, the reformists were not anti-Spaniard, nor anti-Spain, nor even anti-Catholic, but antifriar. In their eyes the friars were the obstacles to Philippine progress. The expulsion of the friars was the most radical of their demands. They also sought a free press, suffrage, freedom of speech, the right of assembly, the free exercise of human rights, and freedom of commerce. The propagandists campaigned for the assimilation of Filipinas as a province of Spain so that Filipinos would be considered as citizens, enjoying the same political and civil rights as Spaniards.

The propaganda movement, plagued with shortages of funds and disagreements among its members on strategy, failed to secure the desired reforms and changes. The friars were too powerful, and they used their influence and resources to thwart the aspirations of the Filipino *ilustrados.* Further, Spain also was too busy with its own problems to give attention to the Philippines.

THE KATIPUNAN AND REVOLUTION IN THE PROVINCIA DE MANILA[8]

On July 7, 1892, a secret patriotic society, the Katipunan, was established in Manila. By coincidence, this occurred on the same day that Rizal, who had returned to the Philippines from Europe and Hong Kong, was banished to Dapitan, on the island of Mindanao. The founders of the Katipunan were led by Andres Bonifacio and Ladislao Diwa. A secret society patterned after Freemasonry (to which many Filipinos had affiliated) and La Liga Filipina (a secret civic society founded by Rizal on July 3, 1892), the Katipunan was dedicated to the awakening and liberty of the Filipinos, by force if necessary. For four years, from its founding in 1892 until the outbreak of the revolution in 1896, the Katipunan zealously guarded its secret existence. During this time, it carefully expanded its membership, initially in the districts of Manila and neighboring towns, and subsequently in some provinces in Luzon and the Visayas, in preparation for revolution against the Spaniards.

The Katipunan was, in the beginning, a society mainly of common people. Urban and mainly Tagalog, they mostly came from the districts of Tondo and Trozo, which housed the poorest Filipinos. Train lamplighters and conductors, poor fishermen, factory workers, sailors and laborers, pot makers and duck raisers, even town police forces *(carabiñeros, cuadrilleros)* became members. Intelligence work was provided by janitors in business firms, clerks in government offices, vendors in public markets, and servants of Spanish families as well as barbers and workers in newspaper offices. There were also members from Binondo and Santa Cruz, including about a hundred from the middle class—a doctor, schoolmasters, clerks, shopkeepers and merchants, and artisans and mechanics—many of whom were Chinese *mestizos.* From Spanish lists of captured revolutionaries it appears that those who joined the Katipunan included all ages, from 16 to 60 years old.

Katipunan activity spread to adjacent towns in the Manila area and in Morong to the east, where senior Katipunan members did the work of recruitment. Admission to the Katipunan required passing difficult initiation rites. Those who became members took considerable risks in view of the vigilance of the authorities, especially the friars, who were becoming increasingly suspicious of unusual gatherings in their parishes.

By the time of the outbreak of the revolution in August 1896, membership had soared to the thousands, including some women. The wives of members were unhappy about their husbands' nightly disappearances for initiation rites or secret meetings, so a women's chapter was established in mid-1893, and wives, daughters, or sisters of Katipunan members were admitted, being acknowledged as helpers and partners. The women performed important roles—they served as watchers in the outer room while secret meetings were held in the back room. They also kept valuable documents and small arms on their persons. Some provided food and refuge to fellow members. Emilio Aguinaldo's wife founded the Red Cross in 1899, which gave valuable support to the revolutionary army. Women members were also trained to ride horses and to fire guns and, on many occasions during the revolution, joined husbands and sons on the battlefield. Women combatants led battles in Cavite, Laguna, Batangas, Bulacan, and the Ilocos. Agueda Kahabagan in Laguna was the only woman general in the revolutionary army.

The Katipunan resorted to many ruses to throw off the brutal Guardia Civil, which intimidated the civilian population by making summary arrests at any time of the day or night. On occasion, Katipunan general meetings were held under the guise of a pilgrimage. Meetings and initiations to membership were also held under cover of sponsored dances and other festive gatherings. October to May, the dry season in the country, then, as now, is fiesta time, and so gatherings of people could be camouflaged by festival events. A particularly important example was the August 23, 1896, massing of Katipunan members during the fiesta of the town of Malabon in the Provincia de Morong, adjoining Manila. This was just a few days before the opening of armed conflict. The patron saint of Malabon, San Bartolome (St. Bartholemew), is represented as a bolo-wielder. The bolo (fittingly called *sangbartolome* in Tagalog) was the principal weapon of the Katipunan members. Malabon on fiesta day became filled with fair stalls selling all kinds of blades. It must have had a record sale of bolos during the fiesta, and Bonifacio's "bolo men" apparently passed through Spanish checkpoints without arousing suspicion.

Propaganda materials were distributed to members more conveniently when that new invention, the bicycle, became available in Manila. Katipuneros rode them in order to recruit outside Manila. Ingeniously, some propaganda on the Katipunan was passed around in original cigarette wrappers, thereby escaping detection by the Spanish authorities. The printing and distribution of the Katipunan paper, *Kalayaan* (Freedom), in March 1896 apparently resulted in a rush to membership, with hundreds joining nightly.

Eventually, Filipinos of various social classes, geographical regions, and ethnic and linguistic groups joined the Katipunan. As membership spread from the Manila suburbs to nearby provinces in Luzon, it came to include both the local *principalía* and the peasantry. By March 1896, with the distribution of the *Kalayaan* newspaper, Katipunan members could be found in the provinces of Bulacan, Cavite, Nueva Ecija, Morong, Batangas, Pampanga, and Laguna.

There are various figures on Katipunan membership. The range is from 15,000 to 43,000 by mid-1896, not counting the families and civilian population in the various towns who were sympathizers of the Katipunan. There are no credible official Katipunan or Spanish government records, however. Whatever the actual number, it is evident that Katipuneros easily outnumbered the Spanish forces, consisting initially of 3,005 Spanish officers and men, supported by 14,654 Filipino junior officers and soldiers (95 percent of the fighting men). By some estimates, they outnumbered the Spanish forces by as much as 20 to 1. Bonifacio's Katipuneros, however, were crudely armed—with daggers, bolos, spears, lances, a few rifles and guns, and *anting-anting* (amulets), while the Spanish military had rifles and bayonets, cannons, river barges, and warships, albeit antiquated.

The increasing reach across classes and regions of an anticolonial movement led to a far greater surveillance and policing of civilian life. Informers for the authorities included the friars, who reported on the people in their parishes. In fact, by late 1895, the Katipunan essentially was no longer a secret society. Between May and July 1896, the Guardia Civil of Malabon, Pasig, Novaliches, and San Mateo and the Guardia Civil Veterana (operating only in Manila, composed of retired Guardia Civil) had been going around, from house to house, with a list of names and arresting suspected individuals in Bulacan and Batangas. The people believed it was no longer safe to wear short, red trousers or a red *saya* (long skirt for women) as red was the color of the Katipunan flag. Anyone dressed in this color would be arrested and probably sent into distant exile, without trial or sentence.

An extra level of repression was created in 1895 with the establishment of a secret police service, the Cuerpo de Vigilancia y Seguridad. This had the task of gathering intelligence reports on life in Manila. It closely watched the activities of suspected persons—Freemasons, deportees, *filibusteros,* and suspected rebels. It also kept track of foreigners in Manila, including Chinese, Japanese, British, Americans, and Germans. It collected rumors; intercepted communications or letters coming to and leaving the Philippines; monitored opinion from the press; collected and confiscated revolutionary writings; and documented and took photographs of arrested revolutionaries. It also centralized all information coming from specific official and ecclesiastical agencies. After hostilities broke out, the Cuerpo established a corps of inspectors and agents (which included not only Spaniards, but Filipinos) that functioned from December 1897 until August 1898, when the Spaniards surrendered Manila to the Americans.

The overt stage of the anticolonial revolution began soon after August 23, 1896. On that evening, Filipino revolutionaries, led by Andres Bonifacio, gathered at Pugadlawin on the outskirts of Manila and signaled their decision to end Spain's oppressive rule by tearing up their *cedula* identity document, the mark of their vassalage to Spain. This event is commemorated in the Philippines as the "Cry of Pugadlawin" and has remained the symbolic outbreak of the revolution. Open hostilities then began, and there was no letup in the fighting through September and October.

The Spanish authorities responded by instituting a reign of terror. Frightened Spanish residents called on Governor Blanco to exterminate the rebels and conduct wholesale executions. The Spanish government conducted lightning raids, mass arrests of rich and prominent men (and a handful of women), and seizures of property. Those rounded up were detained either at Bilibid Military Prison, the dreaded Fort Santiago, or the Asilo de Huerfanos (on the Isla de Convalencia on the Pasig River). Arrested were some of the top leaders of the Katipunan, a number of prominent members of La Liga Filipina, Freemasons, and ordinary common people. Servants of suspected Katipuneros were questioned on the activities of their employers. Prisoners were brutally tortured to extract confessions and to force them to give out names of revolutionaries

More than 4,000 prisoners were reportedly arrested only a few days after the outbreak of the revolution in Manila. Hundreds were shipped to exile in the Marianas or the Spanish penal colony in Africa (Fernando Po Island). By the end of 1896, a total of 998 persons (some figures are higher) had been ordered deported. And beginning in September 1896, the first of almost daily public executions in Bagumbayan would take place. Those executed included Filipinos of all classes—common people, wealthy businessmen, professionals, and priests. The executions were not limited to those arrested and sentenced in Manila but included detainees from the provinces, who were brought to Bagumbayan. Filipino officials, *mestizos*, and even members of the police were arrested, particularly in Tondo and Pandacan, areas that were described as being deserted.

Arrests, torture, and executions also took place in the provinces. The Spaniards reportedly massacred innocent poor people and peasants in two towns in Bulacan. The Guardia Civil in Ilocos (in northwest Luzon), in the presence of Augustinian friars, inflicted horrific torture on nine Filipino priests. The friars, on occasion, administered the torture themselves, with the knowledge and permission of the bishop and the ecclesiastical governor of the diocese. This was done to extract confessions from them regarding an alleged plan to assassinate all Spanish authorities in the province.

The governor general had sought to trivialize the "disturbance" as the work of only 500 persons in Novaliches (a suburb outside Manila)—bandits who had come down from the mountains because they needed food. This propaganda obviously had little effect. With alarming rumors circulating among the Spaniards of a Katipunan plot to capture Manila and massacre its Spanish inhabitants, feverish efforts were made to strengthen the city's fortifications. The city's drawbridges, which had not been raised since 1852, were put in working order to seal Intramuros from the revolting Katipuneros. Arms were distributed to Spaniards in Intramuros, and soldiers reportedly went about with sabers and bayonets displayed. The presence of Filipinos in Intramuros, working in such jobs as domestic servants and cooks, made the Spaniards fearful of being murdered in their homes; in response, there was talk of an order to prohibit these employees keeping and using any sharp or pointed knives that might serve as weapons. The Spanish residents of Manila closed their offices and shops, frightened by all the various rumors. The business center in Escolta and Rosario (in Binondo), normally bustling with activity and brightly lit, closed its stores.

Outside Intramuros, there was the same atmosphere among the colonizers of fear and uncertainty. The Luneta, described by a French visitor as "where they shoot men in the morning and give band concerts in the evening," was normally a crowded, park-like area. Now, however, it was empty and dark. Streets and plazas were deserted even before sunset, as they were also in Caloocan, Pateros, and Taguig, where battles between Spanish forces and the revolutionaries had been fought. Houses were closed and windows shut; at night, they were pitch dark. People were jittery and nervous, assuming that every loud noise meant bullets flying in their direction. Children were not to be seen playing in yards or streets. Public markets, even on Saturdays, were empty (as in Pasig). Many townspeople sought refuge in churches and *conventos* (the residences of parish priests), hoping that the massive walls of these structures would protect them, both from the Spanish guns and the attacks of Filipino revolutionaries. In areas where battles had occurred, broken fences and scattered corpses, mostly in working clothes, added to the general sense of dread.

There was a noticeable movement of people to Manila. Most Spaniards from Ermita and Malate and other foreigners moved to Intramuros, obviously expecting better security there. The influx included the governor general, who abandoned Malacañang Palace, his official residence by the Pasig River. Despite restrictions on Filipino residence in Intramuros, there were also crowds of peaceful natives who swarmed into Intramuros, seeking safety from the battles in Manila's suburbs. Many of them apparently had not been aware of the revolution until fighting occurred.

Just as there was a wave of people coming into Manila, so there was a more noticeable movement among Filipinos, including Katipuneros, away from the city. They evacuated to provincial towns north and east and even to more inaccessible mountain and forest areas like Caloocan and Novaliches. Some lived in caves and makeshift forts, as in San Mateo and Marikina. Students lodging in Manila returned to their homes in the provinces as schools were temporarily closed. It was estimated that some 20,000 people left Manila after the outbreak of the revolution.

In general, foreigners in Manila were not harmed, at least during this early period, and business seemed to carry on as usual. It appeared that not all areas in the city and nearby places were directly affected by the fighting. Nevertheless, Europeans, estimated to number about 400, prepared contingency plans to evacuate Manila in case the revolutionaries attacked the city. The British sent two warships, the French and Germans one each, and smaller native boats stood ready in the Pasig River to transport evacuees to the ships anchored in Manila Bay. Some Chinese also sought refuge in Intramuros, but about 5,000 of the wealthy among them, afraid for their safety and property, fled to Hong Kong. Those who remained were politically indifferent; they offered their services to the Spanish but only in self-defense. A small group of 10 Japanese residents in Manila, mostly owners and employees of trading companies or bazaars, married to Filipinas and sympathetic to the Katipunan revolution, complained of harassment from the Guardia Civil Veterana. The Guardia searched their shops at all hours looking for guns and made their lives impossible and dangerous.

During the first four months of the revolution (August–December 1896), many Spanish families fled to Hong Kong, and some went back to Spain. This prompted the civil governor of Manila (who was himself quite hysterical) to order that all passports or identity papers be presented for approval before anyone could leave the capital. This stopped the mass flight to the British colony.

There was reason for the hysteria—Manila was defended by a small garrison consisting of 700 Spanish artillery men and about 2,500 Filipino soldiers of doubtful loyalty. Many of the Filipinos as well as Spanish *mestizos* in the Spanish army eventually deserted to the revolutionaries.

In order to assist the Spanish military in rounding up Filipino revolutionaries, Governor Blanco established a volunteer militia *(Voluntarios)*. This counted among its members prominent and wealthy businessmen, lawyers, judges, landlords, poor employees, and even friars as reserve officers. To the tune of "Marcha de Cadiz," they drilled daily at the grounds of the Augustinians and Recollects in Intramuros. They also patrolled the suburbs. Demonstrations of loyalty to the Spanish crown came from native volunteers from several provinces—Pampanga, Tayabas (now Quezon Province), Ilocos, Cagayan, Pangasinan, and Cebu. They sent not only men, but also money and weapons, food and medical supplies, and even horses for the Spanish army.

The Manila *Voluntarios* and several guerrilla units of Spaniards were reported to have abused Filipino civilians in Manila and the provinces. The abuses included illegal searches of private homes, brutal treatment of suspected persons, rape of daughters of Filipino families, and looting of private property. The extent of these abuses forced the governor general to declare that anyone found guilty of such crimes would be punished by death.

At the same time, there were reports of almost daily encounters in various provinces in Luzon (not all provinces in the archipelago were active in the revolution), in which Spanish troops reportedly took no prisoners and shot down or bayoneted rebels and noncombatants alike. The victims were said to include women and children. It is true that some children also joined the revolution, at times acting as couriers and lookout sentries; the youngest recorded was a boy of 10 in San Rafael, Bulacan. In Cavite, Emilio Aguinaldo was served by a young aide who died in battle in Noveleta. One Spanish officer boasted that he had ordered the execution of two revolutionaries whose combined age was less than 20 years: As he put it, however, "they just knelt down; in spite of myself, I could only admire the way they faced death so early in their life."[9]

Atrocities were also committed by the Filipino revolutionaries, sometimes on Europeans mistaken for Spaniards or on Chinese merchants. Spaniards were reportedly maltreated everywhere they were found, including the friars. There were, however, occasions when the friars were spared and allowed to flee. This was generally the result of an early warning by loyal parishioners, mostly women.

The projected Katipunan assault on Manila did not materialize. The Katipunan had scheduled an attack for August 30, but failures of coordination prevented it from being launched. Bonifacio's Katipuneros then engaged the Spanish military in a series of clashes in Manila suburbs and nearby towns, but these ended mostly in Filipino defeat and retreat. August and the following months were the rainy season, and torrential monsoon rains, high humidity, swollen rivers, and muddy grounds made operations more difficult. In December 1896, Bonifacio and his forces withdrew to the province of Cavite.

The situation relaxed somewhat among the Spaniards in the city after the Katipunan retreat. At that time, also, a new governor general, reportedly an able militarist, Governor General Camilo de Polavieja, arrived in Manila. The city even became festive with the arrival of troop reinforcements from Spain. They were received with delirious celebrations: street parades, extravagant banquets, and fiery speeches denouncing the enemy as cannibals and wild beasts. On such occasions, Filipinos and *mestizos* in Intramuros were compelled to show their own enthusiasm for the Spanish troops; those who failed to do so were arrested.

After Cavite was recovered by the Spanish in May 1897, life in Manila returned almost to normal. Schools reopened. Luneta, once again, was a crowded park for the traditional relaxed walk known as *paseo*. For the crowds, there was the return of free entertainment provided by the Regimental Band. Novelty stores in Binondo were stocked with imported luxury items and imported foods for what was hoped to be a happy Christmas season. The first movie house opened in Manila in 1897 near the Escolta—the Cinematógrafo. Four theaters in Manila's suburbs staged popular *zarzuelas* by Filipino and Spanish artists and classical operas by visiting French, English, and Italian opera companies. Newspapers, though strictly censored, continued business as usual, reporting that everything was under control.

Despite the rhetoric of life as normal, there were regular battles between Spaniards and revolutionaries in the provinces, arrests of Katipunan members and Freemasons in Manila, and yet more troops arriving from Spain. In the midst of the Christmas season in 1896, José Rizal, charged with "rebellion, sedition, and formation of illegal societies," was shot by firing squad in Bagumbayan in the early morning of December 30. He did not want to be shot in the back because, as he told the officer in charge of the execution, "I am not a traitor, either to my own country or to the Spanish nation!" Rizal's martyrdom had serious repercussions for Spanish rule in the Philippines. His character and fortitude touched the hearts of many ordinary people, people who had not necessarily supported the revolution to that point. His name became the rallying cry and inspiration of the Philippine Revolution, and he was to remain the greatest hero of Filipino nationalism.[10]

LIFE IN THE PROVINCE OF CAVITE—HEARTLAND OF THE REVOLUTION[11]

The call to revolution went out to all 18 towns of Cavite on August 31, 1896. Practically the entire province responded, with one town after another falling to rebel control. Cavite was the most successful rebel front and, excepting the arsenal, naval base, and isthmus, was liberated from Spanish rule by December 1896.

The success of the revolutionaries in Cavite owed much to improved military leadership. The Cavite generals knew enough to build trenches in strategic locations, and they made better preparations for battle (more and better weapons). Importantly, they had the all-out support of the civilian population—men, women, and children; schoolmasters; priests; *principales;* and townspeople. As a result, Aguinaldo, a better military commander than Bonifacio, won battles where Bonifacio did not.

It has been said that the revolution against Spanish rule was more intense in the Tagalog provinces, where friar lands *(haciendas)* were found. These included Bulacan, Laguna, Morong, Batangas, and Cavite. Of these, Cavite was the most militant. The province had the most extensive friar *haciendas*—45,000 hectares (out of a total land area of 250,000 hectares) of the richest and most productive cultivated lands. These lands were owned by Dominicans (Naic and Santa Cruz de Malabon), Augustinians (San Francisco de Malabon), and Recollects (San Juan de Imus). The livelihood of Caviteños depended on land and agriculture. The Katipunan leaders in Cavite were landowners, and the fighting men were their rural farm workers and poor relations, all with shared grievances against the friar *haciendas.* Some families who, in their opinion, had been dispossessed of their lands illegally had withdrawn to the mountains and forests. From there they had been carrying out revenge against the Spanish authorities and their minions. Cavite had developed a reputation as the *"madre de los ladrones"* (center for brigands or outlaws). Some of them joined the revolution. It was therefore not surprising that Caviteños asserted their rights of ownership over the friar *haciendas* after the province came under revolutionary control. In October 1896, Cavite would be the first province from which the friars were expelled from their *haciendas.* Lower and fairer rents were paid to the revolutionary government, and the people fought hard to defend their properties.[12]

In a revolutionary war, the distinction between civilian and soldier is blurred. Thus in Cavite, many townspeople provided moral and material support as well as food and shelter to revolutionaries. In many cases they were related by birth: The families of the Katipunan leaders, including the mother of Emilio Aguinaldo, opened their granaries to the nationalist soldiers. Civilian relatives also served as spies, extracting valuable information from the Spaniards. Agueda Esteban, wife of General Artemio Ricarte, made frequent trips to Manila as a courier to procure supplies needed for the manufacture of gunpowder and bullets. Men, women, and children learned to scavenge and gather empty cartridges and unexploded shells after each clash with Spanish gunboats and land artillery. These were used in the making of recycled ammunition. There was a factory for bullets and another for gunpowder in Imus, where church bells were melted into cannons. The munitions factories were operated by two resident Chinese. Civilian women also risked their lives to bring food to the battlefield and to care for the sick and wounded.

There was something of a fiesta spirit among the Caviteños after the Spaniards were driven from the province, although they were fully aware that the war was not over. Local people enjoyed dances, picnics under the trees, gambling, and cockfights. Indeed, up to January 1897, Cavite experienced normalcy, with weddings and baptisms being held, even while occasionally being disrupted by bombardment and artillery fire from the Spanish fort and arsenal. Christmas 1896 was not quite as joyous as usual: The traditional rites of the season were observed, but with the constant Spanish cannonading only muffled by loud band music. Noticeable in the Catholic masses celebrated during these festivities were the sermons delivered by Filipino priests, exhorting parishioners to dedicate themselves more ardently to the cause of the revolution.

It has also been said that in Cavite, even among the revolutionary leaders, there was not the strong hostility to friars in general that was particularly noted among Katipuneros from Manila. The spirit in Cavite had always been very religious—attendance at Mass was generally high, more so during fiesta days, and recitation of the Rosary in the church was common in all local towns. The revolutionary leaders themselves ordered all fighting men to hear Mass regularly. Prayers were said before impending military operations, and after victories, there were prayers for thanksgiving. Masses were also ordered for those who died in battle, including for Spaniards because they were also Christians.

While there were instances of maltreatment of the friars in Cavite, in general, they were treated with courtesy and reverence. Numerous local officials, and even military leaders, allowed friars to escape before military encounters. This was also true, but to a lesser extent, in other provinces in the Philippines, especially in northwestern Luzon and the Bicol provinces, where women as well as revolutionaries sometimes interceded on behalf of their Spanish parish priests. Vacant parishes in those areas were taken over by Filipino priests. The support of these priests contributed in rallying the people to the revolution.[13]

As a result of the liberation of Cavite from Spanish rule, many refugee families and Katipunan leaders from Manila and nearby provinces evacuated to the province. They were referred to by the Caviteños as *alsa-balutan* (those who packed up and moved). They were somewhat grudgingly welcomed because it seemed they had come to Cavite only to save their lives. In November 1896, thousands of men and women, young and old, came loaded with all their possessions to the "Little Republic of Cavite." These refugees included whole families from many places and, from Muntinlupa, almost the entire town. The townspeople of Malibay (Pasay) also came en masse with their pueblo head, accompanied by their *banda de música* (band of musicians), the ornaments and standards of their church, and the image of their patron saint.

Town band with bamboo musical instruments, Visayas. (University of Wisconsin Library Digital Images Collection (SEAiT).

The refugees strained the resources and provisions of the province, causing tremendous hardships on everyone—combatants and civilians alike. To ensure the supply of food for all, people were ordered to go back to farming wherever possible, not only to provide food for themselves, but especially for the revolutionaries. People were encouraged to plant rice as well as root crops and corn in anticipation of renewed war.

Coastal towns restarted fishing in safe waters. Markets also flourished once again, especially in the towns under rebel control and where refugees from Manila and nearby areas had settled. Bacoor became a veritable central market, where goods from Manila and its environs could be found, including gunpowder, but not cigars, cigarettes, and liquor, all of which were prohibited.

In mid-February 1897, Governor General Polavieja started an all-out offensive to recover Cavite from the revolutionaries. He had, by then, newly arrived Spanish reinforcements with superior firepower, limitless munitions, bountiful provisions, and warships and gunboats in Manila Bay. The Spanish offensive in Cavite and the nearby provinces of Batangas and Laguna was a costly operation, both in resources and men. Aside from casualties of war, many of the Spanish soldiers had to deal with malaria and dysentery. The offensive started with a massive, three-day bombardment of the coastal town of Noveleta. The revolutionaries retreated with men, women, and wounded soldiers. Other towns subsequently fell into Spanish hands with a heavy toll, especially on the side of the revolutionaries. Internal rivalry, personality clashes, disagreements about governmental organization, and regionalism led to division in the ranks of the Katipunan. By May 1897, the Spaniards had recovered the province, and Aguinaldo and his men had retreated north to Biyak-na-Bato in Bulacan.

Every report of Spanish victory was greeted with joy by residents of Manila, especially the Spaniards in Intramuros. Houses displayed the Spanish flag and were decorated with the colors of Spain. From morning until night, bands of musicians would march through the streets of Manila. In dealing with captured revolutionaries and the civilian population, the Spaniards burned or destroyed churches, homes, storehouses, work animals, and farm implements. In some towns, civilians were massacred, and women were raped, including those who had sought refuge in the churches. It was not surprising that some townspeople and fighting men reportedly defected to the Spanish side, lured by Spanish promises of food and safety.

As the Spanish advanced, there was a renewed wave of refugees all over the province, moving from one town to another. As revolutionary control weakened, some refugees from Cavite towns under bombardment and artillery fire sought safety in neighboring Laguna province. They moved en masse via pushcarts or riding on livestock. When they reached a safer town, many had to sleep in the plaza and the streets as the homes of residents overflowed with refugees. There was a continuous procession of dazed civilians seeking lost husbands, wives, and children and looking for places to stay. Many refugees relocated in the hills and isolated barrios, surviving on root crops, fruits, and vegetables.

The Spanish offensives in southern Luzon—Cavite, Batangas, Laguna, and Tayabas—resulted in a subsistence crisis, especially in Cavite and Batangas, as continuous warfare depleted food supplies. During the Spanish offensives in 1897, no planting or harvesting of rice could be done. The situation was aggravated by the lack of work animals and the poor health and lack of stamina of farmers, who were also the fighting men. Thus Cavite's supply of food diminished, resulting in hunger, malnutrition, diseases (malaria, dengue, dysentery), and, in many instances, death. It took a long while before people returned to the towns and even longer to resume sowing and planting. In western Batangas, the food crisis was even longer lasting. It reached its peak in 1898, but it lasted up to the pacification of the province by the American military forces in 1902.[14]

THE REVOLUTION SPREADS IN LUZON

Besides Manila-Morong and Cavite, the Revolution in the early stages was most active in the six provinces of Laguna, Batangas, Bulacan, Pampanga, Tarlac, and Nueva Ecija (the eight rays on the Philippine flag represent Manila-Morong, Cavite, and these six provinces). All were placed under martial law and declared to be in a state of war by Governor General Ramon Blanco on August 30, 1896. Somewhat later, the revolution would also spread to Tayabas, Bataan, Zambales, Pangasinan, the Ilocos, La Union, and Mindoro Island.[15]

Despite the ebb and flow of conflict caused by Bonifacio's withdrawal to Cavite in December 1896 and Aguinaldo's retreat to Bulacan in May 1897, it may be said that there was constant warfare in these six provinces. Typically, armed bands would assemble and take possession of a town, the Spanish forces would attack, and fierce battles would be fought; the site would be strewn with corpses, the rebels would retreat, and the Spaniards would retire.

There was widespread destruction and many casualties among the civilian population. Often this was the result of both deliberate and indiscriminate Spanish actions. Not only were many villages reduced to ashes and crops of unripe rice wantonly destroyed, but also, fields could not be tended because of the risk farmers faced of being seized by the Spaniards as spies. Central Luzon was the rice basket of Luzon, but because of Spanish depredations, food shortages were experienced even there.

As the rainy season of 1897 progressed, both sides found warfare exceedingly difficult. Raw Spanish troops were hard put to replace the dead, wounded, and diseased—increasingly, these reinforcements consisted of boys, poorly trained, poorly dressed, ill-fed and unpaid for months. The revolutionaries were in no better shape, hampered by large numbers of casualties; a lack of effective weapons; a shortage of provisions, especially food for the soldiers; disease; and a lack of medical facilities. No one side won decisive victories.

The first phase of the revolution ended inconclusively. Both sides were willing to negotiate a truce, which was concluded in December 1897. Aguinaldo agreed to go into voluntary exile in Hong Kong after the Spanish government indemnified him and his revolutionary junta with an initial amount of 400,000 pesos (US $200,000).

There was rejoicing on both sides with the cessation of fighting. Aguinaldo was hailed by his sympathizers, who sent him off to Hong Kong, complete with a ball in his honor. The Spaniards of Intramuros celebrated the end of 16 months of war with a *Te Deum* (Thanksgiving Mass) amid the pealing of church bells and lively band music. The month of January was filled with festivities—there was an open-air theater, bands marching everywhere, and card tables for games of chance.

The truce did not end the hostilities—both sides entered the agreement in bad faith. Neither was really willing to abandon hostilities, and both were biding their time and marshalling resources. There were reports of new cruelties committed by the Spaniards, especially by the Guardia Civil Veterana, who were secretly seizing and killing men without charges ever being laid. Persons implicated in the revolution were rearrested on trivial or trumped-up accusations. Execution of suspects took place, and only a few special pardons, rather than a general amnesty, were given. The revolutionaries, for their part, mounted scattered rebel attacks against Spanish garrisons during February, March, and April 1898 in Manila, Cavite, and various Luzon provinces.

THE SPANISH-AMERICAN WAR[16]

As tensions between the United States and Spain grew over Cuba early in 1898, Assistant Secretary of the Navy Theodore Roosevelt sent the Asiatic Squadron to Hong Kong. Clearly, if war with Spain broke out, there would be tactical advantages from attacking Spain's Philippine possession. But this was also an era of imperialism and an era in which proponents of sea power were embracing doctrines that advocated forward bases for the projection of power. The Philippines would provide an ideal base for the projection of American sea power into the western Pacific.

The American navy was as yet untested, however, and the Asiatic Squadron lacked land warfare capability to wrest the Philippines from its Spanish possessors. Accordingly, Aguinaldo and his revolutionaries were seen in Washington as potentially useful. In meetings with American consuls in Singapore and Hong Kong, Aguinaldo was encouraged to imagine an alliance with the United States against Spain (Aguinaldo was later returned to Manila on board one of Dewey's ships after the Battle of Manila Bay).

The start of the Spanish-American War in April 1898 resulted in a general stampede among civilian families wishing to get away from Manila. Many fled up the Pasig River toward Laguna de Bay, which lies beyond the suburbs. Americans and other foreign families in Manila took refuge on board foreign ships in Manila Bay. Others paid exorbitant passage money to leave for Hong Kong, with Chinese leaving once again by the hundreds. Trade in and with Manila came almost to a standstill, with the commercial district of Binondo being worst affected.

The American Asiatic Squadron was commanded by then commodore George Dewey. Upon the outbreak of hostilities, Dewey was immediately ordered to attack the Spanish fleet in the Philippines. When Dewey's squadron entered Manila Bay, Spanish women and children were driven off to the nearby villages, while male Spaniards, from the highest to the lowest, and some loyal native auxiliaries as well, hastened to assure the governor general that they would stop the enemy from landing in Manila or die trying. However, the Battle of Manila Bay on May 1, 1898, resulted in the total annihilation of the decrepit and outmoded Spanish navy. Admiral Dewey occupied the Cavite fort, arsenal, and isthmus, and blockaded Manila Bay, pending the arrival of American landing forces.

Upon Aguinaldo's return to the Philippines on May 19, he immediately resumed the revolution. With Dewey in control of the Spanish facilities in Cavite town and port, the rest of Cavite almost immediately came under Filipino control. The revolutionaries then surrounded Manila, preparatory to attacking the Spaniards in Intramuros.

The Spanish authorities were willing to yield neither to the Filipinos nor to the Americans. When Admiral Dewey requested permission to use Spanish telegraph lines, the Spanish refused. Dewey thereupon cut the cables; this was to have enormous significance later on.

Dewey strictly enjoined Aguinaldo's troops from attacking Intramuros. Moreover, as American expeditionary forces began arriving from June 1898 onward, American military commanders compelled Aguinaldo to yield positions around the city to the American troops.

Increasingly convinced by such behavior that the United States was preparing to take over sovereignty of the Philippines from Spain, Aguinaldo sought to preempt the Americans. Thus the Filipino revolutionaries declared Philippine independence on June 12, 1898. This date is celebrated today as the Philippines's National Day. Aguinaldo began seeking foreign recognition of the new government, and a revolutionary congress was convened in September 1898 to draft a constitution. An education system was initiated in October 1898 with the creation of the Universidad Literaria de Filipinas and the Burgos Institute for secondary and technical education. On January 23, 1899, the Philippine Republic was formally inaugurated at Malolos.

The declaration of Philippine independence did not prevent the Spanish authorities from surrendering Manila to the American forces. The two sides negotiated an agreement that excluded the participation of Aguinaldo's forces. The Spaniards were terrified that the Filipinos would avenge themselves by plundering the city and murdering all the colonizers. To preserve the fiction of an honorable defeat, they arranged for a mock battle to precede the surrender. This all took place on August 13, 1898. Following this, General Wesley Merritt declared that the United States was "in possession" of the Philippines and announced the establishment of a military government.

The surrender might not have taken place, however, had the cable lines not been cut. Deprived of immediate communication, neither side knew that on August 12, a Protocol of Peace was signed between Spain and the United States. Had the Spanish and American forces in Manila known that hostilities had already ended, the Spaniards would have had no need of a mock battle to preserve their honor, and American commanders would have been hard pressed to justify an attack on Spanish forces, feigned or otherwise. This would have changed the entire course of modern Filipino history.

Despite the creation of military government in August 1898, it was at that point by no means certain that the United States would take over the Philippines. Even after the surrender of Manila, Spain continued to claim sovereignty over the Philippines and hoped to maintain its rule in at least part of the country. And a Filipino army was in de facto control of much of the land.

Spain and the United States began treaty negotiations in October 1898. These excluded any representative from the Aguinaldo government. In December 1898, they would conclude in the Treaty of Paris. Well before this point, U.S. president William McKinley had decided on annexation of the Philippines. A number of elements undoubtedly factored into U.S. thinking. There was concern at what other powers might do if the United States did not step in. There were proponents of American expansionism who viewed takeover of the Philippines as "dictated by destiny." There was a belief that Filipinos were incapable of self-government. McKinley's own rather strange explanation was that after falling on his knees in prayer, he came to believe it was the duty of the United States to "Christianize and civilize" the Filipinos.

The Treaty of Paris granted sovereignty over the Philippines to the United States in return for a payment of $20 million to Spain. Even then, matters were far from settled as there was strong opposition in the United States to this imperialist venture. Indeed, a majority of senators opposed the treaty until, 36 hours before the scheduled vote, hostilities broke out between Filipino and American forces in Manila. With the hostilities presented to the U.S. public as the result of Filipino aggression, the treaty annexing the Philippines passed the Senate by one vote in February 1899.

The situation on the ground had changed considerably over the preceding months. With Aguinaldo's return, the provinces had risen en masse against the Spaniards. Between May and December 1898, Spanish forces surrendered to the revolutionaries in one place after another, including Pampanga, Tayabas, Zambales, Mindoro Island, Tarlac, Pangasinan, Nueva Ecija, and the Ilocos provinces.

Part of the Filipino success was due to the fact that they now had more and better arms (some purchased in Hong Kong), the military commanders were more experienced, and the revolutionary army was becoming better organized and disciplined. Further aiding the cause was the resumption of normal civilian life, and though foodstuffs were expensive, in most areas, there was no longer a danger of famine. Moreover, provinces liberated from Spanish control were organized into civilian town governments, with officials popularly elected.

In most areas the turmoil of battle was brief, though chaotic. There was much burning and pillaging of churches and other property, with streams of smoke reportedly seen daily rising from the valleys. Although Spanish garrisons sometimes offered resistance, Spanish prisoners were captured by the thousands. The prisoners were treated well and were eventually released and repatriated to Spain.

The revolution also spread to the Visayas, although there the Spaniards offered more resistance. In April 1898, Cebu rose in revolt. Led by men of the commoner class mainly seeking food, Cebu City, especially the commercial section, was burned to the ground. The Spaniards regrouped, however. Spanish government soldiers raided private houses, brought Filipino families by force into the public square, or conducted them to the cemetery for summary execution. In some towns outside the city where people were killed, villages burned, and standing crops destroyed, there were food shortages.

This was but a temporary setback for the revolutionaries. In June 1898, the revolution was revived, starting in Sudlon, a Cebu suburb. With no Spanish reinforcements coming from Manila after its capitulation to the Americans, the revolutionary movement gained control over the rest of the island outside of the city. A civilian local government was organized, formally recognized by Aguinaldo. Isolated, the Spanish authorities eventually withdrew from Cebu City.

In some areas in the Visayas, there was minimal fighting because the Spanish forces were very small, and the friars and Spanish residents had fled. With the loss of Manila in August 1898, however, the Spanish relocated their capital to Iloilo and sought to maintain control of the southern Philippines. Filipino pressure and the Treaty of Paris facilitated the capitulation of Iloilo to the Filipino revolutionaries in December 1898.

Thus by the time of the Philippine-American War in February 1899, revolutionary forces controlled virtually the entire country, except for Manila and Cavite town and port. In Manila the Americans exercised jurisdiction over Intramuros and from Binondo on the right bank of the Pasig River up to Malacañang Palace. In this area, American rule was implemented, and by the end of August 1898, refugees began returning in large numbers from Hong Kong. Trading operations in Manila were resumed. With freedom of the press guaranteed by the American military authorities, newspapers began publication—the Spanish *El Comercio; La Independencia* and *La Republica Filipina,* both revolutionary publications; two American newspapers, *The Manila American* and the *Manila Times;* and a host of periodicals. The American army started the task of cleaning up Manila's streets, enforcing sanitary regulations, and collecting taxes, sometimes in a harsh and authoritarian manner that offended Filipinos, who resented being called "niggers." Meanwhile, in the streets, public cafes, and drinking saloons (many of them on the Escolta, which were eventually closed because of drunken brawls), the situation was enlivened by frequent altercations between Spanish, Filipinos, and Americans.[17]

THE PHILIPPINE-AMERICAN WAR (1899–1902)[18]

The Philippine-American War broke out in the evening of February 4, 1899, "Black Saturday," when an American sentry fired on a Filipino patrol, which responded in kind. Prior to that, and subsequent to the signing of the Treaty of Paris, President McKinley, on December 21, 1898, had already issued his Benevolent Assimilation Proclamation. This declared that the United States would assume control and disposition of the government of the Philippines. American military commanders were instructed to extend American sovereignty over the entire country.

Despite rising tensions on the ground, American military commanders did not act until the Black Saturday clash. When hostilities erupted, the initial encounters resulted in heavy casualties among Aguinaldo's soldiers, and large numbers of men, women, and children were killed. Indeed, the military superiority of the U.S. Army was obvious. Aguinaldo relied on a regular army, still in a formative stage, consisting of approximately 25,000 men. In addition, there were two irregular groups—the territorial militia and the Sandatahan, essentially the old Katipunan, armed with bolos. The regular army had the rifles and fought in the main battles, while the territorial militia and the Sandatahan were used as reserves or in raids, ambushes, and hit-and-run assaults. Although effective against the demoralized Spaniards, compared with the Americans, the Filipino forces were inferior in numbers, poorly armed, and badly disciplined. They were composed of a motley group of volunteers, veterans of the Spanish army, Katipuneros, and provincial forces—mainly townspeople led by *principales* who had joined to fight against the U.S. invasion. There was also a scarcity of funds and military supplies, the most critical shortage being of rifles and cartridges. There were repeated appeals for arms to be shipped from Hong Kong, but with the treasury empty (taxes could not be collected regularly or efficiently) and the ports blockaded by American warships, no shipments could be delivered. The navy blockades also ended interisland trade in foodstuffs and commodities.

The American army, which included officers and troops recently tested in fighting in Cuba, had seasoned commanders who, in many cases, were veterans of the Civil War and the Indian Wars in the United States. It was steadily built up from 20,851 in January 1899 to 54,200 by May 1900. In December 1900, the peak strength was 74,094 officers and men.

The Filipinos had no defense against naval gunfire, which shelled Filipino positions from Manila Bay, resulting in confusion and the death of combatants and civilians alike. The initial strategy adopted by the U.S. Army was to secure Manila from the rebels; this was done by the end of February 1899. Makati, Mandaluyong, and San Juan del Monte were reduced to ashes. The Chinese quarters in Santa Cruz also burned down. Paco Church, which sheltered refugees and revolutionaries, was completely demolished.

The American forces then moved northward toward the Republic's capital in Malolos, Bulacan. Filipino and American forces engaged in conventional warfare at the battalion or brigade level. Much fighting was done along the Manila Railroad, which was controlled by the Filipino troops. Towns were burned, both by the Americans who took them and by the Filipinos who retreated from them. In the midst of battle, many Filipino households hoisted white flags to indicate their peaceful intentions. Everywhere, hundreds of men, women, and children sought refuge in swampy lands, carrying all their household goods. Malolos fell to the Americans at the end of March 1899.

Malolos Church and Convent, capital of Malolos Republic, 1899. From José de Olivares, *Our Islands and Their People*, vol. 2 (New York: N.D.F. Thompson, 1899). (Photograph digitized by Rita M. Cacas, Archives Specialist, National Archives and Records Administration, College Park, Maryland.)

From this time on, Aguinaldo retreated from one provincial capital to another, all the while pursued by the American military. In the battles, invariably, the Filipinos were defeated by superior American firepower and numbers, and casualties on the Filipino side were heavy. There was continued burning of towns by both Filipino and American combatants, and those food supplies in granaries and warehouses were confiscated or sometimes destroyed. This led to severe shortages among ordinary civilians. Townspeople fled to outlying barrios, leaving many towns empty; trade and farming were also badly disrupted.

In November 1899, Aguinaldo shifted to a new strategy of guerrilla warfare—"fighting in the boondocks." Filipino troops moved in smaller bands, engaging American units in small fire, then disappeared into the woods. To further mobilize the people, old Katipunan chapters were revived, acting as a shadow government for the Malolos Republic. Townsfolk in every Luzon and Visayan town provided the guerrillas with food and other provisions, cover and shelter, medical assistance, and intelligence and courier services. Still, forced contributions were at times imposed on the pueblos, and on occasion, private properties were seized. The resulting hardship and resentment undoubtedly provided a strong incentive for people to accept the alternative American occupation.

Between May and October 1899, some leading members of the Malolos government had begun to abandon the war and advocate acceptance of the American offer of autonomy. Recognizing the unfavorable course of the war, Aguinaldo circulated a message on August 31, 1899. This allowed civilians who had left their towns now to return home, even in areas under American control. His only request was that such people observe the strictest neutrality and highest patriotism in dealing with the enemy.

On March 23, 1901, Aguinaldo was captured in a mountainous region of Palanan, Isabela Province (Luzon). On April 1, he took an oath of allegiance to the United States. Others in the Aguinaldo government who did not take the oath were exiled to Guam, a practice borrowed from the Spaniards.

Despite the capture of Aguinaldo, three revolutionary generals remained in the field—Luciano San Miguel in Bulacan and Morong (now named Rizal province); Vicente Lukban in Samar; and Miguel Malvar in Batangas and Laguna. The guerrilla war intensified in these three areas. The U.S. Army maintained garrisons in the pueblos where local governments had been installed. In practice, the town officials served both the American regime and the guerrillas, who coerced them to support the war through blackmail, intimidation, or threat of execution. To counter this, the American military declared pueblo residents, especially the *principalía*, to be guerrilla sympathizers or accessories unless they overtly and actively helped the occupation regime.

Beginning in 1900, the war between the U.S. military and the Filipino revolutionaries deteriorated into a truly inglorious affair. There were accounts of American cruelties, including torture, execution of prisoners, and indiscriminate killing of men, women, and children. Atrocities, however, were committed by both sides—Filipinos and Americans—against each other and against the civilian population when no cooperation was forthcoming.

The greatest Filipino resistance to U.S. domination was in the provinces of Samar and Batangas, followed closely by Laguna and Tayabas. Resistance in Samar, Batangas, Laguna, and Tayabas was crushed by forcing people into "reconcentration" camps or "zones of protection" for months to prevent them from aiding guerrillas. In 1902, there were some 300,000 Filipinos in the zones of protection of Batangas and Laguna. Outside these zones, houses; crops; gardens; poultry and livestock; boats, if any; and food stores were ruthlessly and systematically destroyed. Elsewhere, scorched-earth tactics were used in regions where guerrilla resistance was strong, as in Abra; this led to the depopulation of the entire province.

In Samar, the controversial Balangiga Massacre took place on September 28, 1901. Studies indicate a complicated interplay among Balangiga townspeople, American pacification forces, and revolutionary guerrillas, further intensified by local perceptions of American behavior, especially toward women. The immediate cause of the violence was an order given by the

Women prisoners of war in Batangas, Philippine-American War. (National Archives.)

U.S. company commander to round up all males as forced labor to clean up the village. This led, in due course, to the bolo-armed townspeople of Balangiga, posing as laborers, setting upon Company C of the 9th Infantry, causing 45 dead and 22 wounded. The U.S. reaction to the attack was a kill and burn campaign in southern Samar, lasting from October 1901 to January 1902.

It took the U.S. Army in the Philippines three years (1899–1902) to "pacify" Filipino revolutionists, alternating between what American historians call "the carrot of benevolence and the stick of military force." The pacification took much longer than American commanders in the field had expected and was at great cost: About 20,000 Filipino combatants dead, about 5,000 American military dead, plus some 250,000 civilians killed, not just from direct action, but also from the ravages of war, including pestilence, disease, and hunger.

Some Filipino rebel leaders and populations accepted more readily than others the inevitability of American rule. In pacified provinces and municipalities, schools were established that were initially taught by American soldiers and officers. Peace and order was maintained by local police forces. As early as May 1899, municipal elections were held, and qualified Filipinos were elected to municipal and provincial positions. The first provincial government was organized in February 1901 in Pampanga. The first American school in the Philippines was built by the military authorities on the island of Corregidor shortly after the Battle of Manila Bay, and by January 1901, a centralized public school system was readied.

In May 1899, the Philippine Supreme Court was created, composed of nine justices, six of whom were Filipinos, with a Filipino appointed as chief justice. In September 1901, three Filipino *ilustrados* were appointed to the Philippine Commission, which exercised legislative and executive functions in the national government in Manila. It can be said that the resistance to American rule in some areas collapsed as American policy and action fulfilled some of the demands of Filipinos who took up arms against Spain—that is, the right to participate in running the affairs of their country.

With the capture of Vicente Lukban in Samar and the surrender of Miguel Malvar in Batangas, civil government was established throughout the Philippines on July 4, 1902, and the Philippine-American War was officially terminated. However, guerrilla activity continued in numerous areas throughout the archipelago. There were also postrevolutionary peasant movements, religious and millenarian in character, which surfaced in various forms in twentieth-century agrarian protests. Fierce fighting also took place in Muslim Mindanao and Sulu until 1913, although this resistance was unrelated to the Philippine Revolution.

The United States was compelled to return "infested" areas to military authority. Reconcentration camps were restored for brief periods in Albay, Cavite, Batangas, and some parts of Laguna and Rizal. After the Brigandage

Act of 1902 was passed, those engaged in armed activity were defined as brigands and outlaws, and depending on the gravity of their offense, they were subject to death. Many were executed. Under the Sedition Law of 1901, the formation of a secret society was, in extreme cases, also punishable by death. Advocating Philippine independence orally or in writing was cause for fines or imprisonment.

THE RISE OF MODERN MANILA[19]

After the capital was occupied by the Americans, modern Manila began to emerge, even while the U.S. military was fighting Aguinaldo's army. Parks, promenades, thoroughfares, and new buildings were constructed. An immense ice factory was erected on the south side of the Pasig River, and Clarke's ice cream became available at a joint ice cream parlor, candy shop and café set up at Plaza Moraga in Binondo. The first government scholars were sent to the United States. The Colegio Filipino was established, the first private, nonsectarian university, founded by Mariano Jhocson and later named the National University. The first American teachers also arrived in the Philippines in June 1901 to staff the public schools, which were being opened all over the pacified areas. In 1901, the first automobile, a "Richard," was brought to Manila. The first hanging also took place. For better or for worse, the American period was underway, and henceforth the struggle for independence would be fought solely in the political arena.

NOTES

1. John Leddy Phelan, *The Hispanization of the Philippines*, Madison: University of Wisconsin Press, 1959; also O. D. Corpuz, *The Roots of the Filipino Nation*, vol. 1, Quezon City, Philippines: Aklahi Foundation, 1989.

2. Corpuz, *Roots*, vol. 2, chaps. 12–13; Eliodoro G. Robles, *The Philippines in the Nineteenth Century*, Quezon City, Philippines: Malaya Books, 1969; Benito J. Legarda, Jr., *After the Galleons: Foreign Trade, Economic Change and Entrepreneurship in the Nineteenth-Century Philippines*, Madison: Center for Southeast Asian Studies University of Wisconsin, 1999.

3. Corpuz, *Roots*, vol. 2, chaps. 13–14; John Foreman, *The Philippine Islands: A Political, Geographical, Ethnographical, Social, and Commercial History of the Philippine Archipelago, Embracing the Whole Period of Spanish Rule, With an Account of the Succeeding American Insular Government*, Manila: Filipiniana Book Guild, 1980 (offprint copy of 1906 edition, chapter 21); Gilda Cordero-Fernando, ed., *Turn of the Century*, Quezon City, Philippines: GCF Books, 1978 (articles of Teodoro A. Agoncillo, Nick Joaquin, and Doreen G. Fernandez, pp. 22–65, 68–85); Edgar Wickberg, *The Chinese in Philippine Life, 1850–1898*, New Haven, CT: Yale University Press, 1965.

4. Corpuz, *Roots*, vol. 2, chap. 15; Foreman, *Philippine Islands*, chap. 22.

5. Edmund Plauchut, "La Algarada Caviteña de 1872," Articulo IV, Serie de Las Islas Filipinas, in *Revue des Deux Mondes*, 1877 (translated from *La Solidaridad de Madrid*, Manila: Imprenta Manila Filatélica, 1916); Nick Joaquin, "Jose Burgos: How Filipino was Burgos?" in *A Question of Heroes: Essays in Criticism on Ten Key Figures of Philippine History*, Makati, Philippines: Filipinas Foundation, 1977

(pp. 7–24); John N. Schumacher, S. J., *Father Burgos, Priest and Nationalist,* Quezon City, Philippines: Ateneo University Press, 1972.

6. David R. Sturtevant, *Popular Uprisings in the Philippines, 1849–1940,* Ithaca, NY: Cornell University Press, 1976; Reynaldo Clemeña Ileto, *Pasyon and Revolution: Popular Movements in the Philippines, 1840–1910,* Quezon City, Philippines: Ateneo de Manila University Press, 1979.

7. Corpuz, *Roots,* vol. 2, chap. 16; John N. Schumacher, S. J., *The Propaganda Movement, 1880–1895,* Manila: Solidaridad, 1973 (Quezon City, Philippines: Ateneo de Manila University Press, 1997, revised edition); Leon M. Guerrero, *The First Filipino: A Biography of José Rizal,* Manila: National Historical Commission, 1971; José Rizal, *Noli Me Tangere and El Filibusterismo,* trans. M. Soledad Lacson-Locsin, edited Raul L. Locsin, Makati City, Philippines: Bookmark, 1996.

8. The Provincia de Manila included Manila of today, Caloocan, Las Piñas, Malibay (Pasay), Mariquina, Montalban, Muntinlupa, San José de Navotas, Parañaque, Pasig, Pateros, Pineda (Pasay), San Felipe Nery, San Juan del Monte, San Mateo, San Pedro Macati, Taguig, and Tambobong. The Provincia de Morong (Rizal province today) was a politicomilitary district under Manila and comprised the towns of Angono, Antipolo, Baras, Binagonan, Bosoboso, Cainta, Cardona, Jalajala, Morong (capital), Pililla, Tanay, Taytay, Teresa, and Quisao. Being closest to Manila, these towns were most active during and most affected by the revolution against Spain and the war with the United States.

9. Andre Bellesort, *One Week in the Philippines,* (November 1897), translated by E. Aguilar Cruz, Manila: National Historical Institute, 1987, p. 65.

10. On the revolution in Manila and life in the city and environs during this period, see Corpuz, *Roots,* vol. 2, chap. 17; and Foreman, *Philippine Islands,* chap. 22. Also Teodoro A. Agoncillo, *The Revolt of the Masses: The Story of Andres Bonifacio and the Katipunan,* Quezon City: University of the Philippines, 1956 (reprinted by University of the Philippines Press, 1996, chaps. 1–10); Bernardita Reyes Churchill and Francis A. Gealogo, eds., *Centennial Papers on the Katipunan and the Revolution,* Manila: Manila Studies Association, 1999 (articles of Isagani R. Medina, pp. 1–13, 45–56); Bernardita Reyes Churchill, ed., *Revolution in the Provinces,* Manila: National Commission for Culture and the Arts, 1999 (article of Motoe Terami Wada, pp. 44–55); Joaquin, *Question of Heroes,* articles on José Rizal and Andres Bonifacio, pp. 53–102; Joaquin, "Red as in Revolution," in *Turn of the Century,* pp. 22–47; Onofre D. Corpuz, *Saga and Triumph: The Filipino Revolution against Spain,* Manila: Philippine Centennial Commission, 1999 (chaps. 1–4); William Henry Scott, "The Nine Clergy of Nueva Segivia," in *Cracks in the Parchment Curtain and Other Essays in Philippine History,* Quezon City, Philippines: New Day, 1982 (pp. 178–207); Gregorio F. Zaide, *Manila during the Revolutionary Period,* Manila: National Historical Commission, 1973.

11. On the revolution in Cavite, see Corpuz, *Roots,* vol. 2, chap. 17; and Corpuz, *Saga and Triumph,* chaps. 5–7; Foreman, *Philippine Islands,* chap. 22; Agoncillo, *Revolt,* chaps. 11–16; also Joaquin, *Question of Heroes,* article on Emilio Aguinaldo, pp. 105–32; Joaquin, "Red as Revolution"; see also the following participants' memoirs: Emilio Aguinaldo, *Mga Gunita ng Himagsikan* [Memoirs of the Revolution], Manila: Philippine Centennial Commission, 1998; Manuel Sityar, *Revolución Filipina, Memorias Íntimas,* trans. Trinidad O. Regala, Quezon City: University of the Philippines Sentro ng Wikang, 1998.

12. Dennis Morrow Roth, *The Friar Estates of the Philippines,* Albuquerque: University of New Mexico Press, 1977.

13. John N. Schumacher, S. J., *Revolutionary Clergy: The Filipino Clergy and the Nationalist Movement, 1850–1903*, Quezon City, Philippines: Ateneo de Manila University Press, 1981 (chaps. 1–4).

14. See Reynaldo C. Ileto, "Hunger in Southern Tagalog, 1897–1898," in *Filipinos and Their Revolution, Event Discourse, and Historiography*, Quezon City, Philippines: Ateneo de Manila University Press, 1998 (pp. 79–116).

15. Corpuz, *Roots*, vol. 2, chap. 18; and Corpuz, *Saga and Triumph*, chaps. 6–8; Foreman, *Philippine Islands*, chap. 22; see also Florentino Rodao and Felice Noelle Rodriguez, eds., *The Philippine Revolution of 1896: Ordinary Lives in Extraordinary Times*, Quezon City, Philippines: Ateneo de Manila University Press, 2001; Churchill, *Revolution in the Provinces*.

16. Brian McAllister Linn, *The Philippine War, 1899–1902*, Lawrence: University Press of Kansas, 2000 (pp. 3–5); see also H. W. Brands, *Bound to Empire: The United States and the Philippines*, New York: Oxford University Press, 1992.

17. Corpuz, *Roots*, vol. 2, chaps. 18–19; and Corpuz, *Saga and Triumph*, chaps. 9–15; Foreman, *Philippine Islands*, chap. 23; Teodoro A. Agoncillo, *Malolos: The Crisis of the Republic*, Quezon City: University of the Philippines, 1960 (reprinted by the University of the Philippines Press, 1997); see also Elmer A. Ordoñez, *The Philippine Revolution and Beyond*, 2 vols., Manila: Philippine Centennial Commission, 1998.

18. Corpuz, *Roots*, vol. 2, chaps. 18–19; and Corpuz, *Saga and Triumph*, chaps. 9–15; Foreman, *Philippine Islands*, chap. 23; Agoncillo, *Malolos*; see also Ordoñez, *Philippine Revolution and Beyond*; Corpuz, *Roots*, vol. 2, chaps. 19–20; Foreman, *Philippine Islands*, chaps. 24–27; see also Samuel K. Tan, *The Filipino-American War, 1899–1913*, Quezon City: University of the Philippines Press, 2002; Bernardita Reyes Churchill, *Resistance and Revolution: Philippine Archipelago in Arms*, Manila: National Commission for Culture and the Arts, 2002; "Proceedings of the National Conference on the Filipino-American War, November 15–17, 2000," in *Kasaysayan, Journal of the National Historical Institute* 1–3, September 2001, pp. 24–29, 68–78; 1–4, December 2001, pp. 1–15, 70–82, 172–179, 199–209.; Rolando O. Borrinaga, *The Balangiga Conflict Revisited*, Quezon City, Philippines: New Day, 2003; Resil B. Mojares, *The War against the Americans: Resistance and Collaboration in Cebu, 1899–1906*, Quezon City, Philippines: Ateneo de Manila University Press, 1999. For American perspectives on the war, see Leon Wolff, *Little Brown Brother: How the United States Purchased and Pacified the Philippine Islands at the Century's Turn*, Mechanicsburg, PA: Bookspan, 2006; Stuart Creighton Miller, *"Benevolent Assimilation": The American Conquest of the Philippines, 1899–1903*, New Haven, CT: Yale University Press, 1982; Brian McAllister Linn, *The Philippine War, 1899–1902: The U.S. Army and Counterinsurgency in the Philippine War 1899–1902*, Chapel Hill: University of North Carolina Press, 1989; and Glenn Anthony May, *Battle for Batangas: A Philippine Province at War*, New Haven, CT: Yale University Press, 1999.

19. Foreman, *Philippine Islands*, chap. 28; Luning Bonifacio Ira and Isagani R. Medina, "What Will They Think of Next?" in *Turn of the Century*, pp. 217–18.

SELECTED BIBLIOGRAPHY

Churchill, Bernardita Reyes, ed. *Revolution in the Provinces*. Manila: National Commission for Culture, 1999.
    Collection of papers on the Philippine Revolution in 1896 and the Philippine-American War in 1899 in various areas of the archipelago.

Corpuz, O. D. *The Roots of the Filipino Nation.* 2 vols. Quezon City, Philippines: Aklahi Foundation, 1989.

The two volumes cover the entire Spanish colonial period in the Philippines (1565–1898).Volume 2 deals with major developments in the nineteenth century, ending with the revolution against Spain and the war with the United States.

Ileto, Reynaldo Clemeña. *Pasyon and Revolution: Popular Movements in the Philippines, 1840–1910.* Quezon City, Philippines: Ateneo de Manila University Press, 1979.

Discusses Philippine popular movements and radical peasant brotherhoods, including the Katipunan Revolution, with an emphasis on their definition of the concept of *freedom.*

Linn, Brian McAllister Linn. *The Philippine War, 1899–1902.* Lawrence: University Press of Kansas, 2000.

Provides a comprehensive study of military operations in the Philippines during the Philippine-American War; using the vast military records found in U.S. depositories, and dispels what he feels have been the misunderstandings and historical inaccuracies of this "forgotten war" in American history.

May, Glenn Anthony. *Battle for Batangas: A Philippine Province at War.* New Haven, CT: Yale University Press, 1999.

Provides an account of the life of revolutionaries and civilians in Batangas, where there was a very strong resistance to the pacification efforts of the U.S. military.

Miller, Stuart Creighton. *"Benevolent Assimilation": The American Conquest of the Philippines, 1899–1903.* New Haven, CT: Yale University Press, 1982.

Tells the story of the Philippine-American War and America's reactions to its imperialistic venture in the Philippines.

Mojares, Resil B. *The War against the Americans: Resistance and Collaboration in Cebu, 1899–1906.* Quezon City, Philippines: Ateneo de Manila University Press, 1999.

Presents the Filipino perspective of the war against the Americans in one area in the Philippines—Cebu Island in the Visayas—and details the dynamics of Cebuano society during the war up to 1906, reflecting "the making of local society" at the turn of the twentieth century.

Phelan, John Leddy. *The Hispanization of the Philippines.* Madison: University of Wisconsin Press, 1959.

Examines pre-Spanish Philippine society at the time of Spanish contact and looks at how Filipinos reacted to Christianization and hispanicization of Philippine culture.

Rodao, Florentino, and Felice Noelle Rodriguez, eds. *The Philippine Revolution of 1896: Ordinary Lives in Extraordinary Times.* Quezon City, Philippines: Ateneo de Manila University Press, 2001.

Collection of historical essays on various aspects of the Philippine Revolution of 1896 by Filipino and foreign historians; essays look into the circumstances of the outbreak of the revolution and the resultant consequences for all parties concerned.

Sturtevant, David R. *Popular Uprisings in the Philippines, 1849–1940.* Ithaca, NY: Cornell University Press, 1976.

Presents a historical survey of peasant movements and rural rebellions in the Philippines from 1840 to 1940, including the period of the Philippine Revolution and the Philippine-American War.

Wickberg, Edgar. *The Chinese in Philippine Life, 1850–1898.* New Haven, CT: Yale University Press, 1965.

Provides a history of the Chinese in the Philippines during the second half of the nineteenth century, during which time significant economic developments took place in the country where the Chinese played a major role.

Zaide, Gregorio F. *Manila during the Revolutionary Period.* Manila: National Historical Commission, 1973.

Provides a good summary background of life in Manila before the outbreak of the revolution, taking the story up to the Truce of Biyak-na-bato in December 1897.

THREE

The Wars of Meiji Japan: China (1894–1895) and Russia (1904–1905)

Stewart Lone

The most powerful image of Japanese society over the past thousand years has been the samurai warrior. This suggests that the military and war has exerted a major impact on the life of civilians. That the military from the eleventh century took actual control of politics, while leaving in place the emperor as a ceremonial ruler, is true. However, from the beginning of the seventeenth century, the samurai became a closed elite; broadly speaking, one was born a samurai, was legally prevented from engaging in other occupations, such as business or farming, and civilians were forbidden from bearing arms. Thus the military and civilians were clearly separated. Moreover, from that time until the mid-nineteenth century, war played no prominent role in the lives either of civilians or, indeed, of the samurai. In fact, the period of hegemonic rule by the Tokugawa military family (1600–1868) was characterized by policies to avoid war. This is why civilians were disarmed, why the Tokugawa skillfully manipulated allies and enemies to maintain a balance of power within Japan, and, under the policy known as *sakoku,* or "closed country," why they shut out virtually all foreigners over the entire period. Thus for the two and a half centuries up to the 1860s, the Japanese people never directly or indirectly experienced war with a foreign state or a full-scale conflict within Japan.

The origins of modern Japan's first international wars, with imperial China in 1894–1895 and Tsarist Russia in 1904–1905, are linked. They go back to the 1860s, when civil war erupted in Japan in response to the intensifying pressures of Western gunboat diplomacy. The victorious group of samurai and aristocrats became the government under the Meiji emperor, and the period from 1868 to 1912 is known as the Meiji era. Under the banner of self-strengthening, the new government opted to reinvent every aspect of Japanese society, including politics, the law, education, the economy, and military service. This was a conservative revolution; that is, it was overseen by existing elites, and its principal aim was national security, rather than individual, or even group, freedoms.

Japan's army commanders had always seen, and in the twenty-first century, continue to see, the status of Korea as a paramount concern. The famous phrase used by General Yamagata, the prime minister of Japan facing the first Diet, or parliament, in 1890, was that Korea was like "a dagger pointed at the heart" of Japan; whoever controlled Korea could dictate Japan's future. Thus the belief at the time was that Japan could not be strong in any real or lasting sense unless it dominated Seoul. In mid-1894, Japan fabricated a pretext for war with China, traditionally the protector of Korea in a classical Confucian relationship. This was in order to drive out Chinese influence from the Korean peninsula. After eight

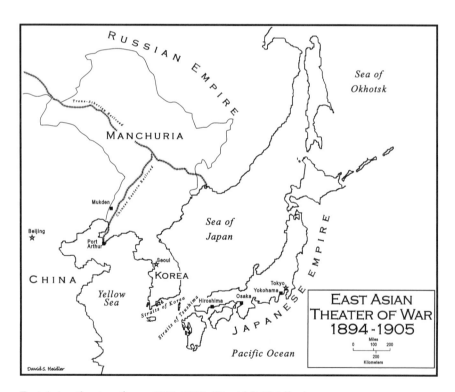

East Asian theater of war, 1894–1905. (David S. Heidler.)

months of reluctantly engaging in war, China submitted and, in return for peace, gave Japan money for its war expenses, territory in the form of Taiwan, and an uncontested position of authority in Korea (this position was quickly squandered after Japan intruded brutally and clumsily in Korean court politics). Following its defeat in 1895, China's own authority in Asia and along its own borders was further weakened by Western imperialism. As part of this, Russia was given rights to build railways in Manchuria, the region of northeastern China that borders Korea. When, in 1900, the Chinese people revolted against foreign encroachment, Russian forces became entrenched in Manchuria. This only strengthened Japan's fear of a Western power absorbing Korea, and when negotiations in 1903 to bring about a Russian pullback from the Korean border were unsuccessful, the Japanese military decided on a preemptive attack before the Russians could further consolidate their forces. This war lasted from February 1904 to September 1905. At its conclusion, Japan was regarded internationally as a great military nation, but the reality was that its economy and society were impoverished and utterly exhausted of war.

CIVILIANS AT WAR

The battleground for both of Meiji Japan's foreign wars was largely in Korea and northeast China; that is, both were fought outside of Japan but very much within its wider neighborhood. This meant that the war was physically close, but homes were never directly threatened. As a result, civilians had a choice as to how much they engaged with the war, for example, whether or not to be active in functions to aid the military or celebrate its victories, or even whether or not to read about the war or view the images presented for public education and consumption. Where the two wars differed most obviously was in their scale and duration. Put simply, the war against China was relatively brief, cost Japan little in terms of money or lives, and was characterized by an uninterrupted series of army and navy triumphs. By contrast, as the Japanese commanders admitted at the start of 1904, the chance of any kind of clear-cut victory over Russia was only 50-50, and the conflict was always going to be hard, costly, and unsatisfactory. Inevitably, those to bear the greatest hardships and feel the deepest dissatisfaction were the ordinary people. The differing scale of the wars in human terms is evident in the bare figures of men involved. In 1894–1895, the Japanese forces numbered about 240,000; total losses in battle were 1,200, with another 10,750 dying of illness. In 1904–1905, the Japanese military was about 1.1 million; of these, some 370,000 men suffered death, injury, or disease. A further telling comparison is that in each war, one of the decisive battles was in Manchuria at Port Arthur (modern Lushun): In 1894, the Japanese army took the port in a single day with only 200 wounded; in August 1904, it lost 15,000 dead and wounded in just the first five days of what was to be a five-month siege.

One thing to state at the outset is that the justification for both wars was widely accepted in Japan. Against China, the distinction made in public opinion and in Japanese propaganda overseas was that here was a war between backwardness and progress, between primitivism and civilization. Indeed, the same rhetoric was used later against Slavic Russia. The political parties were generally loud in their support of the war, as was the media and the civilian intelligentsia. The principal exception, as Japan industrialized and became a colonial power after 1895, was a small group of socialist thinkers who protested and published against the Russian war, but their activities were heavily policed, and their leader, Kōtoku Shūsui, was arrested. In 1894, according to Ōhama Tetsuya, a popular historian of war and society, the single most vocal group of Japanese asserting the righteousness of the war was, in fact, the Japanese Christians. Notable among these was the respected Christian intellectual Uchimura Kanzō (late in that war, a Christian group in Yokohama obtained army approval to donate 250,000 Bibles to the troops at the front, that is, more than one copy for every man in uniform).[1] Buddhist temples and Shinto shrines also gave unconditional support to both wars, conducting services for victory, commemorations for the dead, and sending priests to the front. In terms of direct civilian participation through newly created militia, however, the Japanese authorities made it absolutely clear that in modern war, there could only be one organized and centrally directed military. Consequently, those civilians offering in 1894 to fight alongside the armed forces were ordered to stay at home and work for the good of the nation. Civilian men of conscript age, however, needed in both wars to be ready at all times for the possibility of military service. This extended even to popular sportsmen. In 1894, Japan's leading *sumō* wrestlers were reportedly so concerned that their bulk might slow them on long marches if they were drafted that they began a new regime of conditioning; this involved walking several miles barefoot over hills and valleys before the day's bout. The far greater demands of the war against Russia meant that many more civilian men faced the prospect of being called up at a moment's notice, and so, for them, the war was a time of constant uncertainty.

If we define civilian life as revolving around the production and consumption of food, goods, and services, then the wars of Meiji Japan had a mixed impact. According to the classic study by Giichi Ono, *Expenditures of the Sino-Japanese War* (1922), the most basic purchase for all Japanese—rice—became significantly more expensive only postwar as the influx of money from the Chinese indemnity led to improved standards of living, thus allowing more people to eat more rice.[2] During wartime, the presence of an army in the field may actually have made more food available for the domestic market; although Japanese troops in China relied, in large part, on tinned goods, such as corned beef, they also bought supplies of fresh meat and other foods from local Chinese. Thus while food seemed to dominate the waking hours of Japanese soldiers, the threat of serious food shortage was not widespread on the home front.

What did suffer was the level of any disposable income. The major reason for this is that so much civilian money went into the purchase of government war bonds and donations to the forces. In addition, many people suffered a loss in wages. For example, the construction of new buildings was reduced in 1894–1895 and, in 1904–1905, virtually abandoned. This meant that tradesmen, such as carpenters and builders, struggled to make a living. Makers of small, everyday items, including pots, Japanese-style umbrellas, or lanterns for festivals, also struggled or went broke. Leisure industries that relied on evening customers, such as restaurants and teahouses could only be sure of good profits at times of major victory celebrations. In each war, workers in the textile industry, the cornerstone of Japan's modern economy, were saved only by military orders as winter approached; even with this, a female worker in 1894 might get only 6–10 sen for a day's work.

The ones who benefited from the wars were those directly and consistently supplying military needs. Thus war was a boon for the canning factories; against China, they could not keep pace with demand, despite working day and night, and a male worker in Hiroshima, the collection point for all Japanese forces heading to the front, saw his wages rise between August and October 1894 from 35 sen a day to 50 sen (a female worker enjoyed a 50 percent increase from 10 sen to 15 sen).[3] Elsewhere in Japan, there were also good profits for traders in the vicinity of army barracks. These all did well from providing the soldiers with food, drink, and accommodation. In fact, there were so many soldiers and army laborers at the various gathering places across Japan—20,000 soldiers and 10,000 army laborers, for example, in the northern city of Sendai in November 1894—that temples were often used as temporary inns as well as stables for army horses.

Others went with the troops in search of profit. Thus an entrepreneur from Osaka took a mobile bath on wheels to the Japanese troops in Korea in 1894 and did excellent business. Many urban rickshaw pullers, whose civilian customers simply disappeared in war, found alternative work with the army (there were 154,000 laborers with the army in the China war). Once in Korea and China, however, the job was hard and dangerous. Indeed, civilians working at the front suffered illness and death to an unusual level, but the military leaders were indifferent; they took the view that laborers were motivated by wages, not patriotism, and therefore deserved no special treatment. The wages, however, were not overly generous; in 1894, they were 40 sen per day, while in Japan, then rose by another 10 sen upon arriving overseas.[4] In return, army regulations required a laborer to pull a heavy load for 12 hours a day, avoid indiscipline or drunkenness, and also present an acceptable appearance! In the war against Russia, there were relatively fewer rickshawmen willing to accept these conditions. Overall, the meaning of war for most Japanese workers in the 1890s and 1900s was a tightening of economic life and insecurity about the future. This insecurity about work was also shared by soldiers facing demobilization at the end of each war.

One of the areas of daily life affected most adversely by wartime was consumerism of goods other than the basic foods. At this time, consumerism remained low level. This is evident from the range of advertising in local newspapers. More than any other commodity, advertisements in the 1890s–1900s were dominated by medicines, mainly for headaches and stomach pains (but also for more serious ailments, such as impotence). The common luxuries tended to be tobacco and alcohol. These, however, especially cigarettes, were also among the most popular gifts from the public (and from the emperor) to the armed forces. One urban patriotic group in 1895 listed its total donations to the military as 25 barrels of sour plums *(umeboshi)*, 90 liters in volume of biscuit, 1,000 pairs of socks, 130 hand-towels, and 50,000 cigarettes. On the home front, there was a suggestion, common to many wartime societies, that luxury was the enemy. Thus, early in 1904, there was an official campaign of austerity urging civilians to demonstrate their patriotism by avoiding all indulgences. As soon as wartime taxes were raised on these luxury items, however, there was an even greater incentive to show one's patriotism by smoking and drinking, even to excess. In a similar way, retailers competed to legitimize their products by linking them to the war effort. In 1894–1895, one could buy "Gold Kite Medal Sake," "Great Victory" hair clips, and confectionary decorated with patriotic symbols; restaurant menus offered dishes with military names, and clothing and hair styles were titled "victory" or "glory."

Against Russia, the vastly greater length and cost of the war meant that ordinary people had even less to spend. Yet the post-1895 economic boom, fuelled by the war indemnity from China, had altered living standards and lifted expectations. This meant that there were more products competing for less business and, consequently, fighting even harder for attention. Thus, for example, Kao Soaps claimed in its wartime ads in 1904–1905 that "the two most important things in war are hygiene and economy," and naturally, it promised both to its consumers. Kirin Beer, by contrast, declared that "soon Korea and Manchuria will be outlets for Kirin Beer," a slogan that seemed to imply that Japan's military mission was less about civilization or progress and more about taking Japanese spirits to the mainland. In the straitened market of 1904–1905, there was also greater discounting by retailers. Those selling commemorative pocket watches offered half-price to servicemen and students; dealers in funeral goods (for whom business was suddenly very good) offered discounts to the families of dead soldiers and sailors; even tickets for the popular comedy theater and vaudeville were cut by half.

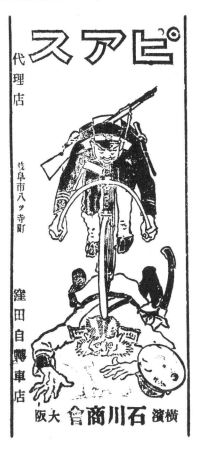

Patriotism and commerce: Pearce bicycle advertisement, April 1905. (*Gifu Nichi Nichi Shimbun.*)

In the villages of Japan, where the majority of people remained, the broad impact of war was twofold. In the early days of conflict, the first impact was the need to provide men for the armed forces and horses for military transport. A vast number of horses was essential for an army in modern war, and so this was an ongoing and heavy exaction on the rural community. Once these initial needs were met, however, life was divided between tending the fields of rice or other crops and dealing with the unceasing demands for purchases of war bonds and donations of money and goods to the war effort. These demands were already heavy in the relatively small war against China: In the first issue of war bonds in 1894, the five denominations ranged from 50 to 5,000 yen, the cheapest in the second issue later that year falling to a still daunting price of 20 yen. During the war against Russia, the enormity of the war expenses was more than the Japanese public could afford, and in order to keep fighting, Tokyo had to borrow heavily overseas at punitive rates of interest.

The successive issues of domestic war bonds and the nationwide campaigns for donations were devastating to the finances of many rural Japanese. Prefectural officials pressured village heads, and village heads pressured villagers, to purchase bonds and donate goods, such as straw sandals and blankets (at the beginning of the war, the army issued a list of acceptable donations, starting with foods, then clothing, and ending with medical supplies). Local civic groups, generally consisting of the better-off members of the community, also encouraged and pressured villagers to contribute with money and goods. The message was then reinforced by priests at the Buddhist temples. There was also the burden of collecting money to help local families with men either killed or injured in war or simply away at the front. Once again, even the relatively easy China war shows the level of hardship for rural civilians. At that time, something like one-third of military families, in villages and towns, were in need of financial assistance from their neighbors. There was no single nationwide system of aid, so the experiences of military families varied from place to place. In the prefecture of Kanagawa, just south of Tokyo, an official report in 1895 showed that in the more desolate villages, there was so little money left over for charity that some military families were actually on the verge of starvation. While this may have been the case in poorer villages, the norm was still for military families in rural Japan either to suffer or to become indebted to their neighbors during wartime. There was also the long-term social and economic impact, especially from 1905, of sick, wounded, traumatized, and disabled troops being sent back to their homes.

For rural Japan as a whole, the one-way flow of wealth from village to the war effort meant that the traditional cycle of celebration, either at harvest times or on other feast days, was reduced or broken. Exceptions were made for the New Year, still celebrated by many in 1895 according to the old lunar calendar, and for the Meiji emperor's birthday (November 3—now the national holiday "Culture Day"). As a general statement, however, village life was much harder, more sober, and far more austere in war, even though Japan was repeatedly victorious on the battlefield.

WOMEN

In the 1890s–1900s, one of the revolutionary social changes for women in Japan was increased access to the middle levels of education (women were not admitted to the universities). This meant greater literacy, self-confidence, and an awareness of events around the globe. However, they had no political rights. Indeed, women were legally prevented even from attending political meetings until the 1920s. Upon marriage, a woman also forfeited all legal rights and took the status of a minor; that is, all decisions had to be made with the consent of the husband. In terms of occupation, the choices largely were to remain in farming, work in the textile industry, perhaps help in a family-owned shop, or join the service industry by working in restaurants, tea shops, or so-called pleasure quarters. The wider possibilities of the department store, modern office, women's journals, cafes, bars, and tourism were all really developments of the 1920s. As neither of the conflicts against China and Russia quite reached the scale of total war seen in World War I, there were no major openings at that time for women to replace men in industry or administration. The one area where war did open new arenas for activity by civilian women was in nursing.

The popular image of the female nurse underwent a shift as a result of war. As late as 1904, there were still stories of a mercenary attitude in some local hospitals; incoming civilian patients were warned by nurses that the quality of the care they received depended on the size of the tips they offered. This obviously deterred poorer civilians even from approaching a doctor or nurse. The wars of Meiji helped to give a new romanticism and respect to the job of nursing. In 1894–1895, there were so few casualties from battle that the military probably did not need many nurses. However, as a demonstration of national unity and of a modernity comparable to the West, there was political value in having women attend the sick and wounded. Thus against China and more so against Russia, civilian women were mobilized as nurses at the front and at army hospitals in Japan; they also provided basic medical care and comfort for troops at railway stations.

Taking the lead in organizing civilian nurses was the Japan Red Cross. This was an association in which males greatly outnumbered females and whose president was an imperial prince. Yet it was the nurse that became its greatest popular symbol. As the rhapsodic lyric of a wartime song "Fujin Jūgun no Uta" *(Women Attending the Army)* put it, "So gently nursing / Her heart the color of the Red Cross." According to historians Sharon Nolte and Sally Ann Hastings, the Japan Red Cross began formally training women as nurses from 1890, provided a small number of trained nurses for the military in the war with China, and within the first six months or so of the war with Russia, had already dispatched more than 2,000 nurses into military service.[5] During the wars, the nurse was exalted as a selfless caregiver (while men were excused by their injuries for letting themselves become dependent on women). It was said that soldiers returning to Japan wrote first to the nurses at the front rather than to their families.

The idealized image of the nurse was somewhere between a mother, an elder sister, and a wife, with the balance more toward sensitive than sensual. However, the military authorities were constantly afraid that men might be distracted by these "angels of mercy" and forget their duty. In November 1894, the Japanese press reported with dismay the first case of a love affair at the Hiroshima Army Hospital between a cavalryman and a youthful-looking nurse of 31 named Nakajima Aiko. A popular nickname for brothel waitresses was "Red Cross member" (while dancing girls were fondly described as "the army band"). This made it difficult for women to separate themselves from their sexuality and be accepted solely for their work. It should also be mentioned, however, that it was an open secret in 1905 that many soldiers being sent back for treatment were, in fact, suffering from sexually transmitted diseases, assumed to have been contracted, as in 1894–1895, among the prostitutes at Hiroshima. Thus the reality of life and work for civilian nurses may have been less about tending the wounded hero and more about applying swabs to suppurating organs.

One of the wider social roles for women in wartime Japan was in organizing support for the war effort. This role was especially pronounced in the conflict with Russia. One of the earliest, and subsequently largest, female groups of any kind was the *Aikoku Fujinkai,* or "Patriotic Women's Association." This had been founded in 1901 by the sister of a leading Buddhist cleric. Early in 1905, it claimed a national membership of 360,000, with an imperial princess as its president. The association presented itself as the most active body through which women engaged themselves on a regular basis in supporting the war. This support took various forms, but the most common activities were to provide refreshments and small gifts for passing troop trains, to raise donations from local communities, and to offer help and comfort to the families of servicemen.

There were some civilians, however, who attacked the association as elitist—restricting itself by membership fees to women from the middle class and above—and also as ineffective. There were stories of class prejudice shown in its attention to the needy and of failures of organization in achieving any kind of result. One local branch was mocked when it received an American visitor; this was on the grounds that the reception was probably among the highlights of the branch's wartime contributions. There were other, smaller and more localized patriotic women's groups that accommodated even geisha in their ranks. The various groups overlapped in their ambitions and methods. This led to hostility and rivalries, for example, over which one could raise the most money or gather the most blankets for the military. In the Russian war, this led to a public backlash against all civic groups for appearing to sacrifice the interests of ordinary people to their own reputations.

YOUTH

Japan was distinctive in Asia in the 1890s for having a centralized, compulsory elementary school system. It began in 1872, the same year as the introduction of military conscription. The two were clearly designed to complement each other, with all pupils learning about routine, discipline, and service and male pupils being provided with military role models in textbooks. The system allowed the Meiji government to ensure that all children had basic literacy (although sometimes this did not last much beyond school age) and a shared understanding of nationalism. With these two skills alone, any government would be able much more efficiently to mobilize a society for war.

The development of school systems in the nineteenth century, in Japan and elsewhere, brought a major change to the nature, pace, and social definition of childhood. The fact of being at war, however, brought a new sense of theater and excitement into the classroom. The war, its battles, and the men at war were used extensively in lessons from history to geography, ethics, physical education, and music. In 1894–1895, the central education ministry distributed songbooks with lyrics and tunes of glory and patriotism (the emperor Meiji also penned some war songs, though the titles, such as "The Great Victory of Pyongyang" and "The Great Victory of the Yellow Sea," were rather dull). The same was true in 1904–1905. Schoolchildren studied the maps of the battlefields, learned the names of towns and cities across Korea and Manchuria, wrote letters to local troops at the front, and were given a sense of pride in being Japanese subjects of a powerful and victorious emperor. In the general domestic propaganda of 1894–1895, in particular, it was the emperor who was identified with the guidance of the war effort and the protection of the nation. Both wars also gave a boost to children's journals, increasingly filled with stories of the military and heroism. One of the most respected from this period was *Shōnen Sekai (Youth World)*, published from 1895, although an equivalent for girls, *Shōjo Sekai,* appeared only after the war with Russia.

Primary schoolchildren were consistently brought into contact with war, at school, in their songs, their games, their toys, and their reading. In addition, they were taken in school groups to two sites of intense emotional power: the railway station and the funeral. At Nagoya station, one of the major stops between Tokyo and Hiroshima, an army officer was told in the winter of 1894 that school groups, each of about 40 pupils, had been organized into one-hour shifts to clean the uniforms and boots of officers. Such duties were probably unnecessary but no doubt were intended to give the children a feeling of special contact with the officers. At major railway stations the architecture of the building and the separation of train and platform also gave a powerful sense of theater, which moved children and adults alike. At Nagoya, a band played rousing music without cease, and each troop train departed to the accompaniment of cries of *banzai* and martial songs from the assembled well-wishers.

If the railway station was generally a site of energetic noise and high spirits (at least until the sick and wounded began to return), the funerals of the military were naturally somber and relatively quiet rituals. Once again, school groups were often taken to the ceremony along with other civic representatives, such as members of patriotic associations, and contingents of local officials and police. In joining this assembly the children were made to feel that they, too, had a role to play in society. They were also witnesses to the communal respect that was accorded those who gave their lives in war. Having said that, the funerals could be long and tiresome, even for adults, as one dignitary after another made the same speech of condolence. Moreover, there were so many dead in 1904–1905 that children may actually have come to understand the uglier reality of war rather than the glorified image in their textbooks.

One of the ideas common to societies at war is a concern with the health of children; in an age in which war is seen as inevitable, even desirable, the natural assumption is that the children of today will be the soldiers of tomorrow. Japanese officials were already concerned before the China war about the lack of height of young men; in 1891, in the Azabu district of Tokyo, the average height of draft-age males was only 156 centimeters. While it was impossible in the short term to make taller children, the Education Ministry in late 1894 issued a directive to increase the physical strength and endurance of Japanese boys. This brought about a major change in the Japanese approach to schooling. Henceforth the curriculum shifted its emphasis from cultivation of the mind to cultivation of the body. This involved more classes in physical training. In response, suppliers of goods to primary schools began making wooden rifles for use in exercises. For their part, teachers were encouraged to toughen the male pupils in winter by ensuring that they did not linger by the fire or wear too many garments (the same regime was applied later to Emperor Hirohito as a child). Early in 1895, there was a move to reform boys' clothing, making the sleeve closer fitting so as to improve movement in physical training classes (in 1905, the Education Ministry considered making the same change to girls' uniforms, but there was public criticism that it would be unfeminine and inappropriate to their expected role in society). Moreover, it became common for primary schools to mark a military victory or other major celebration with a sports meeting (*undōkai*), often conducted at a local *Shintō* shrine.

One of the means by which schoolchildren were involved in the war effort was through play. In the war against China, some schools got together to stage a re-creation of a recent battle. In these the male children of one or more schools were divided into camps of Japanese and Chinese soldiers; female children were arranged into teams of Red Cross nurses; and a local site was chosen to represent a stronghold that, inevitably, must succumb to the brave Japanese. Those pupils who "fell" in the attack (presumably on cue) were stretchered away to the waiting Red Cross girls. Teachers assigned themselves the role of commanding officers and thus quietly reinforced their own authority. Some of the playful re-creations of war attracted large crowds of local people, for whom this was the closest to war they were to get, but for whom also a happy ending was guaranteed. A large-scale example, late in 1894, was at the town of Ōgaki in central Japan. There 1,600 pupils from six local elementary schools played out a battle between the Red Army of Japan and the White Army of China. The audience watching the children of the Red Army storm and take the local castle (borrowed for the event and representing a stronghold in China) was said to exceed 3,000 people from the town and its surroundings. The war against Russia was also re-created in mock battles, but here the far greater public tension and suffering was reflected in a much more serious attitude to play. As one teacher later wrote, in order to make the game "real," he convinced his pupils, aged about nine, that the Russians had seized a port on the Japanese mainland and were even now advancing into the heartland. Consequently, they should assemble before daybreak on Sunday and march off with their bamboo rifles to do whatever they could to assist the Japanese troops. He later heard that at least one child had left home telling his parents he expected not to return alive. The children also had more trouble in their war games of 1904–1905 because the enemy was less distinct. As the same memoir explained, the children had never seen a Russian and had difficulty imagining him; the only thing about which they were certain was that Russians were tall, and so, at this school, the children asked their teachers to play the role of the enemy.

A common error in writing about education and war is the assumption that children simply accepted whatever they were told. In the war against Russia, there were so many troop trains passing along the main lines that some children spent almost as much time at railway stations or standing alongside the tracks as in the classroom. Consequently, some places had to introduce a roster system in order to get the pupils back in school. Also, the education budget in 1904–1905 was cut so heavily in order to divert money to the war effort that much-needed school buildings or facilities were postponed, teachers were encouraged to retire so as to cut the wages bill, and those who remained were given larger classes, more hours of teaching, and, in some cases, had to endure a cut in wages— 30 sen a month for teachers at some common elementary schools, 92 sen at higher elementary schools. Moreover, both staff and pupils were pressured regularly to donate money to the military. In other words, the wartime hardship of schools and teachers, while it may have been presented as part of their duty, was still a reminder to children of the misery of war. At school they sang the war songs approved by the Education Ministry, filled with sentiments of destroying the enemy, even if it meant sacrificing themselves. However, children were not simply blank sheets upon which adults might write their own script. As one letter to a local newspaper noted, "A victory ceremony with a parade of children singing military songs is all very fine but I feel a special joy when I see a handful of lazy, tongue-tied little kids walking along singing, 'Japan won, Russia lost!' "[6] Notwithstanding the criticism that they were lazy (which suggests that the schools were not doing the job expected of them by the government), the children being observed and praised in this letter had a certain honesty about them, shedding war of all its ideological trimmings and reducing it to the basics.

It is worth noting also that many of the primary schoolchildren for whom war was play in 1894–1895 became the teenagers of 1904–1905. Yet the social commentary on teenage Japanese in the Russian war was uniformly critical. Again and again, there were comments from members of the public that young people, then and in the postwar years, were weak and unreliable. This was a criticism made especially against males. They were accused of lacking seriousness or motivation, of "decadence," a term that implied an unhealthy concern with sex, and of being more concerned about their clothing and hairstyles than patriotism. Indeed, to some observers, young men appeared listless and effete, while young women were becoming more self-confident and physically assertive. These criticisms suggest that a wartime education, perhaps especially one in which victory is so easily obtained, as against China, has little long-term impact. Indeed, it may be that turning war into a game in 1894–1895 actually undermined the seriousness with which children viewed it in their later years.

MEDIA

In mobilizing and maintaining cohesion in any society in modern war, literacy and the media are essential. By the time of the Sino-Japanese War, there were national and local newspapers across Japan. At the start of hostilities, the major newspapers sent about 40 war correspondents to the front. The press was able to use telegrams to speed up the flow of information about events at home and overseas (in the major cities of Tokyo and Osaka, rudimentary telephone systems were in place, but these were extended only after the war). One major impact of this flood of news was the issuing of extras, sometimes morning, noon, and night. This gave work to many boys who became specialists in selling papers in the street.

One of the leading newspapers in Japan in the 1890s was the *Yūbin Hōchi Shimbun*. Its print run rose from 13,000 copies a day in 1887, to 140,000 copies in 1904, and to 300,000 just three years later. During the China war, the *Yūbin Hōchi* and other national and local papers underwent various forms of restructuring. This was in order to encompass more news, more illustrations, and, in the case of the now renamed *Hōchi Shimbun*, to use a style of writing more accessible to all social classes. One caveat to all of this is that there were pockets of Japan that were outside the main arteries of communication. It is said that at least one village in central Japan in 1894 was quite unaware the war had started for the first five months of hostilities. While there was military censorship of the war correspondents and of the press, the literate citizenry, and even the illiterate who heard talk about the news, could follow the war in often surprising detail. Thus, for example, a letter from an army sergeant, written only days after the November 1894 massacre of Chinese civilians by Japanese troops at Port Arthur, was printed one month later by his local newspaper in Ibaragi prefecture. This openly told of "a mountain of [Chinese] corpses in the famous city streets, and a river of blood."[7]

One of the senses in which Japanese daily life in both wars was modern is in the prevalence of the image. The difference between the two conflicts, however, rests in the nature of that image. In the war with China, there were really two forms in which people could see the war. The one that has survived to the present is the bold, colorful, but also highly imaginative visualization of war in the woodblock print, very similar in style to what we understand now as manga. There were about 3,000 different prints issued during the war, averaging about 10 a day. The public tended to favor the latest rather than the best. Along with scenes of battle, civilians also wanted to be shown something of the reality of war. Thus there were prints of troops in camp doing the simple, ordinary things, such as cooking meals or keeping warm. In the battle prints the usual image was of a mass of Japanese soldiers overrunning a rabble of Chinese. In these prints the Japanese forces were distinguished by the modernity of their uniforms, the efficiency of their movement, and the resolute expressions of their faces (a feature that also separated the Japanese from the Chinese was the manliness of their moustaches).[8]

The second main channel through which ordinary people could visualize the war was in the magic lantern show. These, as the name partly suggests, were a means of casting an image impressed on glass through a light and onto a large screen. The image, of course, did not move as yet. This meant that war unconsciously was understood by people as static and frozen. Actually, this may have been a more honest portrayal of war at the time, especially in the winter of north China; temperatures there were so low that a man riding a horse could easily find his legs frozen, and the hairs of a horse's mane could be broken off like icicles. Ordinary civilians in the mid-1890s, however, were not expecting movement; the moving picture was only just then being developed in France. Consequently, the magic lantern shows exerted a fascination for many people, and it was routinely said that crowds of several hundred would pack school halls, public buildings, or even village temples whenever a show was held. The force of this appeal is evident in one case in 1894. A textile factory owner threatened his female workers with a fine of 10 sen (a good day's wage) if they left the factory at any time outside the agreed rest period. Hearing of a magic lantern show locally, 13 women pooled their money, paid the fine in advance, and went off to join the audience. The slides of war scenes were available for purchase; in one advertisement, 20 large slides could be had for about six yen, with smaller ones at half the price. There were civilians who bought a set of these slides and traveled about the villages of their county during the war, not to make profit, but to provide information (and entertainment) to villagers.

By 1904, moving pictures were already coming to dominate the modern worldview of many urban Japanese. There was already a handful of commercial filmmakers in Japan, although they mostly filmed scenes of geisha dances (also the most popular image on postcards). Footage of war had been shown in Japan, starting with the Spanish-American War of the late 1890s, the Boer War from 1899, and the Boxer War in China, in which Japanese troops fought alongside those of the Western powers. It was, however, the Russo-Japanese War that saw newsreel and dramatic re-creations of battle occupy the newly established cinemas of Japan. The film, of course, was silent, but there were recordings of music to provide a melody to the drama, and there was also a narrator, or *benshi*. The success or failure of any showing depended on his ability: A skillful *benshi* could whip up the passions of an audience.

Film of the front was obtained from both Japanese news cameramen and from foreigners, especially the French company Pathé. One of the subjects that most interested Japanese civilians was the day-to-day activities of the ordinary soldiers; the enemy rarely made an appearance, except when dead or wounded. To their credit, it is said that Japanese audiences were saddened by images of enemy dead and were both proud and pleased to see films of wounded Russians being treated by Japanese medical teams. In contrast to later wars, for example, the U.S. forces in World War II, images were also shown of Japanese corpses; this seemed to meet the public demand for truth, not lies. One of the leading historians of early cinema in Japan, Peter High, quotes the newspaper *Kobe Shimbun* of June 21, 1905:

Unlike the false "real footage" of the battle which has been coming into the country, this was definitely shot on the actual battlefield. . . . The fact that it is not organized into any clear sequence, like the phony footage, makes it all the more profound. A real battlefield is all confusion and without any apparent logic.[9]

As genuine film of the war fell in short supply, there were Japanese filmmakers who followed the lead of others in staging war for the camera. This was done using a few extras to stand in for the Russian army and a few fires to emulate the smoke of battle. While audiences may have tolerated the illusion of war when it was clearly intended to be fictional, they resented any attempt to fool them. Indeed, what is obvious from contemporary reports is just how critically aware Japanese audiences were in 1904–1905. They were quick to spot and complain about fakes or false advertising. It may be that their definition of modernity was as science, reason, and precision and that this acted as a shield against the excesses of jingoistic exploitation.

MATTERS OF DEATH

One of the aspects of daily life often influenced by war, of course, is death. Figures in the local press in 1894 showed that the average life expectancy for

Japanese was just 36. This was compared to an average of 40 for the French, 37 for Britons, and just 35 for the Dutch. In other words, life in Japan, as in Europe and elsewhere, was short, and death was common. The main reason for this brevity of life was the high rate of infant mortality. In Japan, a glance at any schoolroom would show when the harvest had failed because there would be the empty places of those children who had not survived.

One constant threat to life in Japan, irrespective of war or peace, is natural disaster. This is a mix of earthquakes, typhoons, floods, and landslides. In 1894, just before the start of war with China, a significant earthquake hit Tokyo, killing about 20 people, injuring another 300, and damaging nearly 4,000 buildings, including major government institutions. Within the first months of war, another earthquake hit the northern prefecture of Yamagata. Reports said that nearly 694 people were killed, another 600 injured, and over 2,500 homes completely destroyed. Meanwhile, a typhoon and flood devastated several other regions; in the prefecture of Shimane, there were more than 100 deaths, nearly 1,000 homes destroyed, and another 15,000 either damaged or under water. The government in Tokyo, however, pleaded that it could offer no relief as all available monies were being consumed by the war effort. Moreover, it insisted, were it to help the citizens of one disaster, then it would have to help the victims of others. Thus it used the idea of sacrifice in war as justification for leaving people to their own devices: this extreme conservatism in social welfare was to be a feature of the Meiji government until its final years. However, insofar as the Home Ministry also announced late in 1894 that there were more than 150,000 cases of dysentery and 35,700 deaths from an ongoing epidemic, it would be fair to say that daily life for Japanese during this "soft" war was pockmarked with disaster, disease, and death.[10]

Neither of the two Meiji wars directly increased the immediate level of civilian death within Japan, although hundreds of civilians laboring for the army died at the front, often through illness. Where the indirect impact was felt was in the loss of so many young men in uniform. This was particularly true in 1904–1905. During the earlier war, military funerals were a rare event, and there was never any major threat to population growth. Against Russia, however, regional newspapers were filled with the names of local men killed in battle, and military funerals became commonplace. In fact, army regulations in 1905 encouraged towns and villages to rationalize the process of funerals by holding joint ceremonies for two or more war dead. These regulations also specified that funerals should be held according to *Shintō* or Buddhist rites and that those arranging the funeral should aim for simplicity and cost cutting (as part of this, it was stated that guests arriving before or after the ceremony should be given no refreshment). While prefectural, municipal, and village officials, plus the police and civic groups, all made political capital out of their regular attendance at military funerals, the costs of the ceremony generally fell on the bereaved family, albeit with assistance from relatives and their community and with consolation gifts of money from the mourners. For the long-term loss of a husband or son, however, no war pension could be adequate compensation. Even worse was where a man returned with a major disability or grave psychological damage.

One area of civilian society that benefited from war, both in victory celebration and in funeral commemoration, was religion. Buddhist temples and *Shintō* shrines, along with Christian churches, all sought to demonstrate their patriotism by organizing donations of money for the forces and sending missionaries to the front. A popular saying in Japan is "born *Shintō*, die Buddhist," and it may be that civilians went to temples both to mourn the war dead and to give thanks for those who avoided death; at shrines, which were associated with virility, fertility, and prosperity, they celebrated the military's triumphs (often with a great deal of sake). In the war against China, it could be said that shrines were the greater beneficiaries; against Russia, it was the temples.

Before heading to Korea or China, soldiers sought Buddhist amulets for divine protection; those from the famous temple at Narita, now beside Tokyo's international airport, were seen as especially effective. Wartime displays and competitions of martial arts by Japanese males were generally held at shrines all over Japan. Major exhibits of captured enemy goods, such as flags, uniforms, and spears, were held at the Yasukuni shrine in Tokyo (with traveling exhibits also at museums or prominent places, such as castles, elsewhere in Japan). In 1905, a mass memorial service for Japan's war dead was also held at the Yasukuni shrine. This was unusual in that it took place while the war was still in progress. This suggests that the toll of war dead was so heavy that the military and government felt the need to arrange a special ceremony in order to validate the losses to date and attempt to maintain public support for the losses to come. It also suggests that the people's readiness to continue sacrificing themselves, their men, and their wealth was in decline as the death toll mounted.

SEX

In Meiji Japan, prostitution was both legal and accepted; this was very much a society dominated by men, and the so-called pleasure quarters of the towns and cities were often the sites where men gathered not only to enjoy the company of female entertainers, but also to socialize with each other. Against China, the threat of defeat hardly existed, and so prohibitions on matters of sex were very loose. Indirectly, the diversion of monies to war bonds and the military caused some loss of customers for brothels. The major exception to this, of course, was where the customers were actually from the military. According to the diary of one soldier in 1894, the city of Hiroshima was rife both with prostitutes and with sexually transmitted diseases. This was despite severe punishments for those soldiers found to be diseased or even visiting brothels.[11]

The massively greater demands on life and the economy of the Russian war led, inevitably, to a far greater impact on matters of sex. First, the brothels in many cities and towns were badly hit, both by the general wartime culture of austerity, but even more importantly because, apart from the wealthy elites, there was so little disposable income in the pockets of would-be customers. The saying in 1904–1905 was that brothels enjoyed good times on two occasions: one, when there was a victory to celebrate, and two, when local government assemblies were in session. For ordinary prostitutes the system generally was that a customer would pay a candle fee; once the candle was finished, so was he. The geisha, by contrast, were often called out to a restaurant by patrons in order to pour drinks, flatter male egos, and perhaps sing or dance in a lilting manner. The overall loss of income for sex workers was probably greatest at the higher end of the industry; even a minor individual loss, however, could be devastating for the poorer women. Thus figures for December 1904 showed that there were 22,178 licensed prostitutes in Japan, plus 26,226 geisha. The former had increased by 3,502 since December 1903, while the latter had declined by 1,905.[12] The significant increase in women in the sex and entertainment industries was in larger cities with an army presence, especially Osaka and Hiroshima. By contrast, the number of prostitutes was declining in smaller towns across the country, and brothels were closing their doors. One effect of the wartime downturn was for women to drop out of the licensed system and move into working the street. The decline in the figures for geisha also suggests that some at the upper level of the sex industry either retired, often into running bars or restaurants, or, in order to survive, accepted a drop in status to the level of ordinary prostitute.

One of the newer industries of Meiji Japan retailing sex, in war and in peace, was commercial photography. Actually, advertisements for erotic photos, usually legitimized by emphasis on their artistic qualities, often appeared in local newspapers. One reason for the growth of this business was the improved technology of cameras. The Kodak Box Brownie, so simple to use that it was originally marketed at children, appeared at the turn of the century. Also, during the Russo-Japanese War, the first color photographs were being tested. The authorities, however, were so nervous about the state of Japanese society and so afraid of losing control of morality that they instructed the police to crack down on any illicit trade in erotica. In part, the fear was probably linked to rumors that ordinary young women, not simply prostitutes, were trying to earn money by posing for the backstreet photographers. The main market for these photos, however, appears to have been the troops at the front in Manchuria, and there was at least one example of a well-meaning patriot sending nude pictures to the army as a donation to the war effort. The police, however, were generally seen as hapless either in discovering the whereabouts of photographers or in suppressing the covert trade in immoral pictures.

The Government efforts against the pest and geisha.

Wartime criticism of authorities, 1905: Misdirected police morality campaign attacks the "cat" and lets the "mice" run free. *(Tokyo Puck* journal July 1905.)

LEISURE

Leisure is largely acceptable in wartime insofar as it emulates the virtues of war; that is, it promotes health and strength and enhances the competitive or combative spirit of the public. Thus in the war against China, there was an increased popularity among young men for sword practice (even though modern war revolved around guns large and small). Similarly, against Russia, there was a boom in the number of young people practicing *kendō*. For schoolchildren, sports days, mainly involving running, were another frequent break from the confines of the classroom. Regardless of war, the two holidays that were observed fully and without controversy were the emperor's birthday on November 3 and the New Year. On the former, there was an unprecedented level of celebration; on the latter, people in towns and villages observed at least one day of rest.

In 1894–1895, the successive victories on land and sea made war seem like a festival. In 1904–1905, however, the trend was to minimize, but not entirely eliminate, any form of leisure. For example, annual festivals at local *Shintō* shrines were often divested of the side stalls and entertainments that made them truly festive. There was discussion as to whether or not it was appropriate to go flower viewing at the start of spring or summer; even ikebana, or flower arrangement, was subject to criticism as an inappropriate indulgence. In contrast, visits to the cinema and to the theater seemed to pass without comment even if, as was the case in 1904, one of the most popular films of the summer was a French drama on the life of Napoleon. Perhaps it was simply the modernity of the cinema that made it acceptable, whether or not the main feature related to the war. By 1905, there was also growing weariness of a long and unending conflict; ticket sales to theaters and to the *yose*, or vaudeville, at least at the cheapest end

Alternatives to wartime austerity: Ebisu Beer advertisement, 1905. *(Gifu Nichi Nichi Shimbun April 1905.)*

of the market, began to rise in mid-year as theater managers discounted their prices. For individual leisure, there was always the patriotic alternative of alcohol and cigarettes. However, a commercial advertisement for Ebisu Beer in April 1905, while making much of the fact that it was a supplier to the imperial household, nonetheless was strong on relaxation and short on patriotism.

WARTIME HUMOR

In writing the history of any conflict, one of the things that is most difficult to re-create is the sense of trepidation; anyone reading about a war knows the outcome already. In fighting this anxiety, however, it may be that any civilian society (and no doubt any military also) finds comfort in humor. The nature of this humor depends on the progress of the war: Where victory is easy, the humor will be relaxed; where victory is hard or unobtainable, the humor is more likely to be bitter and target figures in authority.

At the outset of war in 1894, local police forces were instructed to prevent gossip and rumor so as to avoid unrest, but for the public, there was no great fear after the initial easy victories. This meant that humor was often casual and sometimes even smug. Examples include newspaper cartoons suggesting new careers for Chinese POWs; these included performing as stage puppets in what looked like the traditional Bunraku theater of Japan or serving as minders to the more demanding children of Japanese families. The satire was also directed at home, for example, teasing the intrepid reporters tramping over mountains and through snow in search of a great story. The army itself was not immune to being mocked. At Hiroshima, a fire destroyed part of a regimental base late in 1894, and when the commander moved his forces several miles away to a place called Enami, local people joked that this was the "conquest of Enami." In 1894–1895, young men going to the brothel areas might call themselves "scouts" going on "reconnaissance." In the war with Russia, one of the new slang terms among geisha included *resupply* when calling for more alcohol, and upon seeing a client who had collapsed from having had too much to drink, they lamented that he had "fallen gloriously in battle."

Those who attempted to force their values on ordinary people were always easy targets; a publication called *Light of the Nation* changed its name during the Russian war to *Temperance News.* Upon hearing this, the metropolitan *Jiji* newspaper responded with an article noting that the great samurai warrior of the sixteenth century, Takeda Shingen (immortalized in the 1980s film *Kagemusha*), got a headache whenever he tried to read the dry Confucian classics; the article then wondered how today's heavy drinkers in the military would react upon reading *Temperance News.* In fact, there was to be a running battle between the advocates of temperance and the rest of Japan, military and civilian alike, during times of war, with the former heavily outnumbered and outgunned by the latter.

One of the things about wartime that may easily be overlooked is how tiresome it can become. Humor was also a form of relief from tedium as well as from the more tedious local savants of war. Thus a series of letters to a provincial newspaper in October 1904 provided a list of "The 100 Fools of Our Time." In first place came "those who talk as if they are experts on the military situation." Second, however, were "men who gawp as women pass by." Others included "those who disparage everything without a reason," "those who blow their noses and stare at the result as if in amazement," and "those who get so carried away talking about the war in the public baths that they scrub themselves raw."[13] What is notable here is the mix of irritants, some related to the war, others simply part of daily life.

The human and financial strain of the war with Russia quickly led to a bitter vein of humor. This was directed at all forms of authority and power, with the exception of the emperor. Leading the trend was a new satirical journal that appeared early in 1905; this was *Tokyo Puck*. Its favorite targets were the wealthy and the arrogant. Thus in various cartoons it showed what was being reported in the press, that is, businessmen and politicians engaging in acts of corruption, such as pocketing monies donated to the armed forces. It also satirized men of wealth who angrily refused to give money to the war effort and, instead, spent it in evenings with the more expensive geisha. Even national heroes were not off limits. *Tokyo Puck* delighted in cataloguing the misery of a welcome home for what was indisputably Japan's great warrior hero of 1905, Admiral Tōgō. In its series of comic images, this included having his hair and beard pulled by souvenir seekers, being blinded by the flash of photographers, and having gallons of celebratory alcohol poured down his throat. For *Tokyo Puck,* but also for many ordinary people, figures of authority were fair game. Thus village heads, bureau chiefs, mayors, and governors were mocked relentlessly. Of one mayor, it was said that his speeches were finally improving with all the wartime practice; *village head* became another term for *idiot.* The public's humor could also be perfectly brutal. One civilian wrote to his local newspaper to condemn bureaucrats for their failure to donate money to the war effort and asked rhetorically, "Have they no heart— I should like to hear the opinion of a vivisectionist!"

The humor could also be quite gentle and self-deprecating. One of the examples here is that of a man who wrote a letter to the forces from his region. In doing this, he took the advice of the local authorities, who suggested that a letter bearing a woman's name might help to brighten a soldier's day. Having signed off as a woman, however, he now found that the soldier to whom his letter had been given had sent him a reply, begging for a photo. To this, the writer had innocently responded, but as he explained, "Now the soldier is probably looking at the photo of me with a beard and wondering, 'what on earth!'"

LAW AND ORDER

The recurring mantra about Japanese civilian society for much of the twentieth century was that it was safe and that violent crime was relatively rare. Anyone reading the newspapers in the 1890s to 1900s, however, would have difficulty accepting this. Instead, assault, murder, and suicide were commonplace events. During the war years, such incidents may have continued; neither of the wars eliminated the mass of rural and urban poor who might be the perpetrators or victims of violence. In fact, in the very first few days of the Sino-Japanese War, there had been a minor rice riot in Osaka when over 100 impoverished workers attacked a wholesale rice dealer and threatened to kill him if he did not cease exploiting his monopoly of the market. One of the perhaps surprising things about Japanese civilians, even in the 1890s, is that they could purchase handguns. An intriguing press report of January 1895 stated that a number of wealthy men in Gifu City in central Japan purchased pistols for self-defense. What is not explained is against whom they felt they must defend themselves. An advertisement from about the same time, however, declared that a pistol is "the best means to defend one's life and property." The implication is therefore that personal violence is seen as a possibility and that the wealthy are at risk of having their wealth removed from them. By contrast, one cannot rely on the police.

A report from late 1894 on the prison population of Japan suggested that jails nationwide were 10 percent emptier than at the war's outset and that most prisoners were reoffenders. In the case of Gifu prefecture, the total figures were 1,057 men and 99 women; of these, 135 were said to have been imprisoned since the war began. In the war against Russia, the Law Ministry acted to reduce prisoner numbers by ensuring that minor offences did not lead to arrest. The figures for February 1905 showed a total of just under 58,000 civilians in jail. This was a decline of about 6,500 over the previous 12 months. One of the most common crimes, for which the penalty could be a hefty fine and several months in prison, was gambling. Gamblers, however, seemed to be impervious to the restraints of war or the legal system and continued to gamble at any time.

The probability, as it may be with all societies, is that thieves and conmen made up the bulk of the prison population, and in times of war, there were clearly opportunities and incentives for both. Houses, for example, were easier to burgle when men were away at the war. Schemes veering on con-artistry included, in 1894, a man who went around to villages where the army had yet to call. Once there, he would tell farmers to cut their losses by selling their livestock to him, even at basement prices, rather than see them requisitioned by the military. The dealer would then sell the animals to farmers whose stock had already been requisitioned and who, consequently, were in desperate need of animals and willing to pay high prices.[14] More obvious cons during the Russian war included a "salesman" who toured villages offering unbeatable bargains on a fine new bicycle, an example of which he proudly displayed to prospective buyers. However, once a deposit was paid, both the salesman and the bicycle disappeared. Conning people of their money in wartime was obviously seen as reprehensible, but public anger was generally directed at business contractors who skimmed money for themselves or, in the case of the major corporation Ōkura in the China war, at businesses that sent tins of food to the battlefront containing stones instead of meat. Small-time crooks in a time of general and even increasing poverty were somewhat understandable; those with wealth who merely sought to exploit the war to increase their riches were regarded with contempt.

IMAGES OF THE ENEMY

One of the longer-lasting consequences of war for a civilian community may be in the persistence of images of the enemy. The accepted belief among historians is that the Japanese people became contemptuous of the Chinese during the war of 1894–1895. This is overstated. There were few Chinese prisoners of war in Japan, and the only indirect encounters for Japanese civilians was in the war prints and press reports. In the prints it is true that Chinese soldiers were usually portrayed either in defeat or retreat. These were mainly battle prints, and so there was no room for Chinese civilians. However, this was not the case in the press reports or letters home of Japanese soldiers. In these it was equally as common for the writer to note the diversity of Chinese civilians, from those of great wealth to those enduring extreme poverty, of the great passiveness of some versus the astounding industriousness of others. Thus in a report from Manchuria, one Japanese journalist could write admiringly of Chinese farmers who rose at 4:00 A.M. to tend their lands and returned only after dark. In addition to working so hard, they subsisted on so little, and in his words, "There probably is no-one in the world blessed with such a spirit of thrift as the Chinese."[15] Other Japanese at the front wrote gratefully that the Chinese people demonstrated goodwill toward them and that Chinese coolies were essential in keeping the Japanese army on the move.

In 1904–1905, the Russian enemy was more visible to civilians in film (although little of this was designed to provoke hatred). Unlike with the Chinese, there were not existing communities in Japanese port cities such as Yokohama and Kobe. There were, however, over 71,000 Russian POWs in Japan by late 1905. Over 22,000 of these were held at just one location—Hamadera at Osaka—although usually, there were anything from a few hundred to about 3,000 captives in any one place. What this meant was that civilians at the main railway stations had a fair chance of seeing the enemy in the flesh. When this happened, sometimes there were taunts but rarely anything more. In fact, some children recalled receiving their first taste of chocolate as a gift from one of the passing POWs. At the city of Nagoya, which held nearly 3,000 Russians, the senior officers among the prisoners were said to receive their meals from the city's best Western restaurant and to walk freely about the streets with a police guard in tow. There was some public outrage and perhaps amusement, however, when some Russian officers managed to visit a city brothel, passing themselves off as Americans. Despite this, it was generally suggested that the frequency of contact between POWs and ordinary people increased over the course of the war and that the nature of this contact was generally amiable.

PUBLIC UNREST

The war with China ended with direct economic and territorial benefits to Japan. This meant more money for industry, communications, commerce, and education. The war with Russia, however, ended with a peace treaty in which the Japanese representative, Foreign Minister Komura, was unable to extract a single dollar for Japan's war expenses. One response among the public to this in September 1905 was to riot in the streets. In the so-called Hibiya riots in Tokyo, police boxes and government offices were attacked, and martial law was introduced. It has long been the common wisdom of historians that this was a demonstration of Japanese ultra-nationalism, that the riots were in defense of Japan's national honor and showed how ready were the people to continue sacrificing themselves for the flag. In reality, the protesters were a tiny minority of the population, and even among their number, it is probable that the real grievance of many was economic rather than ideological. Elsewhere, ordinary Japanese exhibited a range of emotions. Some were pragmatic; they accepted that Japan simply was not one of the world's great powers and had obtained only what it deserved. Others looked for reasons at home to explain the disappointment of the war's end, arguing that Japan itself was a topsy-turvy society in which young men were effeminate and young women masculine; thus in this unnatural world it was only natural that the victor in war should be the loser in peace. Others took refuge, once again, in humor. Among Yokohama businessmen, after news of the peace treaty, a new phrase was created to describe anyone blundering in a major deal: "He did a Komura!"

The people of Japan in the two wars of Meiji were neither unusually militaristic (as was argued then and later by foreign observers) nor unusually

Satire on the Hibiya riots: "Burned police boxes for sale." (*Tokyo Puck* October 1905.)

pacifist (as some Japanese would like to argue of the present). Instead, their ambitions revolved largely around the basics of daily life: adequate food, shelter, and security. After the victory of 1895, they had reason to believe that war could assist them in achieving these ambitions. After 1905, that belief was not to be sustained. Instead, in the wake of the Russo-Japanese War, the people favored economic growth over militarism and greater concern for individual well-being over that of the nation. This was to last through the 1910s and 1920s, the era known as "Taishō democracy," and was only brought temporarily to an end by the Great Depression and subsequent wars of the 1930s.

NOTES

1. On Christian support for the China war, see Ōhama Tetsuya, *Meiji no Bohyō,* Tokyo: Kawade Bunko, 1990 (pp. 50–55). This book was republished in 2004 under the title *Shamin no Mita Nis-Shin Nichi-Ro Sensō.* The donation of Bibles was noted in the *Mainichi News* of 9 April 1895.

2. Giichi Ono, *Expenditures of the Sino-Japanese War,* New York: Oxford University Press, 1922 (pp. 279–84).

3. Figures for wages in 1894 from Hiroshima-ken, ed., *Hiroshima Kenshi: Kindai Gendai Shiryō 2,* Hiroshima, 1972 (pp. 302–4).

4. Something of the life of civilian laborers with the Japanese army in 1894–1895 can be understood from regional histories, for example, Fukushima-ken, ed., *Fukushima Kenshi 4: Tsūshi-hen Kindai 1,* Fukushima, 1971 (p. 915). It is said that some laborers drank heavily to stave off the bitter Manchurian cold in winter and, falling deeply asleep, froze to death.

5. Sharon H. Nolte and Sally Ann Hastings, "The Meiji State's Policy Towards Women, 1890–1910," in *Recreating Japanese Women 1600–1945,* ed. Gail Lee Bernstein, Berkeley: University of California Press, 1991 (p. 162).

6. Anonymous letter, *Gifu Nichi Nichi Shimbun,* 20 October 1904.

7. On Port Arthur, see Katsuda Shishi Hensan Iinkai, ed., *Katsuda Shishi: Kindai Gendai 1,* Katsuda, 1979 (p. 443), quoting the letter of Sergeant Kurosawa, 25 November 1894, printed in *Iharaki,* 25 December 1894. On the reformation of the *Hōchi Shimbun,* see its edition of 27 December 1894.

8. On the war prints, see Shumpei Okamoto, ed., *Impressions of the Front: Woodcuts of the Sino-Japanese War 1894–95,* Philadelphia, PA: Philadelphia Museum of Art, 1983.

9. Peter B. High, "The Dawn of Cinema in Japan," *Journal of Contemporary History* 19 (1984): 36.

10. For press reports of disasters and disease, see *Gifu Nichi Nichi Shimbun,* 1–2 December 1894.

11. Keiichi Hatori et al., eds., *Meiji 27-8-nen Seneki Jūgunki,* Niigata, 1975 (p. 11).

12. For statistics on prostitution and geisha, see *Gifu Nichi Nichi Shimbun,* 18 June 1905.

13. *Gifu Nichi Nichi Shimbun,* 16 October 1904.

14. Tochigi Kenshi Hensan Iinkai, ed., *Tochigi Kenshi: Shiryōhen—Kingendai 2,* Tokyo, 1977 (local government report, 20 September 1894).

15. Inoue Kantarō report, *Gifu Nichi Nichi Shimbun,* 1 May 1895.

SELECTED BIBLIOGRAPHY

High, Peter B. "The Dawn of Cinema in Japan." *Journal of Contemporary History* 19 (1984): 23–57.

Explains the origins and development both of Japanese filmmakers and film audiences from the 1890s.

Holmes, Colin, and A. H. Ion. "Bushido and the Samurai: Images in British Public Opinion, 1894–1914." *Modern Asian Studies* 14 (1980): 309–29.

A very useful survey of Western attitudes toward Japanese society over the period of its two early wars.

Huffman, James. *Creating a Public: People and Press in Meiji Japan.* Honolulu: University of Hawai'i Press, 1997.

The principal authority on the world of Meiji newspapers deals with the press and the wars of 1894–1895 and 1904–1905 in chapters 7 and 9, respectively.

Keene, Donald. "The Sino-Japanese War of 1894–95 and Its Cultural Effects in Japan." In *Tradition and Modernization in Japanese Culture,* edited by Donald H. Shively. Princeton, NJ: Princeton University Press, 1971.

A pioneering essay on war and the arts by one of the leading translators and cultural historians of Japan.

Lone, Stewart. *Japan's First Modern War: Army and Society in the Conflict with China 1894–95.* New York: Macmillan, 1994.

This remains the sole extended work in English on Japanese society during the first of its modern, international wars.

Lone, Stewart. "Between Bushido and Black Humour." *History Today* 55 (2005): 20–27.

A short article for a general readership dealing with some of the sources of wartime discontent and satire in Japanese society during the conflict with Russia.

Lone, Stewart. "Remapping Japanese Militarism: Provincial Society at War 1904–05." *Japanese Studies* 25 (2005): 53–63.

This deals at greater length with three of the sites at which civilians came into contact with the military: the railway station, cinema, and funeral ceremony.

Nolte, Sharon H., and Sally Ann Hastings. "The Meiji State's Policy Towards Women, 1890–1910." In *Recreating Japanese Women 1600–1945,* edited by Gail Lee Bernstein. Berkeley: University of California Press, 1991.

An excellent analysis of official attitudes toward the roles of women, both in war and peace.

Okamoto, Shumpei, ed. *Impressions of the Front: Woodcuts of the Sino-Japanese War 1894–95.* Philadelphia, PA: Philadelphia Museum of Art, 1983.

Okamoto was a leading historian of politics in Meiji Japan. In this heavily illustrated exhibition catalogue he provides an individual explanation for many of the woodcut prints sold to the public during the war.

Ono, Giichi. *Expenditures of the Sino-Japanese War.* New York: Oxford University Press, 1922.

Using official records, this is a classic study of the costs of war and the impact of war on prices, supply, and economic growth.

Shimazu, Naoko. "The Myth of the 'Patriotic Soldier': Japanese Attitudes Towards Death in the Russo-Japanese War." *War and Society* 19 (2001): 69–89.

> Shimazu is mainly concerned with the attitudes toward death of men in the military. Her point is to show the difference between the official mythology of the selfless Japanese warrior and the reality of a very human body of men. This article is part of an ongoing project.

Warner, Denis, and Peggy Warner. *The Tide at Sunrise: A History of the Russo-Japanese War, 1904–1905*. London: Angus and Robertson, 1975.

> Denis Warner is a veteran correspondent of Asia since the 1950s. In this work he and his wife employ Japanese army records to provide the fullest and most readable account of the entire war. In fact, the book was translated into the Japanese language as a complete history of the war.

Wilson, Sandra. *The Russo-Japanese War in Cultural Perspective, 1904–05*. New York: St. Martin's Press, 1999.

> Most relevant to this chapter is Wilson's own essay "The Russo-Japanese War and Japan: Politics, Nationalism and Historical Memory" (pp. 160–93).

FOUR

Urban Life in China's Wars, 1937–1949: The View from the Teahouse

Di Wang

In 1911, the Chinese monarchy collapsed under the combined weight of repeated humiliations by Western and Japanese militaries and the loss of support from provincial elites. In its stead a weak republic was established, which lacked both political legitimacy and a strong central force of its own. As a result, China's political map was fragmented until 1949. Through the 1920s, independent military commanders controlled large regions of China and waged a series of inconclusive wars with each other. By the 1930s, the Guomindang (also Kuomintang), or Nationalist Party, under the leadership of General Chiang Kai-shek, had risen through battle to become the single most powerful political entity in China, yet it still only controlled about one-third of China's provinces. In this way, war and the presence of soldiers intruded to an unprecedented degree in the daily lives of many Chinese.

In 1937, after years of increasing and frequently violent intervention in Chinese affairs, the Japanese army commenced a full-scale war with the Chinese republic. In response to this invasion the government, under the Guomindang (GMD), adopted a strategy of trading space for time; this meant that within a year, Japan controlled most of China east of a straight line from Manchuria in the north through Beijing, the central city of Wuhan, and down to Guangzhou in the far south. Until 1945 and Japan's defeat, the GMD abandoned its political capital in Nanjing and its industrial base in Shanghai and relocated to Chongqing in the far western province of Sichuan. Other institutions, such as several hundred factories and colleges, along with millions of refugees, also were physically relocated by road, river, and rail from the occupied north, east, and south of China to the western hinterland. The isolated upper Yangzi region in west China became known as the "Great Rear Area" (Dahoufang). It also became, for the first time, the center of China's, or at least free China's, politics, economy, and military (about 60 percent of all Chinese lived in free China during the anti-Japanese war). At the center of this mass wartime relocation of institutions and people were the provinces of Yunnan and Sichuan. This chapter focuses on daily life in Chengdu, the capital of Sichuan, and, in particular, on the most important and frequent site of communal interaction: the teahouse.

The Chengdu plain is both remote from China's crowded east and surrounded by mountains. Until the early twentieth century, this made traveling from the eastern coast extremely difficult. It also obstructed any attack by the Japanese during the War of Resistance of 1937–1945. Across the plain itself, there were numerous walled cities and busy market towns. Unlike north China, where farmers lived in villages for protection, the country people of the Chengdu plain were scattered. Their farmhouses and temples were surrounded by bamboo trees, prompting one Western

Japanese occupation of China, 1937–1945. (David S. Heidler.)

missionary to write, "From hilltops the view over the plain is a panorama of groves interspersed with charming vistas of green or golden fields according to the season."[1] The English traveler Isabella Bird, in the 1890s, wrote that Chengdu "has a superb climate, ranging from the temperate to the subtropical; a rich soil, much of which, under careful cultivation, yields three and even four crops annually of most things which can be grown." It also held vast natural resources, "forests of grand timber, the area of which has not even been estimated; rich mineral resources, and some of the most valuable and extensive coal-fields in the world."[2]

Urban Chengdu was among the country's largest inland cities. In 1910, its population was 335,000; in 1937, 468,000; and in 1949, 658,000. It was also beautiful. Before her arrival, Bird had heard from others that Chengdu was "among the finest cities . . . a second Peking." Harvard Professor Ernest Wilson even thought that Chengdu was "probably the finest city in the whole of China," while a Japanese observer noted that the architecture of Chengdu revealed a "classical atmosphere" like that of Kyoto.[3]

Chengdu is an ancient city. During the Three Kingdoms period (220–280 A.D.), it was the capital of the state of Shu. During the Tang Dynasty in the eighth century, it prospered greatly. However, decades of war in Sichuan between 1622 and 1681 left the local economy devastated and its cities, including Chengdu, badly damaged. Things were gradually restored in the early Qing (pronounced "Ching") Dynasty, 1644–1911. This was the result of domestic commerce and reconstruction, not outside influences. Indeed, until the late Qing, the West had only a negligible influence on Chengdu; Isabella Bird wrote in 1899 that the city owed "absolutely nothing to European influence." During the 1920s, the great Chinese writer Ba Jin, in his autobiographical novel *Family*, described Chengdu as a model of conservatism and despotism, a complete contrast to the modernism and freedom of Shanghai.[4] Such a belief, of course, reflected the radical thought of some new and Western-influenced intellectuals who blamed Chinese tradition for bringing the country to the brink of ruin. However, both critics and supporters of Chengdu agreed that it retained a much more traditional culture than the cities of coastal, northern, and even central China.

The War of Resistance was a turning point in the street life of Chengdu. After war broke out, people still used the street for daily life, but now there was the constant threat of Japanese air raids. As in peacetime, commoners were the major occupants of public space, which served as market, work site, stage, shelter, and social center for the lower classes, many of whom were refugees from the coastal regions. The one place to which virtually all classes of civilians headed at some point during the day was the teahouse. The teahouse, as a microcosm, reflected the larger Chinese world, both in peace and war.

TEAHOUSE LIFE DURING THE WAR

The street, an expansive space that accommodated all sorts of people, was the major arena for public life. By comparison, the teahouse was a much smaller public space, but it also attracted people of all trades. It undoubtedly served primarily as a place for leisure and social discourse, yet it also assumed almost all the roles of the street, from marketplace to stage. Furthermore, the teahouse provided a comfortable environment that was unaffected by bad weather and conducive to hosting activities, such as hobby clubs, business transactions, and even quasi-civil courts.

Even in war, the pursuit of leisure permeated everything and was actively encouraged, at least by those with a commercial interest. As a sign posted by a tea and wine shop advised, "Work hard for reputation and work hard for profit, but find leisure time to drink a cup of tea; work hard for thinking and think hard for working, but seek happiness to sip a little wine." Local people joked that their hometown was a city of the "Three Plentys": plenty of idlers, plenty of teahouses, and plenty of lavatories![5]

Who patronized the teahouses of Chengdu? A guidebook from 1938 and a travel note from 1943 list two categories: the "idle class" (*youxian jieji*) and the "busy class" (*youmang jieji*).[6] The idle class in Chengdu, as commonly understood, was the leisure class: local scholars, absentee land-lords, retired officials, and other elites. The busy class included those who had to work for a living. The busy class in the teahouse could be classified into three groups. First were those who used the teahouse as a theater, such as local opera performers and storytellers. Second were those who used the teahouse as a place to transact business, such as merchants, fortune-tellers, doctors, and artisans. Third were those who used the teahouse as a market, such as peddlers of food and sundries and day laborers. We must recognize, however, that here the terms *idle* and *busy* are used very loosely. Although the idle class was often used to describe those who could sup-port themselves without having to earn a living, it was never formally defined as an independent class, and its members could come from vari-ous economic backgrounds. In Chinese cities, both a rich person and a poor person who had nothing to do were generally considered idlers. Nonetheless, these two terms properly represented the two groups that gathered in the teahouse and shared a common public space.

The Japanese bombed Chengdu furiously during the second year of the war, and residents were constantly subjected to air raids. Some areas just outside the city wall became gathering sites, and many teahouses were built to serve these displaced people. Many crude and simple teahouses emerged on both banks of the Fu River near the New South City Gate. One was called the Village on the River and drew many patrons because of the scenic beauty of the river and the enormous trees and thick bamboo that surrounded it. The teahouse had two areas: The front was open air with square tables and bamboo-armed chairs, while the rear was covered and had wooden tables and chairs. In good weather, both areas would be crowded with customers. When an air raid sounded and people left town, the teahouse became even more crowded. Prior to the war, women, especially younger ones, were not supposed to appear in the teahouse, but during the war, this teahouse served many fashionable young women, who sat and mingled with men while drinking tea, chatting, reading, or playing cards. These female customers were treated as equals and, no doubt to the owner's joy, attracted more men, who wanted to see the well-dressed women.[7]

Chengdu people also used teahouses as reception rooms for meeting friends. Because most common people had small living spaces, they felt more comfortable socializing in a teahouse. It was the site where one expected to bump into friends. An elderly editor recalled that during the 1930s and 1940s, there was a special teahouse for intellectuals where he met his writers to assign and receive articles, thereby saving both postage and time. Many residents made decisions about their daily lives in teahouses. Some occupations, social organizations, and students used teahouses as meeting places. The Sleeping Stream Teahouse became a gathering place for students, extremely crowded on weekends and holidays. While intellectuals favored the Cultural Teahouse, teachers gathered at the Crane Singing Teahouse. Even rickshaw pullers, second-hand goods traders, and latrine cleaners had their own teahouses.[8]

Teahouses filled not only cultural and economic functions, but also often played a role in maintaining social stability. An unwritten rule gradually took shape in Chengdu: When conflict arose, people would seek mediators in teahouses instead of going to court. From this, we might call the teahouse a quasi-civil court. Generally, the two parties concerned would invite a leading public figure to a teahouse to hear their case. Of course, disputes solved in the teahouse were usually over issues of daily life, such as slander, debts, property rights, and even assault, so long as no death was involved (otherwise, it would have to be handled by the district magistrate).

Normality in war: The teahouse. From Hollington Tong, ed., *China After Seven Years of War.* (The Macmillan Co., NY 1945.)

Because this occurred regularly, some men, usually the heads of powerful local secret societies, became professional teahouse mediators. In his short wartime novel, *In the Fragrant Chamber Teahouse (Zai Qixiangju chaguan li)* in 1940, Sha Ding described someone who was invited as a mediator to oversee "drinking settlement tea":

Master Xin is a degree holder of the last civil service examination in the Qing, and had been a commander of a local militia and a leader of the Sworn Brotherhood Society for ten years. He retired eight years ago, and has seldom involved himself in local affairs since then, but his opinion is still as influential as when he was the militia commander.[9]

Settling disputes was not always simple. Where two parties refused to compromise, the teahouse could erupt in violence, with furniture being damaged or a fight leading to injury or even death. When this happened, street officers and the neighborhood headman would deal with the situation. The teahouse owner would expect compensation from the disputants for his losses.

One of the most direct consequences of war for the lives of civilians was the heightened politicization of everything they said or did. Disputes could be seen as evidence of national disunity and weakness; leisure could be attacked as indifference to the sacrifices of others. The political, social, and economic conflicts of war were played out in the teahouse. Although teahouses filled people's ongoing needs in terms of leisure, business, and public life, they became an arena of political struggle or were forced into the political orbit. This was true both in the War of Resistance and in the later civil war of 1945–1949 as the GMD tried to impose its authority on local people and suppress any rival beliefs or activities. From this point of view the teahouse could be considered a political stage, where, especially in wartime, all kinds of people and powers played roles in the unfolding drama of modern China.

DEBATES OVER WARTIME DAILY LIFE

The teahouse was a symbol of daily life. It was central to the routines of individual or small group patrons. It was not a site for a mass rally, a demonstration of group physical strength, or displays of military-style efficiency. In fact, it functioned according to its own publicly created sense of time, and its space was narrowly communal rather than broadly national. To reformist elites and the GMD government, this made it the focus of constant attack. The basic point of their criticisms was that when the very fate of the nation was at stake, people should devote their money and energy to saving the country, rather than spending them in the teahouse. Critics often tried to shame customers by comparing the hours spent idling at teahouses with the plight of soldiers fighting on the battlefields. These criticisms, however, seem to have been ineffectual; according to the essay "The Social Situation in Wartime Chengdu" published in 1938, the second year of the Japanese invasion, Chengdu residents seemed to care little about the war. No doubt, ordinary civilians believed a war of resistance was just (although they had less sympathy for the ensuing civil war between the GMD and communist armies), especially when they heard of the many atrocities committed by Japanese soldiers against innocent Chinese. However, they had reason to be cynical about the GMD government; even Chiang Kai-shek admitted that many GMD officials were lazy, corrupt, and unpopular. This may help to explain why, as the essay asserted, sitting in the teahouse was "surely Chengdu people's pastime." Despite this, it urged those who were selfish and insensitive to wake up and care more about the fate of the nation.[10]

Another essay condemned the so-called Chengdu phenomenon, in which central areas such as Warm Spring Road and Main Mansion Street had more than 10 teahouses crowded day and night; what this suggests is that daily life was able, in small ways, to resist the varied pressures of wartime. The essay criticized some "boring and idle people" for sitting in a teahouse the whole day "without rhyme or reason." The writer observed that "teahouses have recently become weird places where waitresses publicly flirt with customers and even charge four to five times more for tea served in private rooms." Another article published that same year also condemned the prosperous entertainment trade at a time when so many were struggling with the effects of wartime inflation.[11] In fact, the greatest impact of war on the daily lives of Chinese was soaring inflation. The GMD largely financed its wartime expenditures by printing more and more money, which thus progressively lost its value (China's leading financiers had refused to relocate their money to the west at the start of war). According to a political cartoon for the period 1937–1949, 100 Chinese dollars in 1937 would buy two oxen; in 1941, a sack of flour; in 1945, two eggs; and in 1949, a sheet of paper. Thus inflation, rising consumption taxes, and the loss of wealth were some of the main trends in the daily lives of ordinary civilians.

Yet, despite all this, a 1943 article "Chatting about Chengdu" could describe a city seeming, in some ways, still to be in peacetime; those with money continued to frequent the splendid shops, while they and others were regularly to be found at entertainment venues and teahouses. Actually, one of the reasons for this leisure activity was the rapid population increase brought about by refugees from the Japanese-held territories. In the case of Chongqing, the republic's wartime capital, the city's population nearly tripled, and this, according to Lee McIsaac, made it one of the world's most congested cities.[12] In the crowded and unstable conditions of wartime life, people sought to recreate some of the pleasures from peacetime, and few were both so simple and so familiar as spending time at the teahouse.

Along with the wartime movement of peoples, however, an inevitable passenger was disease. In the initial exodus from the Japanese invasion to the temporary capital of Wuhan in 1938, there were major outbreaks of malaria; the result was what one historian of the city, Stephen MacKinnon, has called the largest crisis management campaign in China's public health history to 1949.[13] A point here may be that the teahouse played an essential role in public health by providing boiled water to drink. A further and ongoing problem for the refugees from the more prosperous eastern provinces, however, was their inability to feel at ease in the west. Chinese refugees themselves came to echo the prejudices of some Western travelers to China in the nineteenth century; that is, they were astounded by the filth, squalor, and poverty they witnessed in Sichuan, including the numbers of beggars and the hundreds of people who starved or froze to death in the street in the winter months. Some could hardly believe they were sheltering in part of the same country. Thus, as Lee McIsaac further explains, the eastern refugees were constantly complaining about the conditions of life in their new homes and offering advice to the locals about how to deal with such things as sanitation and rat infestations.

Cultural friction between the self-appointed sophisticates of eastern China and the residents of the west also ranged across differences in speech and habits. One example was a common practice of Sichuan laborers: While working, they wrapped white cloth around their heads in a kind of turban. The use of the color white, which symbolized death in other parts of China, seemed macabre at best to the newly arrived refugees and was later criticized as an undesirable practice by the GMD government.

In addition, there was competition between these so-called downriver refugees and local people for jobs in the relocated offices and industries. In general, the refugees dominated the new government offices and such areas as banking. Consequently, daily life involved interregional conflict, irritation, and frustration. However, over time, there was also an increased mutual understanding of Chinese about other Chinese. A case in point is the exiled artists and writers of Shanghai who began during the war years to take a far greater interest in the lives and customs of rural Chinese. Having said that, the extent of the human dislocation of war meant that many people had lost not only their homes and possessions (something like two-thirds of all structures in Wuhan City, for example, were destroyed by 1945), but also their jobs and any sense of security. Consequently, the teahouse acted as a kind of refuge both for locals and for the actual refugees. For this reason, it was one business that did very well in war, and the saying was that teahouses and similar places of leisure, like mahjong parlors, emerged like "bamboo shoots after a spring rain." Indeed, it was this very success that led Chiang Kai-shek to lament later that "the Chinese revolution would have been successful if people had used the time they spent in the teahouse for the goal of the revolution."

Many elites thought that teahouses reflected the inertia of too many Chinese civilians. A book titled *New Chengdu* claimed that patrons "kill time in the teahouse, telling stories from ancient and modern times, commenting on society, playing chess, gambling, criticizing public figures, and gossiping about private matters and secrets of the boudoir."[14] However, while conservatives attacked teahouse culture for its lethargy and idleness, they did not seem to consider that the very normality and relative peace of the teahouse might have played a major role in limiting popular opposition toward the government and its handling of the war. In fact, those who opted to wait out the war by retreating into the familiar routine of the teahouse were probably the least of the GMD's worries.

Yet there were others who defended the teahouse by emphasizing its positive social function. The custom of frequenting teahouses had a long historical legacy in China and met a real social demand. The most passionate defense of teahouse culture came from the writer who used the pen name Lao Xiang (Old Folk) in his long series "A Discussion of Tea Drinking by Chengdu People," published in the *West China Night News (Huaxi wanbao)* in 1942. He pointed out that drinking tea had always been a part of daily life in Chengdu, where it was "neither cherished nor despised"; indeed, it was a normal and unexceptional part of daily life and had not become a "serious issue until some people began to talk about it." In response to the criticism that people wasted too much time there, the author wrote mockingly, "It seems these critics treasure every minute but sometimes they let the cat out of the bag because they also like to play cards, chat, and watch local operas, spending more time in these activities than people in Chengdu do drinking tea." It seemed to him that those who had different hobbies and preferences tried to avoid attacks on themselves by joining the chorus condemning teahouse goers.

LIFE ON CAMPUS

One of the criticisms of the teahouse to which Lao Xiang responded was that it was the "devil's den" *(moku)* where students ignored their studies. His reply was that educators, instead, should find out why students were dissatisfied on campus and liked to go to the teahouse. Part of the reason here, no doubt, was the dilemma of students who saw themselves as the future hope and leaders of China but were ambivalent at being in school while others were on the frontlines of resistance (students were exempt from military conscription until the system changed in January 1943, but even after that point, they were allowed to finish their courses before being drafted). More than one-third of all China's universities and colleges on the eve of war had been in Beijing and Shanghai. In exile in the seemingly backward western provinces, often without books, which had not survived the exodus, or materials for scientific and technical experiments, the students had to question the value of what they were learning. The traditional stereotype of the scholar in Asia is the thin, pale-faced, sickly young man who reads all night to the detriment of his constitution. In wartime China, however, the lack of food meant that diseases such as tuberculosis and malaria increased among the student body (according to a 1938 study of just over 5,000 students in Chongqing, already fewer than 100 could claim to be in perfect health). The students' diet was poor, and they relied on snack shops, which proliferated around university campuses selling such things as bean curd, noodles, and steamed bread. There was usually no fuel for heating dormitories in winter, and oil was rationed to the point where, at one campus, there was enough for only a single lamp to be shared among 40 student boarders. Chemistry students made a little extra money by manufacturing ink to sell cheaply on campus. At one of the national universities in Sichuan, the students of anatomy were unusually fortunate: They were given their own skeleton when construction work began on a new building over what looked like an old graveyard. Despite government grants, poverty was one of the inescapable aspects of life for nearly every teacher and student in wartime. Clothing was threadbare; one teacher constantly wore a long coat so that his students would not see the holes in his trousers. A few students were relatively well dressed in what they called "Roosevelt suits," that is, blue drill garments donated by the U.S. Red Cross. Teachers managed to subsist with official handouts and by taking on extra jobs. Students had to find their own ways to survive. Historian E-Tu Zen Sun recounts the example in 1941 of National Southwestern Associated University in Kunming, Yunnan province (a wartime creation from several major universities from the east). The saying about its students was that they pawned their winter clothes to buy spring term books and pawned their books in the fall to redeem their winter clothes.[15]

One of the features of student life in wartime free China was the use of humor to alleviate their problems. Many of them had not only relocated to this unfamiliar region with their college, but they had also been separated from their parents, who often remained under Japanese occupation. It is also worth noting that there had been a significant increase in the number of institutions of higher learning, from 108 prewar to 137 in 1944; of these, 22 were national universities and 18 private. So more young people were being exposed to the challenges of tertiary education, even as the world around them was in chaos. Where they targeted their humor was at themselves and, in particular, at affairs of the heart. Thus a male student who developed a crush on a girl was said to be "gliding," to have "taken off" if the girl accepted his affection, and to have "made a forced landing" if the girl abandoned him (if he abandoned her, he was said to have "bailed out"). Someone in a lower class who was attracted to an older student was said to be an "antiaircraft gun" because he or she was aiming for the skies, while the reverse situation was termed "dive bombing."[16]

While schools, colleges, and universities often used makeshift quarters for classes, and sometimes turned packing crates into desks, one of the roles identified by the essayist Lao Xiang for the teahouse was as a place for thinking. He noted that many teahouse goers, including students, were among the least able to protect themselves against inflation; one of the few social activities within their means was to meet friends at the teahouse and converse about all manner of things, "as big as space to as small as a fly; from Aristotle to the shape of a woman's body; and from skyscrapers in New York to the Peace and Joy Temple." While some people discussed topics at random and some conducted business, others just sat alone, reading books. In this, students and ordinary people were not so very different to the café intellectuals of Europe, and Lao Xiang showed how aware Chinese were of other worlds, noting in his essay that "the great French writer Balzac drank foreign tea and coffee while writing his book, *The Human Comedy.*" Apart from students, even commoners might be inspired to do great things while drinking tea; the author states indignantly, "They do not gamble, drink much alcohol, watch local operas, or frequent prostitutes, so who are we to say they have enjoyed themselves too much?"

The value of students to teahouse owners, however, was limited by their poverty. In 1941, there was a case of a teahouse in a rural town in southern Sichuan which remodeled itself in order to attract students from the recently arrived campus. This meant installing a new storefront and bright lights. The lights worked perfectly in attracting students, but after purchasing a single cup of tea, they would occupy the seats for hours while using the lights to study. This meant that more free-spending customers avoided the place because there were no seats. Consequently, the owner sold off his new lights to the university and restored the weak oil lamps he had used before.[17]

THE TEAHOUSE AS A PLACE OF RETREAT

The Japanese invasion of China was intensely brutal. In the early 1940s, Japanese army policy was the so-called three alls: "burn all, kill all, destroy all." Death and destruction were therefore routine experiences in the areas where Japanese forces were active. In free China, there was the chance quite literally to distance oneself from such brutality (at least when the air raids ceased). The teahouse was at least a partial refuge from the war, even if it attracted aggressive debate about whether it was helping or hindering the war effort.

In his essays on tea drinking, Lao Xiang addressed the claim that "mere talk hurts the country." He argued that critics considered the national interest a top priority, but while they despised "mere talking," they never volunteered to go to the frontlines to fight the Japanese and only engaged in empty talk themselves. While intellectuals, students, and women readily volunteered for war work in mobilizing other people and helping out in patriotic campaigns, the life of the soldier in the GMD army was often desperate and brief. Medical care was the exception rather than the rule and was generally unavailable to the 3.5 million men in uniform. In addition, water was so scarce that troops sometimes relied on puddles to stay alive. Those newly conscripted were treated with such suspicion by their superiors that there were cases of such men being roped together to prevent them from running away. The corollary of this is that in addition to the millions fleeing the Japanese, there were also many men on the run from the misery of their own army.

One of the impacts of war was that the language of debate itself could become more abrasive. Thus, in Lao Xiang's essay, he attacked those who insisted that "mere talk hurts the country" by saying that if this were correct, then "teahouse-goers are traitors . . . and should be given the death penalty." He implied that these critics were do-nothings who came to Chengdu after the war, thus suggesting that they too were among the recently arrived refugees from the prosperous east and, because they could not openly criticize the rich and powerful, they found a convenient target in Chengdu's teahouse culture. He concluded with open sarcasm that for them, the best solution would be to "follow Hitler and burn all books of tea."

One of the roles of the teahouse amid the dislocation of war was as a resting place for travelers and traders from outside the city. In fact, despite the disruptions of war, there remained considerable movement of people, goods, and ideas. In part, this was because Japan controlled only the so-called points and lines, that is, the major cities and towns in its area of occupation, plus the lines of communication. Moreover, even from within the occupied area, it was possible, as Sherman Cochran has shown of leading Chinese traders of modern medicines, to negotiate with the Japanese authorities and continue to sell products to free China. Indeed, the war years 1937–1945 have been described as the "golden age" for Chinese-owned new-style drugstores based in Shanghai as they greatly expanded their sales and branched across the country.[18]

Inevitably, however, travel in wartime was more dangerous than in peace; Japanese soldiers were terrified of being ambushed and had little or no Chinese language skills, so any contact with the occupying troops could easily explode into violence. There was also widespread bombing of urban targets by the Japanese air force, especially in the clearer summer months of 1938–1941 (after Pearl Harbor, the Japanese bombers were preoccupied in other theaters of war). This meant that people tried to steer clear of the points and lines. Some of the carriage of goods was entrusted to smugglers, who, at least, had a long tradition of outwitting rulers and rules.

For those on the move it was therefore natural to head for a teahouse. It was a place of warmth in winter, when oil for heating was scarce. It was a place of light, when people could ill afford illumination at home. It was also a place filled with humanity and had its own civilized rhythm, with patrons who regularly went there to drink "early tea" *(zaocha)*, "noon tea" *(wucha)*, and "evening tea" *(wancha)*. In Lao Xiang's essay, such patrons were described as "addicted." What this probably meant was that such people's lives were bound to the routine of the teahouse, and in order to maintain a sense of peace in war, they were more than willing to spend a few cents on a cup of tea.

Lao Xiang also made the point that Chinese cities and towns had yet to find an alternative communal space to the teahouse. As he put it, "If more public spaces are built for appointments and gatherings of friends in the future, people will spend less time in the teahouse. We do not cry out, 'long live teahouses,' but we also disagree that teahouses should be forbidden. When a better alternative emerges, teahouses may fade away."[19] In its wartime capital of Chongqing the republican government was busy with construction projects showing off China's modernity, and so critics opposed teahouses as a vestige of "old society"; even Lao Xiang believed they would be abandoned as society became more progressive. However, their cultural importance was and is so great that Chengdu in 2006 had at least 3,000 teahouses.

What all of this shows is that the daily lives of civilians in wartime China were a constant topic of debate by reformist and traditionalist elites. At the center of the debate was the very question of how civilians should live their lives, spend their money, and use their time. The two poles of the debate essentially came down to freedom of choice and national efficiency. In 1942, the *West China Night News* published a semisatirical contribution to this debate by a man called Ju Ge. In his essay he described a so-called ideal teahouse. This was to be a municipal teahouse in the heart of the city. The teahouse was to have a director and associate director, and all customers were to obey their instructions. The teahouse was to demonstrate its patriotism by serving only Chinese tea, and the quantity of tea leaves in each bowl should, in accordance with modern methods of precision, be standardized: two millimeters per bowl of green tea, five millimeters for red tea, and three pieces for chrysanthemum tea. There would be no limitation in the number of times a bowl could be refilled, but the quantity of water should not exceed 0.5 *sheng* (about 0.56 quart); adding a touch of humanity, it would be legislated that customers who weighed more than 60 kilograms or had walked more than two kilometers under the hot sun could request 0.75 *sheng*. The teahouse should keep fixed, regular hours, opening from 6:00 to 7:00 A.M., from noon to 1 P.M., from 4:00 to 5:00 P.M., and from 9:00 to 10:00 P.M. In a modern world of discipline and lack of sentiment typical of wartime, patrons who stayed longer than two hours would be punished for wasting time. Further, in tune with the rise of modern bureaucracy and the keeping of records, a teahouse goer had to get a permit to drink in the teahouse; this was to certify that he was at least 20 years old and employed and show the reason for his desire to enter the teahouse, for example, that his own home was too small to accommodate tea drinking. Patrons would be required to dress formally, to "straighten their clothes and sit properly," and to sip tea slowly. "Bizarre clothes," "exposing the neck and shoulders," "whispering," "yelling," and especially "loud talking" would be prohibited. All patrons would be required to be at the teahouse at a certain time and would not be allowed to enter late or leave early. Reading newspapers and playing chess would be forbidden. The teahouse should have a radio tuned only to certain programs of the Central Broadcasting Station, such as news and market information. All patrons would exit the teahouse by marching in single file.[20]

Thus the ideal teahouse of 1942 was to operate either like a Fordist factory or, even more pertinently, like a military camp. This would no doubt satisfy Chiang Kai-shek; he had already stated that the model for modern life was (or should be) that of the soldier. From 1934, his government had attempted a campaign known as the New Life Movement to militarize all aspects of civilian behavior, for example, in speech, manners, posture, dress, and habits. This, however, had failed for widespread lack of support. In the same way the ideal teahouse was always destined to remain an ironic fantasy as ordinary Chinese civilians ignored or paid lip service to government directions but retained the teahouse as their own domain.

WORKING MEN AND WOMEN

While the conditions of war disrupted or destroyed many businesses, forced millions of people to move in search of safety, and led to crippling inflation, the ongoing and even increasing popularity of the teahouse meant that it, at least, was one place that offered the chance of work. The shift of peoples from the east to the west also led to new attitudes and expectations, for example, in the employment of women.

One thing that did not change significantly in war, however, was the social respect given throughout Chinese history to masters of their craft. This extended even to waiters in teahouses. An example of this comes from the fall of 1942. One evening, the war hero and noted Christian convert General Feng Yuxiang (famous for baptizing his soldiers with a fire hose), along with several other prominent figures, went to the Bright Spring Tea Balcony in Chengdu to drink tea. He and his companions were also there to watch in action the renowned waiter nicknamed "Pocked-Face Zhou." As soon as they sat down, Pocked-Face Zhou brought to their table a large purple bronze kettle in one hand and a pile of more than 20 sets of tea utensils in the other. He stopped at a distance from the table, placed the saucers precisely in front of each patron, and put a bowl onto each saucer. Although the customers requested many different kinds of tea, Zhou filled their orders without error. He moved two or three feet back from the table and poured boiling water into each bowl. Then he stepped forward and hooked each bowl lid off the table with his little finger and covered each bowl. The process was neatly done in a single step, and not a drop of water was spilled. The observers felt like they were watching a magician's performance. When Zhou received payment, he did not give change back immediately because he was too busy serving others. When the customers were about to leave, however, he gave precise change to each customer without any confusion, regardless of how many he had served. His extraordinary memory amazed patrons.[21]

Chengdu was home to many teahouse waiters like Pocked-Face Zhou, who bore the popular informal title of "masters of tea" *(cha boshi)*. As the phrase suggests, these waiters were far from peripheral figures in teahouses; in fact, they personified teahouse culture. Some called them, among other titles, *tangguan* (officers in charge of a hall), *yaoshi* (young masters), or *tihu gongren* (workers carrying kettles), but "masters of tea" became an elegant name for teahouse waiters. Although there is no doubt that the term was meant partly to be humorous, it nonetheless reflected these workers' great skill and considerable knowledge of tea as well as their rich social experience. These masters of tea were scattered among various teahouses in Chengdu. While there is little literature from the war years on small business–sector workers in general, the fact that teahouses were public places made their workers more visible than others and ensured that anything that happened at a teahouse attracted society's gaze and made its way into the local press and observations of social commentators. This shows again that civilian life in wartime China was a catalogue of many activities and interests, with the war itself having, on occasion, to compete for popular attention.

Most tea servers in Chengdu were male. However, in the late 1930s, a major social change occurred as women began to find employment as waitresses. In traditional Chinese society, women were important contributors to the economy, but they mainly worked at home in handicrafts, such as spinning, weaving, and shoemaking, or in domestic service, such as cooks, wet nurses, and nannies. In rural areas, women also did various jobs on farms. Virtually the only women who earned a living in public places were entertainers and prostitutes, both occupations regarded at best as low class and more generally as indecent. Therefore women entering teahouses as waitresses represented, at least in Chengdu, an important shift in many areas, including employment patterns and teahouse culture, of women's public roles and gender relationships. Teahouse waitresses, called *nü chafang,* emerged in 1937, drawing great public comment because this was a new phenomenon in the city.[22] Local newspapers provided much more coverage of the personal and professional lives of waitresses than of their male counterparts. These reports provide valuable information about waitresses' roles in the workplace and their wider social impact.

The rise of teahouse waitresses in Chengdu was a direct result of Japan's invasion and the forced movement of peoples. Chengdu in 1937 was a conservative and isolated city that enforced greater restrictions on women in public. Although people's attitudes toward women there had changed since late in the Qing era, no previous transformation was as rapid as this one. The influx of refugees from the more urbane east of China brought to Chengdu the relatively open attitudes found in the coastal areas. Also, at the beginning of the war, people tended to concentrate on the national devastation as Japanese forces destroyed towns and bombed such things as university campuses. At this point the perpetuation of traditional morality was less of a priority for elites and the government, and thus the emergence of women in the public workforce, while it fascinated newspaper readers and lovers of gossip, did not immediately emerge as a cultural issue. As a direct result, many upmarket teahouses, such as the Wise Tea Balcony and Three Sages Teahouse on Warm Spring Road, sprang up in the city's most prosperous area. These new teahouses not only provided private rooms to attract customers, but also were the first to hire waitresses. This attracted more male customers, who came to gawk at the novelty of women at work and often to make fun of them. Later, virtually all Chengdu teahouses followed this trend, and waitresses eventually could be found in even the simplest and crudest establishments. A teahouse without a waitress at that point was considered out of fashion and began to lose customers to its rivals.[23]

The women came from a variety of backgrounds, but most were illiterate or barely educated wives from poor families. The popular belief in traditional China was that an educated woman was a liability to herself and her family; women were given respect for being good wives and mothers, and they were expected to find fulfillment of all their ambitions within the family home. This meant that female illiteracy was the norm. One of the great public campaigns during the two wars was for literate women to teach other women to read. Indeed, the rise in literacy of Chinese women is one of the great revolutionary changes of the twentieth century, and the impact of war was central in bringing this about. However, this was to make far more progress under the communist regime following its victory in 1949. During the Japanese invasion, women still had to combat entrenched tradition, despite the social and economic upheavals of war. Thus in a book of propaganda articles edited by the GMD government's own Ministry of Information in 1945 the caption of a photograph of women textile workers could read, "The war has increased the number of women in industry in China, but they still enter factory more or less under family's protest [sic]."

Of course, the reason why women sought new jobs was a virtually unprecedented level of poverty. The drastic increase in the cost of living meant that many men who received monthly salaries often could not even support themselves, let alone their families. According to one observer, the husbands of waitresses were usually petty clerks in government offices, laborers, and soldiers who were away fighting the Japanese. Poverty for many women in the 1920s–1930s was commonplace, and it

Changing work roles for women. From Hollington Tong, ed., *China After Seven Years of War.* (The Macmillan Co., NY 1945.)

was often through borrowing and pawning any and all possessions that they managed, despite great difficulty and repeated humiliation, to feed themselves and their families. The wartime scarcity and inflation, however, meant that far more women were now threatened, while the chance of borrowing or pawning goods had been greatly reduced. In short, war demanded change if women were to survive.

The severity of women's plight in wartime is evident in the way that waitresses chose to overcome intense social pressure, and even harsh prejudice from waiters and other male workers, in order to keep their jobs. The ultimate demise of the waitressing profession in Chengdu teahouses resulted in part from this gender-based hostility. Acknowledging their situation, some people called them "pitiful birds" *(kelian de xiaoniao).*[24] Of course, some fared better than others, and a hierarchy among waitresses soon emerged. In high-class teahouses the waitresses were prettier and in better physical condition because the proprietors were very selective. Waitresses also preferred to work in prosperous teahouses, where they could earn more.[25] These women, who were usually 18–23 years old with demure expressions, typically sported short hairstyles (a style made popular in the movies and commercial advertising of 1930s Shanghai); minimal makeup; what had come from the 1920s to be seen as the national dress for women, the *qipao* or *cheongsam,* with its elegant but sinuous shape; and that global symbol of the modern waitress, the white apron. They generally adopted an innocent expression that, not entirely misleading, suggested to male customers that they had only just emerged into the bright lights of the public arena. In fact, they quickly learned which gestures and tones of voice were appropriate for a particular clientele and used their power to attract male customers. In lower-class teahouses, most waitresses had to live by their wits as they were actually hired by hot towel men or cigarette traders, and their main job was to sell these wares; for a day's work they could expect only 1.5 *yuan,* and they had no security as they were hired only on a day-to-day basis. In addition, they had to recoup any losses out of their meager salaries, which also were based on customer turnover. The one great advantage was that they received free breakfast and lunch. In some simple and crude teahouses, however, waitresses often could not earn enough to survive.[26] Moreover, female workers in a male-dominated society were always vulnerable to economic shifts, and whenever a recession occurred as a result of wartime problems, setbacks in the battlefield, or poor harvests, women were always the first to be made redundant.

The stigma attached to women who worked in public among gatherings of men meant that hooligans often harassed waitresses. Despite this, waitresses found little help or sympathy from local authorities or society at large. To a certain extent, these women could be compared with geisha in Japanese teahouses. However, there was generally a close bond between the proprietors of Japanese teahouses and geisha and between geisha themselves. They lived their private and professional lives as "mothers" and "daughters" and as older and younger sisters to each other. Most of the waitresses in Chengdu teahouses, by contrast, were married women with families to feed and did not have "sisters" to share their predicament. They had no bond with teahouse keepers, so their jobs were less stable, and they were often alone in handling problems at work. Japanese teahouses were located in inner chambers behind closed doors, and drinking tea was more of a ceremonial ritual. Chinese teahouses, however, were far more accessible; the doors were always kept wide open so passersby could glance at everything inside. Many did not even have a door; when they opened in the morning, workers took the wooden wallboards down one by one and put them back up when they closed. Thus workers and patrons could easily move tables and chairs onto the sidewalks. Teahouses were always crowded, noisy, and chaotic places, and fights broke out constantly, even in wartime. There was also little physical space between patrons and waitresses, which made physical harassment a constant threat. While the role of the geisha, whose job was to entertain customers, was clearly defined and socially acceptable, waitresses in Chengdu teahouses were a new and loosely defined social being. Therefore waitresses faced a dilemma: Although their basic role was not to provide entertainment, many patrons expected much more from them than mere service. If waitresses refused to meet the needs of customers through flirting and making jokes, they might offend both their customers and employers; if they behaved as patrons expected, they risked social ostracism for seeming to act like prostitutes. In fact, the image of waitresses was complicated, defined through a combination of job performance and public perception.

LAW AND ORDER

One of the additional duties given to teahouse workers in the wars was to be police informants. In particular, the police were concerned about two kinds of enemy: spies for the Japanese and agitators for the rival Chinese Communist Party. In 1940, for example, the government asked the Teahouse Guild to "stay on high alert" for 120 students from the Resistance University in North Shaanxi province who were heading for Chengdu and Chongqing.[27] The Chinese Communist Party had established the university to cultivate a new generation of leaders in its movement, so the arrival of these highly motivated students appeared as a direct threat to the GMD's authority, and their activities in Sichuan were closely watched. Also in 1940, the Chengdu police claimed that some traitors plotted their activities in teahouses and demanded that the Teahouse Guild provide secret reports about them. The guild had no choice but to cooperate, even if its members were not entirely sure what they were supposed to be reporting; during the war years, the GMD used the term *traitor* to describe anyone who spoke out against it or questioned its regulations.

Official reports show that along with men of all differing classes, hoodlums also often gathered in teahouses. There they taunted waitresses and physically bullied both male and female employees. In 1939, two incidents were highly publicized. In the first a waitress was brutally beaten when she refused a man's advances. The woman was Tang Bingyun. She sold hot towels and cigarettes in the Spring Dragon Tea Garden. One day, on her way out to buy a meal, she was stopped by Zhou Ziming, a local hoodlum. When Zhou attempted to molest her, she rebuffed him and ran back inside the teahouse, but Zhou chased her and assaulted her. When she criticized his actions, he became furious and hit her so hard that she began to spit blood.[28] The other case involved Xie Lizhen, a waitress in the Yuan Garden Teahouse. A patron named Ding grabbed her foot as he pretended to pick up a towel from the ground. She asked him politely to stop. Instead, he savagely bit her as well as her employer when he tried to intervene.[29] Xie was too frightened to resist. Such incidents became a serious issue that threatened waitresses' livelihood.

Waiters were also exposed to danger at work. One day, in August 1943, several local "ruffians" *(liupi)* ordered tea in the Number One Tea Balcony. When served, they told waiter Lü Qingrong they would pay for it later, but they slipped out while Lü was busy with other customers. Lü had to pay for this loss from his own pocket. The next day, the same group returned and did the same thing. When they tried to sneak out, Lü chased them and asked for payment. Claiming that Lü made them lose face in public, they not only refused to pay, but also pistol whipped him, and one of them fired a shot into the air to intimidate bystanders. Those who knew Lü said he was "a trustworthy and kind man" who "never had any trouble with his customers" since coming to work in the teahouse many years earlier.[30] This incident shows that waiters were very vulnerable. They could not afford to cover the costs of customers who left without paying, but if they tried to protect their interests, they risked being assaulted or even killed. Such incidents had happened long before the war, but it may be that the violence of wartime led to a greater brutalization even of civilian life in these years.

One of the reasons for the decline in social stability was the influx of rootless or disaffected people. In a long war these included military veterans who had lived alongside death and brutality. Against men who had already fought the Japanese, the police would always struggle to assert their authority. Moreover, the police themselves appear to have been primarily concerned with political order rather than relatively small social infractions. Thus the authorities closely watched for any sign of political dissent or sympathy for the Chinese Communist Party. A major fear reflected in wartime movies was also the threat of Japanese spies. In comparison, an individual causing an affray was a petty matter, while an organized group of hoodlums was perhaps too much of a challenge for a police force enjoying little social respect or support. The result of this lack of police protection for ordinary workers meant that men and women had to find alternative means of security.

In the case of waiters and waitresses, it was the Union of Teahouse Workers that provided support. In 1939, after investigating the two cases of bullying of waitresses described above, the union appealed to the municipal government to "protect laborers" and "purify social customs." According to its petition, harassment, intimidation, and violence against workingwomen was commonplace. To generate sympathy, the union emphasized the fact that many waitresses were the wives of officers and soldiers fighting on the frontline against the Japanese. These women could barely eke out a living in their husbands' absence, so they went to work in teahouses. Using a very modern political vocabulary, the petition accused hoodlums of "violating women's rights" as well as attacking decency and undermining the morale of the brave officers and soldiers by causing trouble behind the lines.[31]

The union also appealed to the government and society to take a positive view of waitresses: "Now we are experiencing a time when the country depends on the military and the mobilization of all citizens, when even women can go to the front if the nation requires." Therefore the government should support and protect "women's economic independence." The union asked the government to issue a public notice that banned harassment and punished violators. Two weeks after receiving the union's request, Mayor Yang passed the letter to the Sichuan Provincial Police. In his memorandum Mayor Yang repeated the union's choice of words by noting that such behavior was an assault on decency and an abuse of the women's "human rights."[32] In a similar fashion the union, in 1943, investigated the case of the waiter Lü Qingrong and pressured the municipal government for justice.[33] Thus another feature of modernizing China was that as government authority was weakened by conflict or the police were distracted by fears of revolutionaries, spies, and conspiracies, ordinary people were forced to organize themselves far more for self-defense. This occurred at all levels of urban life, from common workers to businessmen.

For the business world it was not individual violence or abuse that was the issue, but rather the government's insatiable wartime demand for revenue. This took the form of increasing, and increasingly insupportable, taxes, even at the same time as the value of money in circulation was being destroyed by inflation. Businessmen across China had already been developing their own modern forms of association to deal with governments, especially since the civil wars of the 1920s. However, the enormity of the anti-Japanese war forced small business owners, such as teahouse proprietors, to enter more forcefully into the political arena and organize protests against tax increases.

A typical example comes from August 1940. At this time the municipal government of Chengdu issued yet another new tax on commerce. In response, the Teahouse Guild called on its members to "never acknowledge this tax and resist to the end." It was agreed that all teahouses would strike if the government began arresting its members (thus also revealing the increased threat of government force in wartime daily life). The guild called for solidarity in the face of this unjust tax and asked its members to condemn anyone who broke ranks. To encourage resistance, the guild also promised to pay the living expenses of any members who were arrested. All participants signed the resolution. In a demonstration of the strength of civil society even in war, the government bowed to this pressure and put the new tax on hold. In the meantime the guild continued to fight its case through negotiation. The guild achieved an acceptable compromise early the next year when the government decided that the tax would be based on a teahouse's classification rather than on the number of tables it had and that the license fee would be paid quarterly instead of monthly.[34]

The guild cooperated with the local government on local affairs; it was clearly in its interest to do so. This was true of all businesses involved in open and legal activities. However, businessmen did not sacrifice all self-interest to the needs of war. In the case of the Teahouse Guild, it could argue that its members were providing an essential service in maintaining the stability of daily life. Thus it fought to protect itself when the government threatened the viability and the reasonable profitability of its industry. Although the government emerged the victor in the vast majority of cases, the guild occasionally prevailed. Teahouses that acted together, as with any other business, had a much stronger voice, and governments were compelled to acknowledge that a war could only be fought effectively with the consent of the people.

THE POLITICIZATION OF DAILY LIFE

The teahouse was a public place intended for rest or conversation. That is why it was such a vital part of civil society. Apart from those who met friends, conducted business, read quietly, or simply drank tea, however, there was a new feature of wartime life, that is, patrons who discoursed endlessly on current affairs; they were nicknamed "teahouse politicians" *(chaguan zhengzhijia)*. In the past a public notice stating "do not talk about national affairs" *(xiutan guoshi)* was posted in many teahouses. By 1943, however, according to an essay actually titled "Teahouse Politicians," loud arguments over politics were heard in the teahouses every day, with these highly opinionated patrons declaiming either that "so-and-so is a great man" or that "so-and-so is plotting a conspiracy." One of the habits of these discussants, apparently, was to claim that they had inside knowledge of things that would never be reported in newspapers.[35] Rumor, it seems, was often the currency of conversation in wartime life.

Some of the civilian elite, and especially the eastern refugees, were contemptuous of the teahouse politicians, seeing them as foolish or even threatening to their own social status. However, teahouse politicians were usually liberals who read newspapers and had strong views. Some earned a positive reputation among local people for sharing news and ideas, while others became objects of ridicule. In general, their base was the teahouse, where they stayed for several hours a day. In action, they behaved like actors on the stage, often making a speech before the other customers. To a certain extent, they could even influence public opinion as these discussions in the teahouse were the only outlet that most people had for expressing their political concerns. There was a risk, however. The police and the government could use whatever was said against the speaker, and there was a constant danger of arrest. The government commonly planted secret agents in teahouses to eavesdrop, and, as noted earlier, it also pressured teahouse owners and employees to report on the political conversations of their customers. Those who dared to criticize publicly the government were punished harshly. A teahouse that failed to alert the police could also be implicated, even to the point of being forced to close. For this reason, some teahouse keepers actively discouraged any dangerous talk. At one teahouse the notice insisted, "If someone asks your opinion, do not talk about national affairs, just drink your tea!"[36]

Regardless of the wishes of nervous teahouse owners, one of the greatest changes to occur in wartime was the invasion of politics into public space. This was largely the work of the government itself and its supporters. Acknowledging the importance of the teahouse in Chinese life, the GMD, in 1941, initiated a plan of propaganda in teahouses. Under this plan, all of the 640 or so teahouses in Chengdu were divided into three classes, with varying types of propaganda to be employed. What was common to this propaganda effort was that all teahouses were now compelled to purchase portraits of the founder of the GMD, Dr. Sun Yatsen (commonly known as "the father of modern China"), plus those of Chiang

The politicization of daily life: Nationalist lectures at the workplace. From Hollington Tong, ed., *China After Seven Years of War.* (The Macmillan Co., NY 1945.)

Kai-shek and other party leaders; also, teahouses were to prepare space for a lectern and blackboard as well as the GMD party flag and national flag. Army officers were subsequently sent around various teahouses to ensure that these directives were being carried out. Initially, they found that none of the teahouses had complied, and the mayor of Chengdu was forced to warn the Teahouse Guild of its members' obligations.[37] Similar political props and lecture campaigns were conducted at other places, such as factories.

New regulations further required teahouses to provide government-selected books and newspapers, thus giving them a kind of wartime library function. The books largely revolved around praise of republican war heroes, GMD ideology, and the denunciation of traitors. The newspapers and the blackboards worked in concert, with the blackboards often carrying weekly summaries of events. In one example, there were three main items: a two-line update on the war in Europe; a brief note of China's diplomatic success in signing a major agreement for a loan from Britain; and an extended description of China's victory over the Japanese at battles in southern Hubei and northern Hunan provinces.[38] The government also directed each police district to set up a large, well-financed, and centrally located "model teahouse" as an example for others; in this, as well as newspapers, posters, and flags, there was to be a radio or record player and maps of Sichuan and the rest of the world. Teahouses were also ordered to place on their walls the so-called citizens' pledge (*guomin gongyue*). This had 12 clauses, most of which focused on serving the nation, never surrendering to or trading with the enemy, and never working with or for traitors. The GMD also dictated that there would be nine categories of slogans to be posted on teahouse walls. These reinforced the ideas of the GMD, the need for people to support the government and work to destroy the enemy, and, in particular, to realize that avoiding military service was the most shameful action a citizen could take.[39]

The purpose of this propaganda campaign was obviously to spread the GMD version of the war among the greatest number of ordinary people. In this way the teahouse actually became both a stage for "saving the country" and a site of information about the progress of the war. There people could learn the latest news from the frontlines as well as stories about the resistance, the ruthlessness of the Japanese invaders, and wartime tragedies. Therefore the war was a turning point in which expressions about politics (rather than free debate) moved from being taboo to being officially encouraged.

As a source of information and a place of patriotic performance, the teahouse worked alongside the more modern venues for wartime entertainment and news. Cinema was already an established part of urban life in China by 1937. The two major centers of film production were Shanghai and Hong Kong. In the early years of the anti-Japanese war, both film centers continued to function—Hong Kong because it was a British colony and Shanghai because part of the city was actually administered by British, French, and American councils. About 200 feature films were made in Shanghai alone between 1938 and 1941. Many of these have been described as politically neutral, often costume dramas based on classical literature or folk tales. A notable addition, however, was China's first ever feature-length cartoon, *Princess Iron Fan* (1941), heavily influenced in its style by the Disney studio. Some of the films from Shanghai or Hong Kong managed to find their way to free China, but not always to favor. *Mulan Joins the Army* was produced in 1939 and shown in Chongqing in 1940. According to the film historian Yingjin Zhang, however, this showing was greeted with howls of outrage by the audience, which felt betrayed, accusing the film's makers of having weakened the patriotism of the famous story and emphasized its romance in order to satisfy the Japanese authorities, even though Shanghai was not then fully under Japanese control.

After 1941, both Shanghai and Hong Kong were taken over by the Japanese, and those films which survived the Japanese censors tended to be apolitical family dramas and romances. By this point, few, if any, movies from occupied China could be seen by people in the west. Instead, they were given patriotic features, plus many newsreels, documentaries, and some cartoon shorts made by companies under the direction of the GMD government. These films were then exhibited across free China by touring teams of GMD projectionists. However, funds and film stock were so scarce under the republican regime that film companies generally had to suspend feature production for several years of the war against Japan.

Popular entertainment, either in the teahouse or the theater, was both politicized and sanitized during the wars. As the editor of the publication *New Chengdu* noted, "In the past, storytellers' language was licentious and plots were bizarre, which unconsciously corrupted the thoughts and behaviors of the masses." After the Japanese invasion, storytellers still used well-known materials as the basis for their stories but inserted patriotic and anti-Japanese themes. In part, this was a natural patriotic response, but it was also essential if performers wished to be heard; the GMD government insisted that plays include patriotic and anti-Japanese terms and content.[40] The responsibility for overseeing scripts was given to a new organization called the Temporary Instructive Committee of the Chinese Nationalist Party for People's Organizations in Chengdu.

A number of these wartime scripts, often combining storytelling and folk songs, have survived. Some recall the history of Japanese aggression against China; some praise the brave resistance movement or commemorate the heroes who lost their lives on the battlefield; some denounce traitors; while some express yearning for the lost motherland and others bemoan the nation's sad situation.[41] Examples include "Recovering the Motherland" *(Huanwo heshan)*, which described China's beauty, vast territory, rich natural resources, long history, and wonderful culture. The "Exposure of Traitors" *(Hanjian timing)* denounced the crimes of the Japanese invaders and exposed eight traitors but warned that there were too many others to name individually. Another script with a similar topic, titled "The Fate of Traitors" *(Hanjian de xiachang)*, declared there would be no mercy for any who were caught, while their families would also be held responsible, forfeiting their property and being permanently branded enemies of the state.[42]

Of course, one of the motivations behind these patriotic programs was to promote business, and the theaters and entertainers knew how to deal with the government for survival. In 1939, folk singer Wang Qingyun applied for a permit to perform folk songs in the Pleasant Wind Teahouse. He claimed that he wanted to spread propaganda to support the government in the War of Resistance. He promised not to perform any "lecherous songs" but to "wake people up to mobilize the nation." In a similar vein, in 1941, three people from Jiangsu province requested permission to perform operas, claiming that the Nanjing National Opera Stage was a source of "noble entertainment" that could only help to rouse the spirit of the Chinese people in order to recover the land stolen by the Japanese. This is not to say that such justifications were false. Rather, it is to emphasize the point that entertainment in wartime had first to be justified by patriotism in order to gain official approval.

ONE WAR ENDS, ANOTHER BEGINS

After 1945 and victory in the nine-year-long War of Resistance, however, people looked for light entertainment rather than politics. Suddenly, a backlog of Hollywood films became available, and people flocked to the cinemas to see such politically innocent fare as *Son of Lassie*. In liberated Shanghai, in 1948, it is said there were about one million moviegoers each month. With illiteracy still at about 80 percent, cinema and theater were arguably more popular than ever. Yet the great carryover of life before and after 1945 was inflation. In 1946, one U.S. dollar was worth 2,020 Chinese dollars; in mid-1948, it bought seven million Chinese dollars. The GMD attempted to reassert control over the economy by restricting imports and by giving support either to its own companies or those of entrepreneurs with links to the GMD leadership. The result of this interference in the economy was simply to restrict yet further the supply of goods and increase the reputation of the GMD and its cronies for corruption and incompetence.

The lives of students from 1945 to 1949 were dominated by a sense of frustration. As the War of Resistance ended, they were preparing to return, along with their universities, to their original cities. However, the GMD was so desperate to reclaim control of the urban east that they sent advance teams who, lacking military and police support of their own, actually employed surrendered Japanese troops to man guard posts and even patrol the city streets. This caused outrage among ordinary Chinese.

Both the GMD and Chinese Communist forces, however, were angling for the best position in what seemed an inevitable return to civil war. In trying to prevent this the students were at the forefront of calls for peace, both in their journals and in their activities, such as marches and hunger strikes. While many Chinese had seen the War of Resistance as just, the same could not be said of renewed infighting, in which, obviously, Chinese went back to killing other Chinese. Thus the students, who were continuing the long tradition of intellectuals speaking out against misgovernment, were no doubt representing the views of many citizens. At Kunming, in late 1945, however, the government set the trend for its dealings with students over the next four years when it used overwhelming force to crush student demonstrations it branded as communist inspired.

The war between the GMD and the Chinese Communists lasted from 1945 to 1949. Much of the fighting, especially in 1946–1947, took place in the north and northeast of the country; the GMD capital, Nanjing, fell in April 1949. Until this time, political talk in public places once again became taboo. Yet with resentment growing even stronger against Chiang's persistent demands of the people to endure and sacrifice against a background of corruption, inflation, and social disorder, chatting in the teahouse became once again the commoners' only outlet. However, the authorities continued their wartime surveillance of public opinion with covert agents embedded among the customers. Thus when patrons became angry and started shouting, the teahouse keeper would say, "Be careful! The walls may have ears."[43]

The government listened to the conversations held in teahouses, but it scrutinized the public meetings held there even more carefully. In particular, the police and local government sent agents to spy on meetings of military servicemen in teahouses. In 1946, for example, the police sent a secret agent to the Sleeping Stream Tea Balcony to investigate a gathering of former classmates in a military school. The investigator reported that a man called Liang Qinghui organized the meeting to discuss the issue of how they could earn a living after being demobilized from the army. The group established an association of classmates and elected Liang Qinghui president, with the job of seeking both economic relief from the government and funds for the construction of war memorials for their classmates killed in the war.[44] The local government, however, reacted nervously and quickly issued a public notice restricting such gatherings:

Under the order of the Sichuan Provincial Capital Police on October 21, 1946, because some military servicemen recently organized gatherings without permission and held meetings in inns and teahouses, a rule from the Military Security Committee restricts such activities in an effort to cut social disorder at its roots. The professional guilds must hereby notify all shopkeepers of inns and teahouses that they should immediately report any meeting of military people in their inn or teahouse to the Bureau of the Military Police. Otherwise, they will be punished harshly.[45]

Government officials were nervous about gatherings of military personnel in public places because they believed this group, with its sense of organization and its familiarity both with violence and the reality of the recent war, could cause more damage than any other. From the available sources we know that most of these meetings were social gatherings and did not have a political agenda. Still, the government after 1945 saw any public meeting as a potential threat. In trying to crush all forms of dissent or even autonomous group activity, however, the GMD merely became more repressive, and as it attempted to dominate what little public space remained in the teahouse, so its legitimacy in the eyes of ordinary civilians continued to evaporate. With this, the GMD's defeat at the hands of the Communist army in 1949 was virtually guaranteed.

NOTES

1. Lewis Walmsley, "Szechuan—That Green and Pleasant Land," in *Canadian School in West China*, ed. Brockman Brace, Canadian School Alumni Association, 1974).

2. Isabella Bird, *The Yangtze Valley and Beyond: An Account of Journeys in China, Chiefly in the Province of Sze Chuan and Among the Man-sze of the Somo Territory* (Boston: Beacon Press, 1987), 10. Original published by John Murray in 1899.

3. Bird 1987: 345; Ernest H. Wilson, *China: Mother of Gardens* (Boston: Stratford, 1929), 121.

4. Bird 1987: 350; Ba Jin, *Jia* [Family] (Beijing: Renmin wenxue chubanshe, 1985). First published in 1932.

5. Zheng Yun, "Yifu duilian de miaoyong [A Smart Use for a Matched Couplet]," in *Chengdu fengwu* [Chengdu Folklore], vol. 1 (Chengdu, China: Sichuan renmin chubanshe, 1981), 82–83; Yu Xun, 73 years old, interview by author, Joy Teahouse, 21 June 1997; Chen Jin, *Sichuan chapu* [Teahouses in Sichuan] (Chengdu, China: Sichuan renmin chuban she, 1992), 32.

6. Hu Tian, *Chengdu daoyou* [Guidebook of Chengdu] (Chengdu, China: Shuwen yinshuashe, 1938), 62; Yi Junzuo, "Jincheng qiri ji [Seven Days in Chengdu]," in *Chuankang youzong* [Travel Notes in Sichuan and Xikang] (Zhongguo luxingshe, 1943), 194.

7. Hai Su, "Chapu zhongsheng xiang [Various Faces in the Teahouse]," in *Shimin jiyizhong de lao Chengdu* [Old Chengdu in the memories of its residents], ed. Feng Zhicheng (Chengdu, China: Sichuan wenyi chubanshe, 1999), 143–46.

8. Hu Tian 1938: 69–70; Yi Junzuo 1943: 194; *Sichuan shengzhengfu shehuichu dang'an* [Archives of Social Department of Sichuan Provincial Government] (Sichuan Provincial Archives, *chuangzong* 186), 186-1431; He Manzi, *Wuzakan* [Five Series of Random Talks] (Chengdu, China: Chengdu chubanshe, 1994), 193; William G. Sewell, *The People of Wheelbarrow Lane* (New York: A. S. Barnes, 1971), 131–132; *Guomin gongbao* [Citizens' Daily], 17 October 1929; Wen Wenzi, ed., *Sichuan fengwu zhi* [Customs in Sichuan] (Chengdu, China: Sichuan renmin chubanshe, 1990), 456–57.

9. Sha Ting, "Zai Qixiangju chaguan li [In the Fragrant Chamber Teahouse]," in *Sha Ting xuanji* [Selections of Sha Ting], vol. 1 (Chengdu, China: Sichuan renmin chubanshe, 1982), 147.

10. *Xinxin Xinwen* [Latest News] (hereinafter *XX*), 29 April 1938.

11. *Huaxi wanbao* [West China Night News] (hereinafter *HW*), 16 June 1941, 23 November 1941.

12. Lee McIsaac, "The City as Nation: Creating a Wartime Capital in Chongqing," in *Remaking the Chinese City: Modernity and National Identity, 1900–1950,* ed. Joseph Esherick (Honolulu: University of Hawai'i Press, 1999), 175.

13. Stephen MacKinnon, "Wuhan's Search for Identity in the Republican Period," in Esherick 1999: 170–71.

14. *HW,* 17 June 1943; Qiu Chi, "Chengdu de chaguan [Teahouses of Chengdu]," *XX,* 7–8 August 1942; Zhou Zhiying, *Xin Chengdu* [New Chengdu] (Chengdu, China: Fuxing shuju, 1943), 246.

15. Quote from Sun in J. K. Fairbank and Albert Feuerwerker, eds., *Cambridge History of China,* vol. 13, part 2 (Cambridge, UK: Cambridge University Press, 1986), 416. Much of this section is drawn from Frank Tao, "Student Life in China," in *China After Seven Years of War,* ed. Hollington K. Tong (New York: Macmillan, 1945).

16. These and other terms are noted in Tao 1945: 114–15.

17. Tao 1945: 118.

18. Sherman Cochran, "Marketing Medicine and Advertising Dreams in China, 1900–1950," in *Becoming Chinese: Passages to Modernity and Beyond,* ed. Wen-hsin Yeh (Berkeley: University of California Press, 2000), 87.

19. Lao Xiang, "Tan Chengduren chicha" [A chat on tea drinking by Chengdu people], parts 1–3, Huaxi Wanbao (West China Night News), December 26–28, 1942.

20. Ju Ge, "Lixiang de chaguan [Ideal Teahouses]," *HW,* 17 October 1942.

21. Li Sizhen and Ma Yansen, "Jinchun lou 'sanjue'—Jia Xiazi, Zhou Mazi, Si Pangzi [Three Bests in the Bright Spring Tea Balcony: Blind Jia, Pocked Face Zhou, and Fat Man Si]," in *Chengdu zhanggu* [Anecdotes of Chengdu], vol. 1, ed. Chengdu shi qunzhong yishuguan (Chengdu, China: Chengdu chubanshe, 1996), 380–81.

22. Lu Yin, "Xianhua nü chafang [A Chat on Waitresses in the Teahouse]," *HW,* 25–28 February 1942.

23. Lu Yin 1942.

24. Lu Yin 1942.

25. *HW,* 16 June 1941.

26. Lu Yin 1942.

27. *Chengdu shi shanghui dang'an* [Archives of Chengdu Chamber of Commerce] (Republican period; Chengdu Municipal Archives) 104-1401.

28. *Chengdu shi zhengfu gongshang dang'an* [Archives of Industry and Commerce in Chengdu] (hereinafter *CSZGD*) (Republican period; the Chengdu Municipal Archives, *quanzhong* 38), 38-11-908.

29. *CSZGD* 38-11-908.

30. *CSZGD* 38-11-984.

31. *CSZGD* 38-11-908.

32. *CSZGD* 38-11-908.

33. *CSZGD* 38-11-984.

34. *Chengdu shi shanghui dang'an* 104-1401.

35. Yu Xi, "Chaguan zhengzhi jia [Teahouse Politicians]," *HW,* 15 January 1943.

36. Ci Jun, "Chengdu de chaguan [Teahouses in Chengdu]," parts 1–2, *HW*, 28–29 January 1942; Lao She, "Chaguan [The Teahouse]," in *Lao She juzuo xuan* [Elected Plays of Lao She] (Beijing: Renmin wenxue chubanshe, 1978), 78, 92, 113.

37. *CSZGD* 38-11-952; *Chengdu shi shanghui dang'an* 104-1384, 104-1388.

38. *Chengdu shi shanghui dang'an* 104-1390.

39. *Chengdu shi shanghui dang'an* 104-1388.

40. Zhou Wen, "Chengdu de yinxiang [Impression of Chengdu]," in *Wenhuaren shiyezhong de lao Chengdu* [Old Chengdu in the Sight of Intellectuals], ed. Zeng Zhizhong and You Deyan (Chengdu, China: Sichuan wenyi chubanshe, 1999), 229; *XX*, 9 April 1938; Wang Qingyuan, "Chengdu pingyuan xiangcun chaguan [Rural Teahouses in the Chengdu Plain]," *Fengtu shi* [Folkways] 1 (1944): 37–38; Zhou Zhiying 1943: 224.

41. *CSZGD* 38-11-1103.

42. *CSZGD* 38-11-1103.

43. Ci Jun 1942; Zhang Zhenjian, "Nanmen you zuo 'Shusan qiao' [An Evacuating Bridge at the South City Gate]," in *Shimin jiyizhong de lao Chengdu* [Old Chengdu in the Memories of Its Residents], ed. Feng Zhicheng (Chengdu, China: Sichuan wenyi chubanshe, 1999), 321–22.

44. *Chengdu shenghui jingcha ju dang'an* [Archives of the Police Force in the Capital City Chengdu] (Republican period; the Chengdu Municipal Archives, *quanzhong* 93), 93-2-759.

45. *Chengdu shi shanghui dang'an* 104-1388.

SELECTED BIBLIOGRAPHY

Esherick, Joseph, ed. *Remaking the Chinese City: Modernity and National Identity, 1900–1950*. Honolulu: University of Hawai'i Press, 1999.
  A collection of outstanding articles on diverse aspects of urban culture. Especially useful for wartime daily life are the pieces by Stephen R. MacKinnon, "Wuhan's Search for Identity in the Republican Period," and Lee McIsaac, "The City as Nation: Creating a Wartime Capital in Chongqing."

Fairbank, J. K., and Albert Feuerwerker, eds. *Cambridge History of China*. vol. 13, part 2. Cambridge, UK: Cambridge University Press, 1986.
  Some of the best summary chapters available on key questions, including E-Tu Zen Sun, "The Growth of the Academic Community 1912–1949" (pp. 361–420), Lloyd Eastman, "Nationalist China during the Sino-Japanese War 1937–1945" (pp. 547–608), and Suzanne Pepper, "The KMT-CCP Conflict 1945–49" (pp. 723–88). Eastman and Pepper have also written major books on their respective topics.

Li, Lincoln. *Student Nationalism in China, 1924–1949*. Albany: State University of New York Press, 1994.
  Explains the role of students in relocating along with their universities at the start of the War of Resistance, their activities during the war, and their opposition, especially in 1945, to the resumption of civil war.

Ono, Kazuko. *Chinese Women in a Century of Revolution 1850–1950*. Stanford, CA: Stanford University Press, 1989.
  A general summary of women's movements over a century, but with only a few pages on the War of Resistance.

Pan, Yihong. "Feminism and Nationalism in China's War of Resistance against Japan." *International History Review* 19 (1997): 115–30.
> Mainly about Chinese women in the communist areas but also mentions women under the Guomindang. The theme, common also to Japanese women in 1937–1945, is to what extent the demands of the nation-in-arms actually improved the rights and freedoms of women.

Spence, Jonathan. *The Search for Modern China.* New York: W. W. Norton, 1990.
> A general history by one of the most respected of all cultural and social historians of China.

Tong, Hollington K., ed. *China After Seven Years of War.* New York: Macmillan, 1945.
> While intended as a work of propaganda, it contains highly evocative chapters by different observers on such things as life in Chongqing, the roles of women, and, especially useful, Frank Tao, "Student Life in China."

Westad, Odd Arne. *Decisive Encounters: The Chinese Civil War 1946–1950.* Stanford, CA: Stanford University Press, 2003.
> The most recent scholarly work on the subject. It focuses largely on the political and military aspects of the civil war, using sources that only became available with the end of the Cold War.

Yeh, Wen-hsin, ed. *Becoming Chinese: Passages to Modernity and Beyond.* Berkeley: University of California Press, 2000.
> Another collection of excellent articles by leading historians of modern China, including Leo Ou-fan Lee, David Strand, Frederic Wakeman, Jr., and Yeh herself. Particularly relevant to the present topic are Sherman Cochran, "Marketing Medicine and Advertising Dreams in China, 1900–1950," and Paul Pickowicz, "Victory as Defeat: Postwar Visualizations of China's War of Resistance."

Zarrow, Peter. *China in War and Revolution 1895–1949.* London: Routledge, 2005.
> Useful in setting the political and military background to the wars from 1937 to 1949.

Zhang, Yinjing. *Chinese National Cinemas.* London: Routledge, 2004.
> Summarizes the activities of film companies during the war years, both in occupied and free China, in addition to describing the plots of some of the major films.

FIVE

Daily Life of Civilians
in Wartime Japan, 1937–1945

Simon Partner

ORIGINS AND COURSE OF THE WAR

Between July 1937 and August 1945, Japanese society was mired in one of the most violent and destructive conflicts in all of human history. Today, military affairs play such a small part in the daily lives of most Japanese that it is hard to imagine the pervasive influence of the military in the early decades of the twentieth century. Japan fought successful wars against China (1894–1895) and Russia (1904–1905), was a treaty ally of Britain in World War I (winning easy victories against German interests in China and the Pacific), and participated with the Allies in the multinational Siberian campaign of 1918–1922. Each of these (mostly) successful campaigns increased the prestige and political power of the military. The military played the leading, and often oppressive, role in governing Japan's formal colonies, Korea and Taiwan. And in 1931, activists within the military were responsible for taking over the northeastern Chinese province of Manchuria and turning it into a puppet state, Manchukuo. It was this last act of aggression that set Japan on a collision course with China and, eventually, the United States and its allies.

The Japanese military was also a major player in domestic politics, not least because the defense budget was so enormous. Until the turn of the 1930s, Japan had enjoyed more than a decade of relatively stable civilian government, with prime ministers and cabinets generally composed of elected members of the Japanese parliament (known as the Diet). From 1930, however, with the global depression bringing misery and fear across the globe, a series of political assassinations destabilized Japan's domestic politics, and for much of the decade of the 1930s, generals and admirals served as prime ministers. Even within the army, there were competing factions, one of which staged a major coup attempt in Tokyo in February 1936 (the famous 2-26 incident). Ever since the introduction of conscription in 1872, the Japanese military had been an increasing presence in the lives of Japanese citizens. During the 1930s, this presence expanded to the point that military matters became an integral part of civilian daily life.

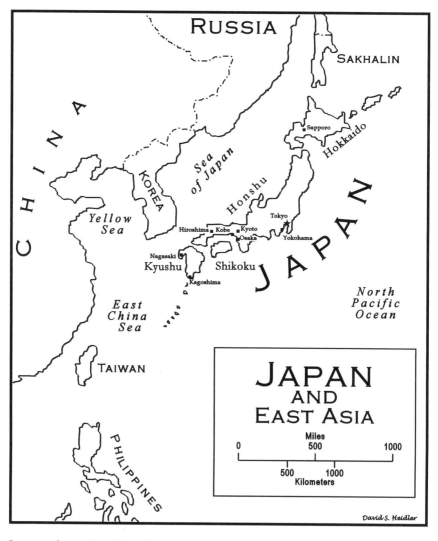

Japan and east Asia. (David S. Heidler.)

This was especially the case after July 1937. At that time, Japanese and Chinese forces clashed at the Marco Polo Bridge, outside the Chinese capital. This was only one of many incidents that had occurred where Japanese and Chinese troops were in close proximity (the Japanese were in Beijing to protect foreign interests in the capital, a role they had played since the 1900 Boxer rebellion). In this case, however, the localized clash rapidly escalated into a full-scale confrontation. Pushed by its own aggressive military leaders, the Japanese government found itself unable to back down, and within a week, Japan and China were at war.

The international community quickly condemned what it saw as Japanese aggression in China, particularly after Japanese planes attacked British and American citizens in the country. The Japanese military leaders undoubtedly hoped that they could rapidly quell the Chinese and establish their domination (as they had done in Manchuria) before anyone could stop them. But the army eventually became bogged down in a grueling war of attrition across vast stretches of Chinese territory.

As late as 1940, the Japanese government continued to hope that it could fulfill its aims in China without taking on the Western Allies. But these hopes were dashed by the continually expanding field of hostilities (in 1938, and again in 1939, there were large-scale and, for Japan, very costly clashes with Soviet forces on the Chinese border), by American sympathy and support for the Chinese, and ultimately, by Japan's own misjudgment of the situation in Europe. Germany's successes in the early stages of the European war prompted Japan to enter an alliance with Nazi Germany and fascist Italy: the so-called Axis. Having sided with what seemed likely to be the victors in Europe, the Japanese government made the fateful decision late in 1941 to attack the United States, hoping thereby to force Washington to withdraw its hand from China and allow Tokyo to make its bid for supremacy over all of Asia. Even at this time, realists in the Japanese government and military rated their chance of success at less than 50 percent.

The apparent ease of Japan's early victories in Western colonies at the end of 1941 and into early 1942 gave the people a brief sense of optimism. By mid-1942 and the battle of Midway, however, the Japanese forces were already on the long path toward defeat. In 1943, the United States devastated Japan's merchant marine and began to starve the home islands of imports. Late in 1944, U.S. bombers began to take apart one Japanese city after another, until there was virtually no worthwhile target left standing. At the opening of hostilities with China in 1937, the government assured its citizens that hostilities would be brief. But those hostilities continued each year to expand and entered a dramatic new phase in 1941. As the mobilization of the Japanese people progressed, goods, services, and increasingly, men of all ages began to disappear from the landscape. In 1945, the urban landscape itself began to be erased, and millions of Japanese began living hand to mouth as refugees in their own country. If mobilization is one of the key words in describing any society at war, then the Japanese people from 1937 to 1945 were constantly forced, for varying reasons, to be on the move.

SPIRITUAL MOBILIZATION, RELIGION, CELEBRATIONS, AND FESTIVALS

In 1937, in spite of the increasing role of the military in daily life, most Japanese people were less interested in Japan's so-called divine mission on the Asian mainland than they were with the everyday pleasures and cares of modern life—factory and white-collar work, movies (Charlie Chaplin's comedies were extremely popular in the 1930s), beer halls, brothels, and baseball. Japan had made a rapid recovery from the slump of 1929–1930, and thanks to strong military demand and a surge of investment in Manchuria and Korea, economic opportunities were plentiful. The plunge into war with China was a shock for ordinary Japanese citizens.

The immediate result of the outbreak of war was an urgent demand for military personnel. Within a month, 500,000 men—mainly reservists and those who had completed one round of military service—had been mobilized. The mobilization caused immediate disruption to countless households; families had to adapt to life without their men, and this meant more responsibility in the home for women. But the effects of the war might have stopped there had it not been for a series of measures taken by the Japanese government to exert control over the daily lives of Japanese civilians. The first of these was the August 1937 launch of the National Spiritual Mobilization Campaign.

Ever since World War I, Japanese military planners had recognized that modern warfare required more than just an effective fighting force. The massive scale and technological nature of war now required that whole populations be mobilized. The entire national economy must be directed to the war effort, and the work, even the private activities, of citizens must support that effort.

The concept of spiritual mobilization was certainly appealing for the Japanese government. It wanted to turn into reality the ideological construction of the wartime slogan (actually inflating the real population figure) of "100 million hearts beating as one" under the benevolent father figure of the emperor. But how, in practice, does a nation go about mobilizing and directing the spiritual lives of tens of millions of people? In the end, the activities of the spiritual mobilization drive were directed into a few, relatively familiar activities.

The first of these was to promote savings. The Japanese government had been organizing savings drives ever since the turn of the century. Saving, it believed, performed two important functions. First, it encouraged thrift and turned citizens away from extravagance—a theme with deep roots in Japanese governance since at least the Tokugawa *shōguns* (1600–1868).

Second, it provided a pool of money on which the government could draw for its own purposes, either by issuing government bonds or by tapping postal and bank funds. In time of war, these two functions were doubly important. War bonds, whether purchased by individuals or institutions, such as banks, were a vital feature of war financing, and reductions in consumption of consumer goods freed essential resources for military production.

The government used all of its propaganda resources—radio broadcasts, newspaper and magazine articles, posters, leaflets, and speeches—to drive home slogans such as "let the housewife save for her family" and "save for yourself and for the state." A more direct impact on the

Government poster for savings campaign. (Japan, Ministry of Finance, undated, reproduced from Hajime Miyoshi, *Nihon no Posutaa* [Japanese Posters]) (Published by Shikōsha, Kyoto 2003.)

ordinary civilian, however, was the government's strategy of assigning specific war bond quotas to prefectures, which in turn passed them down to towns, villages, and ultimately, to neighborhood associations. Citizens who might not feel they had to obey every dictate of the central government still hesitated to shame their own neighbors by failing to participate in the purchase of bonds.

The second major activity of the spiritual mobilization campaign was the organization of rallies and celebrations. Under the auspices of spiritual mobilization, cities and towns throughout Japan held mass prayer ceremonies at *Shintō* shrines and Buddhist temples and celebrated military victories with parades and loud, patriotic music. In the early years of the war these gatherings were often happy and festive. Japanese citizens had—or chose to have—little awareness of the atrocities being perpetrated by their troops in the Chinese capital Nanjing, for example, as they celebrated the fall of that city in December 1937 with lantern parades and brass bands. Moreover, the Japanese press had been filled for years with stories of the internal chaos and violence in China. This meant that Japanese civilians could easily convince themselves that the war was not only just and likely to be brief but also that it might, as their government insisted, actually be a good thing and bring greater stability throughout Asia.

After the attack on Pearl Harbor in December 1941, however, the mood became much more somber. Any comparison of Japanese and American economic strength in journals or newspapers before 1941 always showed an unarguable truth: Japan's resources and wealth were dwarfed by those of America. The mayor of one village wrote that when he heard of the attack, "I felt a chill throughout my body and the flow of my blood reversed its course. The recognition that a great affliction was facing our empire was carved in my heart."[1] The declaration of war was followed by a series of huge rallies in Tokyo, including the "Crush America and Britain" rally on December 10, 1941; the "National Rally on the Propagation of the War Rescript" on December 13; the "Strengthening Air Defense Spirit" rally on December 16; and the "Axis Pact Certain Victory Promotion" military rally on December 22.

Some of the ceremonies linked to spiritual mobilization were held in shrines as a part of the Japanese government's promotion of state *Shintō*. Foreign observers tended to equate both the spiritual mobilization drive and the *Shintō* cult with ultranationalist fanaticism. The American propaganda film *Know Your Enemy—Japan* portrayed the Japanese engaged in frenetic rituals led by robed *Shintō* priests, culminating in ceremonies at which dry-eyed mothers held boxes containing the ashes of their sons (the film assured American viewers that the mothers, dehumanized by their devotion to the cause, "feel no grief").

For any community it is natural to pray at times of great danger. But a great deal of the structure of religious activity in wartime Japan was directed by the state, which considered *Shintō* an ideal medium for the mobilization of religious feeling. As a uniquely Japanese religion, it emphasized the special destiny of the Japanese race. Since the emperor was said to be descended from the sun goddess, he held a special, divine position within the framework of *Shintō*—thus permitting the government to call for extraordinary sacrifices in his name. And the tradition of inducting new gods into the *Shintō* pantheon allowed the government to offer instant divinity to all fallen soldiers. In this, the Yasukuni shrine (built close by the imperial palace in Tokyo in 1869 to honor the dead of Japan's modern wars) was at the heart of religious nationalism. Later in the war, the government began a massive campaign to build great shrines to the war dead in all of Japan's prefectures, diverting volunteer labor to the construction projects, even in the midst of dire manpower scarcity.

It remains an open question whether the state *Shintō* apparatus really succeeded in penetrating the souls of Japan's 70 million citizens in the 1930s–1940s. After the war, many remembered that in their inmost hearts, they had been praying for peace, for a way out of the appalling sacrifices their government was demanding of them—even for the collapse of Japan's militarist government.

The third major activity of the spiritual mobilization campaign was life-style improvement. This was not so much a new departure as the coopting of an existing initiative. The government had launched a national Life-style Improvement Movement in 1920. Its stated goal was "to awaken the people's consciousness, to guide their thinking . . . [to] eliminate waste in clothing, food, and housing, as well as social ceremonies . . . [and to]

1930s postcard of the Yasukuni shrine.

renew people's lifestyles through the chasing out of ostentation and the inculcation of rationality." In spite of this austere agenda, many social activists had seized on lifestyle improvement as a way to help raise the standard of living of Japan's impoverished working class in both town and village. Women activists, in particular, saw it as a way to relieve working-class women of the double burden of productive labor and household duties: Through a rational and scientific approach to housework, perhaps the movement could introduce into the home new amenities (such as modernized kitchens), thus giving women more time, freedom, and ultimately, the chance of greater social status.

Under the spiritual mobilization campaign, however, lifestyle improvement became an increasingly coercive tool for government control of daily life. As the war in China dragged on, the movement's leaders focused on the economic imperative to save resources, to maximize production, and to minimize consumption. Women were told that "victory comes from the kitchen," and in 1940, there were reports of women's groups saving tea leaves either to be reused or sent to the military. Virtually from the outset of war, calls for lifestyle improvement came to echo the harsh tone of the eighteenth-century *shōgunal* edicts against extravagance. One military commentator wrote in 1937, "In normal times, waste is a loss to the family, but not necessarily to society or the nation; but in this emergency, waste is treason against society and the nation. It is a criminal act."[2]

As with any government initiative, the spiritual mobilization campaign engendered its own bureaucracy. The government created a National Spiritual Mobilization Central Committee in October 1937. Seventy-four national organizations immediately joined: They included the Patriotic Women's Association, the Women's Defense Association, the Committee of Patriotic Farmers' Organizations, the National Farmers' Union, and the Patriotic Labor-Farmers' Association. Thus virtually any community organization was now officially allied to the spiritual mobilization campaign—bringing millions of civilians into the movement. Indeed, to the extent that this campaign was successful, its success lay in coopting and incorporating the large number of independent and semi-independent groups and associations in Japan into full cooperation with the prosecutors of the war effort. In 1941, this entire umbrella organization was folded into another government invention for the mobilization of daily life, the Imperial Rule Assistance Association.

In spite of this impressive organizational structure, the government was only too aware of the limited effectiveness of mobilization through exhortation and moral suasion. It was left to the Spiritual Mobilization Campaign's Draconian sibling, the Economic Mobilization Law of 1938, and to the system of councils and neighborhood groups that was created to implement this law to bring about real changes in the daily lives of Japanese civilians.

NEIGHBORHOOD ASSOCIATIONS

One of the most successful traditions of east Asian governance has been in utilizing the principle of mutual responsibility. An extraordinary feature of Tokugawa-era Japanese villages, for example, is that for the most part, they contained no police presence. Villages were held communally responsible for meeting their basic obligations—the village tax quota, labor service, and the reporting of illegal activities, such as Christian worship. How they went about doing so was largely at the discretion of the village leadership. The system was borrowed from the ancient Chinese structure known as *pao chia,* which, for purposes of mutual responsibility, had grouped families into blocks of 100 *(chia)*—roughly equivalent to a village—and *chia* into blocks of 10 *(pao)*. This system derived its strength from the fact that, especially in a society (such as a village) characterized by low mobility, people were much more likely to feel obligation and loyalty to their immediate neighbors than to a relatively abstract and remote entity, such as a government or emperor.

A variant of this system was introduced into Japan as early as the seventh century, and it continued to be used as a technique of social control through much of Japan's recorded history. Even in the absence of government mandate, neighbors found it useful to organize themselves into groups or associations to provide mutual support in activities such as rice planting, roof thatching, and fire prevention. By the early twentieth century, thousands of neighborhood associations and hamlet or ward councils existed more or less independently throughout Japan. The neighborhood associations were typically groups of from 5 to 10 households living in close proximity, while the councils offered membership to all the families in the community. Town and hamlet councils were not a formal part of local administration—villages and towns had elected assemblies for that purpose. But while the latter were restricted to elected members, who were usually a part of the wealthy elite of the community, the town and hamlet councils were open to all—and their assent was generally sought for important local business.

The Japanese government has always been most effective when coopting existing groups for the purpose of government, and the war years were no exception. Government bureaucrats understood that if they wished to extend their control into the daily lives of Japanese citizens, they must penetrate the social groups with which ordinary Japanese interacted—the neighborhood associations and hamlet and town councils.

In 1940, the Home Ministry created new regulations that made membership compulsory in both town and hamlet councils as well as in 10-family neighborhood associations. By the end of the year, there were some 19,000 town and hamlet councils in place and 1.2 million neighborhood associations. The ministry defined the goals of the councils as "to organize and unify people who live in cities, towns, and villages based on the spirit of neighborhood solidarity"; "to organize the basis for planning people's moral training and spiritual unity"; "to cause all national policies to prevail among the people and help national policies be put smoothly into effect in every respect"; and "as regional units of control for people's economic life, to demonstrate their essential function in enforcing a controlled economy and stabilizing people's livelihoods."

Each month, the Home Ministry would issue a series of "thoroughgoing points" to regulate the content of the monthly council meetings. The thoroughgoing points would be sent by the ministry to the prefectural authorities, then passed down to town, village, and hamlet councils, which, in turn, passed them down to neighborhood associations. The neighborhood association was where ordinary Japanese people came into direct contact with the government's administration of the war effort. A relatively marginal institution that had until 1937 existed for occasional communal activities, such as street cleaning, rice transplanting, or fire and earthquake drills, now began to intervene more and more in their individual daily lives. For some, this represented a welcome strengthening of community ties or (for those who became association leaders) a way to increase their local influence. But for many, the neighborhood association was an unwelcome intrusion into the narrow sphere of private life. Neighborhood association activists gained a reputation as busybodies, forever poking their noses into the private affairs of their member families. Any family that diverged from the norm—in clothing, opinion, hairstyles, sleeping and waking habits, or leisure activities—risked rebuke from these neighborhood busybodies. Some neighborhoods even erected roadblocks to control the comings and goings of outsiders—as in the case of one local council, which planted in the street a large illustrated billboard saying "those people with permanent waves will please refrain from passing through this neighborhood." In some cases, children were placed on urban street corners to scold any woman who showed too much concern for her appearance.

Neighborhood associations were charged with a wide variety of wartime activities, including meeting quotas for government savings drives; meeting quotas for donations in money and in kind (particularly metal goods) for the war effort; air-raid drills; distribution of helmets and gas masks; attendance at lectures and rallies to promote the war effort; fire patrols; payment of taxes; and even mail delivery. The associations met once a month (on the eighth, a day declared Imperial Rescript Day in honor of the emperor's declaration of war on that day) in the home of one of the members. NHK, the national radio company, broadcast a half-hour program timed to coincide with the meetings, during which a representative of the Home Ministry read that month's directives.

But of all the neighborhood associations' activities, the most important was the distribution of rations. Even before Pearl Harbor, food was becoming scarce. The war closed off imports and diverted huge supplies to the military in Japan and overseas. As Japan's sea lanes were gradually closed off by Allied naval and air power, supplies dwindled further. When promised rations failed to show up on time, this became a matter of life or death for ordinary people. Members depended on the fairness of the associations' leaders to ensure equitable distribution. But fairness entailed many difficult decisions since some families were inevitably needier than others. And the local nature of the neighborhood association made it inevitable that petty resentments and neighbors' feuds would sometimes intervene.

RATIONING, ECONOMIC CONTROLS, FOOD, CLOTHING, CONSUMPTION

In March 1938, the Japanese Diet approved the National General Mobilization Law, "to apply controls to our human and material resources in such a way that the country can most effectively attain the objectives of national defense in wartime." This law gave the government sweeping powers to control both production and consumption. Increasingly, the government used these powers to divert productive capacity to military production (for example, chemicals were directed away from agricultural fertilizers and into military industries) and to squeeze consumption. One aspect of this was the bleaching of color from the urban street as neon lights were switched off to conserve electricity. Dance halls and other places of amusement were closed, leaving many young women out of work and many young people in general without a place of temporary escape from the war. Most families found themselves doing without, not from loyalty to the goals of spiritual mobilization, but simply because goods and services were no longer available.

Food was, of course, the most important item to come under government control. From early 1941, the government introduced a rationing system for a wide variety of items of food. Rice was distributed to local dealers and to those companies that provided meals to workers. The basic ration was 330 grams per adult per day. Families were issued passbooks, and the rice shop would allow them to take home a 14-kilogram sack of rice two or three times a month, depending on the number and age of family members. The saying in wartime Japan, however, was that there were five colors of rice, varying from yellow to black (white rice became the stuff of dreams for many ordinary people). Ration books were also issued for miso and soy sauce. For most other foods the rations were distributed to the neighborhood association, whose leaders were left with the unenviable task of distributing them fairly. This was particularly hard when, as often happened later in the war, the promised rations were not delivered. Families would rush to the distribution point as soon as word came that rations had been received. At times the weak and elderly were unable to claim their share in time and had to do without. In this way, daily life became literally a struggle for survival.

On the whole, the Japanese people accepted the rationing system as fair. Black marketing and profiteering—major problems in Britain and elsewhere—did not become rife in Japan until after defeat in 1945. Nevertheless, some people cheated, and the authorities did establish a police unit specifically for economic activities. Bending or breaking the rules was most tempting for farmers; they were angered at having to give up the food grown by the sweat of their brow in exchange for government handouts. But urban citizens also tried to work the system; some resorted to feigning pregnancy or invented family members in order to increase their rations.

Along with food, the war drained away the very fabric of civilian life. Almost from the beginning of hostilities, it became difficult to purchase textiles. The materials available (and socially acceptable) were increasingly harsh and dull. With the growing shortage of cloth, the government encouraged families throughout Japan to wear *monpé* trousers, a simple pantaloon made of rough cloth. These were similar to the traditional farm clothes of northern Japan, but in other parts of the country, they were an alien form of dress. From the turn of the 1940s the government first encouraged, then required families to use cloth made of cotton or wool mixed with *sufu*, a factory-produced "staple fiber" made of wood pulp (the word *sufu* comes from the abbreviation of the Japanese rendition of *suteepuru fuaibaa* (staple fiber)). *Sufu* was notoriously weak, particularly when exposed to water, and magazine articles exhorted wives to think of ways to strengthen clothes made with this material.

Ration coupons on clothes were introduced in February 1942, just at the moment when the Japanese military was celebrating victories across southeast Asia. Restrictions on food and now clothing sorely tested any sense of wartime unity. Rural residents were angered once again when they found that they were entitled to only 80 coupon points, while city dwellers got 100. Even for those with coupons, however, textiles were disappearing from the shops even before the system was introduced; Japan's cotton industry depended on raw material imports, and the war meant that import channels were closed. The little cloth that was available was largely requisitioned for the war effort (late in the war, women were asked to cut off any long sleeves and send the material to the military). As a result, new clothing became almost impossible to find from 1941 onward. Wartime magazines were filled with ideas on how to make do. One suggestion was to stitch together several worn-out garments to make a single sturdy outfit. As one reader explained, however, even the thread to sew up rags was no longer available.

In addition to food and clothing a wide range of other goods were rationed, including nails, needles, bandages, shoes, sake, cooking oil, tire tubes, and salt. Families could apply for extra rations in cases of special need—for example, special sake allowances were available for weddings and funerals. Families were issued with an increasing number of ration coupon books for all of these different items, until the system became quite overwhelming (reportedly, some families ended up with more than 35 different books).

As items increasingly became in short supply, their quality declined steeply, and people had no choice but to accept poor substitutes. Soap, for example, was now made of fish oil, which was said by some to be contributing to an explosion of lice by actually feeding the little parasites (again, though, farm wives complained bitterly that urban families got double the soap ration of farm families, even though the former had access to laundry services, had smaller families, and did not have to get their clothes dirty, as did farmers). Instead of leather, cobblers had to make do with whale and shark skin, or even raw squid—which worked well until the shoes became wet! Those lucky enough to own cars had from mid-1938 to rig them up with coal stoves in the trunk if they wanted to supplement the Draconian gasoline ration. Thus while patriotic women's groups worked to train women as car drivers, there were fewer and fewer cars either available or with the resources to be driven.

With all of these restrictions, it is not surprising that most survivors remember the war days as a time of unrelieved misery and hardship. For many, this was true even before Pearl Harbor. It became the norm, especially from 1943, with the loss of Japan's merchant fleet and, for urban residents, it reached a crescendo from late 1944 with the start of U.S. bombing of the homeland. At the outset, so many bombs missed their target in Tokyo and fell in the bay that locals joked the American plan was to kill the fish and starve the citizens. However, the United States had complete control of the skies over Japan and attacked almost every city and town in the country (the ancient capital of Kyoto was exempted by the American government because of its irreplaceable stock of cultural treasures). In a single night in March 1945, for example, 334 U.S. bombers hit Tokyo, destroying 16 square miles of the city center (an animated map of this event features as one of the most powerful exhibits in the present-day Edo-Tokyo Museum). The western coastal city of Toyama, with a population of 127,000, was also attacked with 1,500 tons of bombs on August 1, 1945, with the result that 99.5 percent of the built-up area was obliterated. It is said that U.S. bombing leveled over 2.5 million houses in Japan, leaving 10 million people homeless. Thus city life, and with it, the middle class, which symbolized Japan's modernity and success to 1937, was virtually erased at the war's end.

Still, it is surprising how some members of the privileged class managed to hold on to their creature comforts right up to the end of the war. Some restaurants and bars remained open, and those with sufficient money found ways to circumvent the rationing restrictions. The plump popular entertainer Furukawa Roppa, for example, dwells lovingly in his diary on the steak dinners he was able to eat while performing in cities around Japan and its occupied territories. Another famous entertainer, Shinshō, a master of *rakugo,* the comic monologue, was said to love nothing more than women and sake and, as historian Barak Kushner puts it, "like a true resident of Tokyo, he never let the sun shine on his day's earnings and changed his name sixteen times in a bid to evade creditors."[3]

Moreover, one of the leading historians of wartime and postwar Japanese society, John Dower, has pointed out in a major article, "The Useful War," that at the same time that it brought extraordinary material hardship and decline in consumption for most Japanese, the war also offered economic opportunities to many. Japan had suffered from chronic underemployment in the prewar decades, but during the frenetic industrial growth of the war period, there were jobs for all. And for those who could not make an adequate living in Japan, there were opportunities in Japan's vastly expanded overseas empire. Some of these opportunities were, of course, eliminated with Japan's defeat in August 1945, but much of the underlying structure of economic power actually survived the war, to be revived during the postwar, high-growth era.

MEDIA AND MASS CULTURE

All of the belligerent nations in World War II attempted to use the modern media—newspapers, magazines, cinema, and radio—as vehicles for domestic propaganda. The Japanese government was no exception. Indeed, the cabinet, army, navy, and foreign ministry each had separate information bureaus, which sometimes competed with each other to control and influence the flow of information.

As with any nation at war, the government operated a strict system of censorship. All published and broadcast material had to be submitted to the Home Ministry prior to release. Any mention of troop movements or military activities was strictly controlled (indeed, newspapers and broadcasters even had to suspend their daily weather forecasts for fear of providing useful information to the enemy). In addition, the government censored any material thought to be critical of the war, decadent, or just too "Western." Kissing, for example, was no longer permitted in movies, while the government encouraged tales of martial heroism. The number of newspapers and magazines was drastically reduced through forced mergers and closures, as the government attempted to assert greater control over what people knew and thought.

At the same time, though, the war brought unprecedented demand for information. Everyone wanted to know the latest war news, and newspaper readership climbed dramatically, even as the papers became shorter due to the chronic shortage of newsprint. As Japanese citizens were drawn into the war effort through the government's spiritual mobilization campaign, through town councils and neighborhood associations, and through savings drives and industrial growth, they became connected to the nation in ways that they had never been before. The war years, indeed, brought to fruition the creation of a mass culture that had begun in the 1920s and 1930s.

The *Yomiuri* newspaper was one of the pioneers in this process. The newspaper was purchased in 1923 by a former police chief, Shōriki Matsutarō. Shōriki had a popular touch, and he greatly expanded the circulation of the newspaper by promoting large-scale public events, including baseball. Shōriki was the founder of the Yomiuri Giants (still today a top baseball team in Japan), and in 1934, he brought Babe Ruth and an all-star American team to Japan for a series of hugely popular exhibition matches. Shōriki was the chairman of the influential Cabinet Information Bureau during the war and thus a central figure in the government's information campaigns (he was briefly imprisoned as a Class A war criminal after the war, for his propaganda work).

Shōriki recognized that the public needed spectacle, preferably on a grand scale, as a form of mass mobilization but also as entertainment. After 1941, baseball fell into temporary eclipse due to its unfortunate American origins. But it had such a fan base among ordinary Japanese that a compromise was found by reworking the vocabulary—for example, replacing the Japanized American term *beesuboru* with the properly Japanese (if actually Sino-Japanese) word *yakyū*. One of the reasons for baseball's popularity was that many Japanese enjoyed the dramatic confrontation between pitcher and hitter; it was common to view this as a kind of duel between professional warriors, and hitters were often compared to traditional samurai swordsmen. Indeed, individual confrontation was at the heart of popular Japanese sports, even though the propaganda goal was to strengthen a collective sense of national unity. Thus the sports that were sponsored heavily during the war were those with native origins, especially *sumō* wrestling and *jūdō*.

Japan's sports impresarios had pulled off a major coup in 1936 by winning the 1940 Olympics for Tokyo. Throughout 1937, crews worked on the construction of a vast Olympic stadium near the Meiji shrine in western Tokyo (the site eventually hosted the 1964 Olympics). As the China war bogged down and the European situation deteriorated, the Japanese government bowed to the inevitable and canceled the Olympics (sports teams across Japan were also to be disbanded from 1943). In its place the government offered a different sort of spectacle. The year 1940 was the 2,600th anniversary of the founding of the Japanese nation, according to official mythology. The government organized a series of events throughout Japan to commemorate this anniversary, culminating in a magnificent ceremony at the Olympic stadium. In this, trumpets sounded before a crowd of some 50,000 as the emperor and empress progressed to a pair of gold-painted thrones. The prime minister, Konoe Fumimaro, led the entire assemblage in the national anthem, followed by a speech averring that Japan's mission was world peace. Led by the prime minister, the crowd yelled, "Long live the emperor!" *(tennō heika banzai)*. At the same moment, guns at the Miyakezaka army headquarters, and aboard battleships moored off Shinagawa, roared into life, and sirens sounded all over the nation. The entire event (with, as respect for his divine status, the exception of the emperor's speech) was broadcast live on the radio, and citizens all over Japan joined in the *banzais*. The ceremonies ended with a choir of 3,000 schoolchildren and college students from around the country singing "2,600 Years." Selected in a national contest and already released by major record companies, the song reflected the ambitions of the authorities rather than the realities of civilian life with its refrain, "Glorious Japan / Shining like the golden bird of myth / We celebrate today this feast of the morrow / 2,600 years since the founding / Ah, 100 million hearts are calling!"

Japanese bureaucrats in the late 1930s were influenced by Nazi media policies. Attending the 1936 Berlin Olympics, they had been fascinated by the slick choreography, the hero-worshipping crowds in front of their führer, and the advanced technologies used by the Germans in staging and broadcasting the Olympics. The Nazis initiated a national campaign to put a radio set in every German home, and the Japanese government soon launched a campaign in imitation of this; the goal was "the total mobilization of the people's spirit, as well as . . . the arousal of domestic opinion and of correct thinking."

Radio ownership in 1937 was approaching 40 percent in the cities but had yet to reach the 10 percent mark in rural Japan. A consortium of the army, navy, and Communications Ministry put out posters under their combined names, exhorting people to "[pull] together for the defense of the nation; [listen] together to the radio." Indeed, during the war, the military spokesmen who regularly appeared on the radio, either to inform or delude (as in the catastrophic defeat at Midway, which was reported as a great victory), became media stars in their own right and as famous as the commanders in the field. Along with lectures and advertising campaigns on the value of radio to civilians, the government also repeatedly lowered the license fee, excusing altogether the families of active servicemen. The national broadcasting company, NHK, also built transmitters at close intervals around Japan to improve reception and cut the technological costs of receivers. Still, the cheapest radio in 1942 cost 10 yen, a heavy investment for farmers and factory workers, whose monthly income might be no more than 10 or 20 yen.

By the early 1940s, however, the radio had become an integral part of most Japanese homes (it was to become vital from 1944 as one of the most effective forms of air-raid warning). Its penetration, however, still lagged in the countryside. Many Japanese families woke up to radio calisthenics, listened to the news over their increasingly meager breakfasts, and moved to the beat of the latest popular songs (such as "Patriotic March") as they performed their household chores. Radio content had always been serious since the first broadcasts in the 1920s, so the war years were not a complete departure in tone. There were superficial changes, such as the program "Woman's Hour" being renamed "Home at War Hour." Late in the war, there was public fatigue with austerity and propaganda, and radio shifted to include more entertainment, although this tended to be talks on such things as Zen Buddhism, the tea ceremony, art history, or performances from the kabuki theater. Western music was broadly restricted to classical works of Japan's allies, Germany and Italy. Jazz, whether on radio or on record, was targeted as a form of "spiritual pollution" because of its image as the quintessential American music. Japanese wartime critics described it as frivolous, sensual, and associated with decadent lifestyles. Jazz had been so popular with young Japanese before the war, however, that one of the wartime propaganda campaigns in 1943 was to encourage people to destroy their collection of jazz records. In this way they were being told to liberate themselves from the enemy's culture. In practice, as the work of E. Taylor Atkins shows, musicians, record buyers, and owners of what formerly had been jazz cafes simply evaded the prohibitions by incorporating Japanese and Chinese folk tunes into their music or renaming jazz as "light music." That the beat lingered on is suggested by the comment of one kamikaze pilot late in the war: "How funny to listen to jazz music before going out to kill the jazzy Americans!"[4]

In the evenings, the cinema, despite all the restrictions of war, remained as popular as ever. The government began closing cinemas early in the evening and imposed a 90 percent surcharge on cinema tickets as part of

Spritual purification: Antijazz campaign, 1943. (*Shashin Shūhō,* 3 February 1943.)

a broader effort to restrain the flourishing entertainment industry (toward the end of the war, the government also closed more than 10,000 geisha houses, banned the kabuki theater, and severely restricted variety shows). But cinema was still an important medium for government propaganda. Some of this was conveyed through the newsreels, which were prepared under tight military control and often focused on images of local peoples across Asia welcoming the Japanese forces. But the government also expected feature films to do their part in promoting the war effort. In some cases—such as *The Story of Tank Commander Nishizumi* (1940)—these films were sponsored directly by the government or the military. Others, such as the 1944 film *The Most Beautiful*, directed by Japan's most respected postwar filmmaker, Kurosawa Akira, were privately produced; but this film still contributed to the spirit of wartime sacrifice by its portrayal of women factory workers enduring dreadful hardships in order to produce optical instruments.

One noteworthy feature of Japanese wartime movies is that although many are obviously propaganda, for the most part they do not promote hatred of Americans or other Westerners. Indeed, ordinary Japanese in the 1930s, and even into the war years, in contrast to those in the military, who were trained to hate the enemy, were not naturally disposed to hate Americans. Just a few days before the strike on Pearl Harbor, Japanese cinemas were showing *I Wanted Wings,* an Oscar-winning romantic drama from Hollywood about the training of American air force pilots. Even in Japanese films that were overtly about the war, the enemy was conspicuously absent. Perhaps one reason was the lack of white actors. But the focus of films like *Commander Nishizumi* was more on what was seen as the bravery, purity, and spirit of sacrifice of Japanese heroes than on the desire to kill the enemy. Both *Commander Nishizumi* and *The Most Beautiful* portray a people whose strength, as idealized by the filmmakers, lies in their calm acceptance of suffering. This ideal became the dominant theme of Japanese cinema between 1942 and 1945.[5]

More generally, there are remarkably few signs of anti-Western hatred among civilians in wartime Japan. The newspapers published cartoons of Roosevelt growing devil-like horns. An American flag was painted on a Tokyo street so that civilians could trample (if they looked down to notice) on the national symbol of the enemy. And when the Americans began fire bombing Japanese cities, hatred did smolder amid the ashes. But it seems that the majority of Japanese people continued, if anything, to admire Western culture, which had, after all, played an enormous influence in daily life until the very eve of the war. Japan was experiencing the same processes of social development—and the spread of mass culture—as America, Britain, and Germany. Perhaps this is one reason why American popular culture found such immediate acceptance after Japan's defeat.

October 1941 advertisement for Hollywood's *I Wanted Wings*. (Newspaper *Kyoto
Hinode Shimbun*, 24 October 1941.)

SCHOOLS, CHILDREN, AND YOUTH CULTURE

The Japanese government had initiated a system of compulsory education in the early 1870s, with two major goals. One—influenced by Western
ideas of self-help—was to provide young Japanese with the knowledge
they needed to improve their lots in life. The second was to create good
citizens. In the mid-nineteenth century, few Japanese had a clear idea of
what Japan as a nation, or the emperor, should mean to them. The school
system was a major opportunity for the government to get its message
across to young citizens while still at an impressionable age. Love for
the emperor and duty to the nation became increasingly important com-
ponents of the school curriculum as time went on. After 1937, the army

became increasingly involved in education (an army general, Araki Sadao, was to become education minister in the late 1930s). Although in the past the Education Ministry had jealously preserved its independence, it was now forced to allow army officers to work with bureaucrats in rewriting textbooks and revising the school curriculum toward a much more overtly mythic and militarized view of Japanese nationalism.

Major revisions were introduced in April 1941. Elementary schools were now to be called national schools, and the period of compulsory education was extended from six to eight years. The new curriculum firmly turned its back on "the [Western] view that education is an investment or a path to success and happiness." The new goal of the schools was to "restore the former spirit of Japanese education, nurture the innate disposition of the Japanese people who are the support of the world and the leaders of the Asian league, return to the imperial way, and wholeheartedly promote the Japanese spirit."

Spirit, in general, took precedence over academic achievement. This was convenient, as teachers were in increasingly short supply, and students were in demand for war-related activities, such as so-called volunteer labor, military send-offs, and military drills. The Japanese language, ethics, geography, and history programs were all folded into a new course called National Studies (early in the war against China, history, that is, a strictly nationalistic view of Japanese history, was given special emphasis when it was made compulsory as part of the elite civil service exams). In the new textbooks, topics that were regarded as too Westernized or too decadent were dropped or revised. Thus, instead of what some Japanese cultural critics saw as the frivolous Western concern with surface beauty, for example, the new ideal was "the beauty of death." The emphasis on the mythologies of Japan's divine origin extended across disciplines. One geography teacher was taken aback when his students corrected him: The Inland Sea could not have been created by the subsidence of land that had originally connected Shikoku and the mainland, they insisted, as "our history teacher told us that the gods used that land in ancient times, to build a bridge between Japan and heaven!"[6]

Schoolchildren began spending an inordinate amount of time outside, doing military-style drills and working on so-called volunteer projects. Some aspects of this were probably much more fun than sitting in a classroom (the classrooms were, anyway, freezing cold much of the year as many schools donated their iron stoves to the war effort). Photographs show children laughingly attacking effigies of Roosevelt and Churchill with wooden swords or lying on the ground pretending to be victims of gas attacks. At other times, the drills were harsh—children were made to spend long hours on cold winter days in bare feet and even bare chested. Often, children were called on to help with projects such as weeding roads and banks, cleaning shrine and temple grounds, and even building new airfields. Nor were the holidays exempt: The traditional summer holiday was renamed the "summer training period" and was devoted to voluntary labor.

Children were taught at school to love and revere the emperor. The textbooks portrayed him as the father of the nation, a symbol of benevolence. They were told that at his enthronement, "the emperor kindly said that he would make us happy and make our country prosperous." Every national school in Japan contained a repository—sometimes just a cabinet in a classroom, but more often a small stand-alone shrine on the school grounds—that contained portraits of the emperor and empress and a copy of the Imperial Rescript on Education, promulgated by the current emperor's grandfather. Any time a student walked past the repository, he or she was expected to face it and bow deeply. Several times a year, the head teacher would reverently remove the rescript and ceremoniously read it to the assembled school. These were occasions of deep solemnity. Teachers who misread or stumbled over the words were so shamed that there were even reports of them committing suicide.

Despite the shortages in food, clothing, fuel, and other supplies, Japanese schoolchildren found plenty to amuse themselves against the background of all-out war. Even with the squeeze on consumption, there was a flourishing industry in inexpensive children's toys, such as model airplanes, toy gas masks, and picture playing cards (one educational version were the Greater East Asia alphabet cards, illustrated with scenes from Japan's new possessions). Boys' magazines contained stirring tales of soldiers' heroism or information on territories that were now part of the Greater East Asian Co-prosperity Sphere; children's comics used cartoon characters, such as the dog-soldier Norakuro, turned from a prewar rascal to a wartime leader of men (or, in his case, actually dogs), to instill the values of loyalty and selflessness. Parents, too, enjoyed dressing their sons up in military uniforms for special occasions, such as the *shichigosan* celebration in a child's seventh, fifth, and third years. Children were also called on to see departing soldiers off to join their regiments. The stations were often thronged with crowds of laughing and waving schoolchildren, carrying little Japanese flags and shouting *banzai* to the soldiers.

As Japan became increasingly exposed to American air raids, and urban schools were threatened from the air, cities began evacuating their children to rural areas. Sometimes parents organized these evacuations independently, sending their children back to relatives in the countryside. But in most cases they were organized by local districts and involved whole schools. Many Japanese in their sixties and seventies today remember the evacuations as the defining experience of the war for them.

The children found themselves in utterly unfamiliar environments. The village children with whom they were thrown together often spoke in a strong dialect, and many of the urban comforts the evacuees had always taken for granted—such as tatami straw mats on the floors or simply clean clothes to wear—were no longer available. Life in the village was crowded (many villages were hard-pressed to accommodate their new guests), smelly (farm families still used human manure as fertilizer in the fields), cold (many rural areas of north and west Japan had much more snow than the heavily populated east, and farmhouses were distinctly well ventilated), and dark (if they had electric light at all, most families had just one 20-watt bulb). And of course, the children missed their parents. But they usually adapted quickly, and they soon found themselves playing new games, making new friends, and learning a new way of life as they experienced the cycle of planting, nurturing, and harvest.

Childhood, however, ended early in the war years. Young men and women over the age of 14 were required to register with the National Work Guidance Center for potential labor mobilization, and they were liable to be sent to munitions factories, where there was an ever greater risk of being bombed. In the final years of the war the army and navy accepted volunteers as young as 14. Indeed, the military came to rely increasingly on Japan's youth. More than three-quarters of those who died as volunteer kamikaze pilots were university students (the military preferred to accept arts students rather than scientists and engineers, whom they considered too important to the wider war effort to sacrifice). For those youths who were not conscripted into compulsory labor or the military, there was usually plenty of hard labor on the family farm or in the family business, which was likely to be suffering from the lack of able bodies as men were drafted into the military.

WOMEN, WORK, AND FAMILY PLANNING

As soon as Japan plunged into conflict with China in July 1937, families began losing their menfolk to the military. Japan's combined forces climbed to one million during the early years of the China war. By the time of the attack on Pearl Harbor, they were at three million. Later, in spite of heavy losses of about two million, the total number of men in uniform kept climbing, to a peak of seven million in 1945—that is, 20 percent of the total male population. Earlier in the war, exemptions were still available for those in key professions or those in higher education. But by the end of the war, virtually all able-bodied men under the age of 45 were serving in one capacity or another.

This drain of men left women with a harsh duty. More than half of all Japanese families were engaged in family businesses, such as farming, shopkeeping, or home-based industry. The women had to keep these enterprises going, helped by children and the elderly. As if this were not hard enough, the nation also had a voracious need for labor, in factories, mines, and on construction projects. In the absence of men, Japanese firms began recruiting women to fill these positions. And this, too, was on top of the additional burdens imposed by the war—air-raid drills, savings drives, and volunteer labor, including the activities of the Patriotic Women's Association and the Women's Defense Association.

The Patriotic Women's Association was formed at the turn of the twentieth century and originally comprised upper-class women, but by the time of

World War II, both it and the Women's Defense Association had millions of middle- and working-class members. Indeed, membership in one or the other organization was effectively compulsory.

One of the main responsibilities of members in these groups was to send off departing soldiers with appropriate ceremony. Usually sporting simple white dresses as a symbol of purity, and association sashes as badges of identity, they were especially visible at railway stations, where they manned tables and offered tea and snacks to the traveling soldiers.[7]

In the towns, women's group members would stand on street corners collecting stitches for thousand-stitch belts. These belts, worn around the stomach by soldiers and sailors, were said to offer protection to the wearer through the spiritual power of the many women who contributed to them. At least, they were a demonstration that the people back home cared. The same is true of the comfort packages that women's groups prepared. These contained a variety of items that soldiers might find useful or reminiscent of home: cigarettes, magazines, local newspaper clippings, letters from village friends, candies, soap, razor blades, photos of Japanese film stars, and so on. In the larger cities, many women would purchase these bags in ready-prepared sets available in department stores. In this way the big retailers managed to find a market in patriotism. The more elaborate ones cost as much as five yen, putting them well out of reach of the laboring classes, who made do with the more common, homemade versions.

As the war progressed, women's groups were also increasingly called on to participate in funerals. The ashes of dead Japanese soldiers came home in small wooden boxes, arriving by the thousand on the ships unloading at Japan's major ports. The families of the bereaved were informed of the arrival and, in many cases, traveled to collect their loved one's ashes. The women's groups would greet them at the station on their return and accompany them home. Funerals were usually paid for by the municipality, and they were semiofficial occasions, which the mayor and local officials as well as members of the women's associations would attend. Parents at these ceremonies were expected to show composure and even to thank the gods for allowing their son to die for emperor and country (perhaps this was what gave rise to the myth that Japanese mothers felt no grief). But the women's groups maintained a discreet backup to help the family keep up this appearance.

Women's group members were involved in local defense activities, many of which had previously been undertaken by youth associations or army reserve associations. They included fire prevention and firefighting, air-raid marshaling, town and village improvements, and entertainment. For example, women's groups organized lectures on health, hygiene, emigration, and morals. The lecturers were often local notables, such as school principals, teachers, local agricultural experts, or doctors. Women's groups also helped arrange patriotic ceremonies on national holidays, such as national foundation day, army day, and navy day. Women and girl students were often the mainstays of local concerts or dance performances aimed at raising people's spirits.

Women were also vital participants in the neighborhood associations (the nominal heads of these associations were usually men, but most activities were led by women), and they were key contributors to savings drives, collections for the military, and the donation of metal goods for recycling into munitions. The often-enthusiastic support for these efforts is one indication of the genuine enthusiasm and support for the war effort by many women. In another indicator, occupying U.S. forces conducted a survey in late 1945 of 5,000 men, women, and children to determine the level of their will to fight. The survey found that the fighting spirit was strongest among women, particularly young women, and schoolchildren.

In spite of all the burdens thrown on their heads by the war, women also took advantage of new opportunities. The absence of men gave women an independence that they had never enjoyed before. Women occupied a lowly position in the Japanese family system that prevailed until Japan's defeat: They could be married off or sent out to work at the whim of the family head; they were expected to perform menial household tasks without complaint; and they were the last to be consulted in matters of comfort or convenience. Now, with many family heads fighting in the war, women were able to take independent decisions based more on their own interests. Moreover, the war work they undertook was often paid, sometimes at a much better rate than they had commanded before. Some women therefore gained limited financial independence, although they were still likely to have their wages claimed by the remaining male family members. Moreover, some women enjoyed the responsibility and freedom they felt while undertaking important tasks for the sake of the community—whether in a leading role in the neighborhood association or in putting on an entertainment for the community to keep up morale.

In addition to their added duties in the absence of menfolk, women were also called on to support Japan's imperial ambitions by producing babies. Until the late 1930s, overpopulation had been perceived as one of the great problems facing Japan. Indeed, the population problem had been used as a major justification for Japan's takeover of Manchuria: Japan needed land, the argument went, to resettle its surplus population. But as the Japanese government contemplated a world in which Japan dominated the entire Asian continent east of India, enthusiastic bureaucrats began planning to increase the Japanese population within just 20 years from the current 70 million to 100 million (the number that was already misleadingly used in many wartime slogans).

Early in the war, the government outlawed any method of birth control. It also began offering rewards to women for fertility; the wife of General Tōjō, prime minister from 1941, was one of the major public faces in this campaign. Under the auspices of the welfare ministry, prefectures designated those with 10 or more children as "excellent fertile families," offering monetary incentives (including the prize of free higher education) and producing leaflets with photos of big families with many small children. Of course, the government had to battle with the many disincentives to having more children—the shortage of food to feed more mouths and the absence of men to help make the children in the first place. The general policy of the authorities throughout the war years, however, was to try and limit the use of women as labor. Instead, as Thomas Havens has shown, the goal was always to protect the traditional ideal of women as wives and especially mothers, in stark contrast to Japan's enemies, who, it was argued, were sacrificing the home and family in order to produce munitions.[8] The belief in Japan clearly was that without a strong, stable family, there could be no victory. Thus many of the women who engaged in wartime work were young and single, often aged between 15 and 24. This was the accepted age when a woman could work; thereafter it was seen as normal that a woman should marry, quit work, start a family, and labor for the state in war or peace only through handicrafts or piecework from home.

CRIME AND POLICING

In the eyes of foreigners, Japan was virtually a police state by the late 1930s—similar, perhaps, to the Soviet Union under the ever-watchful eye of the KGB. Of course, this was, in part, because foreigners were kept under special surveillance in the atmosphere of suspicion that prevailed across much of the world. A visitor could get into serious trouble for photographing ships in the harbor or soldiers on parade. Even those staying in remote areas commented on the intrusiveness of the police—requiring residents, for example, to open up their houses for inspection twice a year to ensure that standards of cleanliness were being maintained. The officious and self-important local policeman, his sword trailing along the ground, was a standard element in the portraits of Japan that foreigners sent home.

Some of this was a continuation of long-standing practice: The police had been an authoritarian presence in Japanese lives since the days of the samurai. Nor was it always unwelcome. For the majority of Japanese the police remained a reassuring guarantee of what they saw as the extraordinary safety of their law-abiding country.

But for the small minority who were involved in political dissent, the war years were a time of fierce repression. Socialists, trade unionists, agitators for Korean independence, even old-fashioned liberals or university professors were liable to interrogation and imprisonment, regardless of their wealth or social standing. As the war situation worsened, even more everyday activities—reading foreign books, listening to jazz in a cafe (although one observer noted that the police could not distinguish between Duke Ellington and Mozart), grumbling about the war, even lamenting the loss of a son in the fighting—could bring one under suspicion. A careless comment questioning the mythology of the emperor's divine origins might land the speaker in deep trouble for the amorphous crime of lèse-majesté. All of this meant that the police were stretched to breaking point during the war, and indeed, there was an emergency drive in 1944 to recruit juvenile police, that is, males aged between 16 and 19.

The guardians of correct thinking and of the political status quo were the special higher police (*tokkō*) and the political arm of the military police (*kempeitai*). The military police had sweeping powers to arrest and prosecute in the military courts those suspected of subversive crimes; it was active in policing Japan's overseas possessions (where it was feared and hated) as well as in pursuing domestic crimes. The special higher police focused on rooting out deviant thought, especially left-wing sympathies, within Japan. Indeed, the unit was generally known by foreigners as the "thought police."

John Dower has aptly pointed out that one reason for the high visibility of the special higher police was the very real fear among Japan's governing elite—particularly in the later years of the war—that Japan was on the brink of social and political chaos, perhaps even a communist revolution. Dower's research has revealed that there was a certain amount of disillusion at all levels of Japanese society; this was recognized within the police forces themselves, and officers who read materials on left-wing beliefs in order to understand their enemy also came to see the abuses within the wartime system. The level of wartime cynicism and weariness among ordinary Japanese casts into doubt the mythology of Japanese unity and homogeneity that was symbolized during the war years by the slogan "100 million hearts beating as one."

Police records reveal numerous investigations for careless or critical comments on the war, the emperor, or the social system. For example, a young farmer was imprisoned for six months for saying that the Chinese leader, Chiang Kai-shek, was a greater man than the emperor. Another farmer openly told a village meeting that "being born in Japan is regrettable . . . and I loathe the emperor." A father whose son had been killed in the war was arrested merely for saying, "However much one may speak of the nation, can a parent help but weep?"

The police also kept records of graffiti and seditious writings found in public places or in anonymous letters. These included critical comments on the war and the shortages that went with it, on the social system, and on the emperor. While some were obviously written by communist agitators, others—such as the individual who wrote *stupid* over the imperial crest on a banknote or the 16-year-old boy who was caught writing *I hate the military* on the wall of a public toilet—were presumed to be the thoughts of ordinary Japanese. The police investigated thousands of such incidents, and not surprisingly, they found that antiwar and defeatist comments increased markedly in the final year of the war.[9] In fact, it is easy to argue that ordinary Japanese, from at least the beginning of 1945, were just waiting for the war to end and, with it, the chance to rebuild their lives. This may be why there was such a positive reception to the Allies once they commenced their occupation late in that year.

RURAL JAPAN

At the turn of the 1940s, close to half of Japan's population still lived in rural communities. Throughout the 1930s, rural problems—overpopulation, the oppressive landlord system, and unyielding poverty—were considered among the central political and social issues confronted by the nation. The war brought yet another blow to rural communities; and yet it also offered a vision of how rural Japan might fight its way out of poverty.

The initial effect of the war on Japanese villages was to precipitate a shortage of labor. This was in itself ironic since for more than a century the principal issue in rural Japan was the shortage of land relative to population. The average rural family had six members. The average farm size of between one and two acres might have been enough to feed this many people, if farmers did not have to pay a share of their produce to landlords and the government in the form of rent and taxes. As it was, most farm families had to send some of their members out to work for wages—whether on wealthier farms in the village or in factories in nearby towns and cities. Now, though, with the young men being sent off to war, the remaining family members were hard-pressed to get their crops in.

The effects of the war on rural families may be understood from the experiences of one rural woman, Sakaue Toshié.[10] Toshié was 12 years old in 1937. Her family was in many ways typical of poor tenant farmers in the rice-growing areas of Japan. On their two acres or so of land in Niigata prefecture in Japan's northwest, they grew barely enough to feed themselves. After paying rent and selling some of their crops for cash, they were unable to make ends meet without sending all available family members out to work for money (even then, they often had to hide when their landlord and creditors came calling). These included Toshié's father and mother, who both worked as day laborers on public works projects and on neighbors' fields; her elder brothers, one of whom was a local farmhand and the other a shop assistant in Tokyo; her elder sister, who had been sent out at the age of 10 to work as a maid; and Toshié herself, who, after completing her six years of compulsory schooling, was sent to work as a child-minder for a landlord family in a nearby village.

Toshié's eldest brother was called up in 1937 and served in China, but he came home sick at the end of the next year. The family was able to struggle by without incident until the time of Pearl Harbor, when Toshié was 16 and had just returned after completing her four-year contract. Toshié's sister, Kimié, was home, too. At the age of 18, she had suffered a sudden mental breakdown, and now she needed constant care.

After the attack on Pearl Harbor, Toshié's two brothers were called up almost immediately. Her elder brother had just married, and he left his wife with the family as he went off to rejoin his regiment. Toshié never saw either brother again. One died in the desperate fighting on the island of Guadalcanal and the other of disease in Sumatra. Meanwhile, the family was left to manage as well as it could with two of its men gone. Toshié found herself working as a farm laborer as she tried to help her parents reclaim a flood-prone field near the river that the prefecture had given them for a low annual rent.

The family grew rice, soy beans, a little mulberry, and vegetables. They sold their soy crop for a little cash, and they fed the mulberry leaves to silkworms, which they reared twice a year for a little more income. The rice (which they mixed with wheat, barley, and daikon leaves to stretch it out) and vegetables were the basic sustenance for the family.

Even before the war, Toshié's father had to sell a substantial part of his rice crop to buy necessities and to pay his rent and taxes. Now, with the introduction of the new rationing system, he had to give up virtually his entire crop. The village received from the prefecture a quota of rice to contribute to the rationing supply. Village officers divided the quota among the hamlets, which in turn, divided it by neighborhood group. Because of his poverty, Toshié's father had little say in the allocation. He felt that his own quota was too high given the poor productivity of much of his land—but there was nothing he could do about it. If he failed to provide his quota, he would be shamed in front of the neighborhood group, whose other members would have to make up the deficit. And so, in exchange for their precious rice, the family received ration coupons, which were good only for an uncertain supply of necessities.

The family made up for the loss of their crops by working for wages. The war meant there were plenty of opportunities for paid work. Toshié's father sent her and her sister-in-law off to work in a labor gang on the Niigata docks. They unloaded shipments of coal from freighters. It was grueling work, alongside prisoners of war and other slave laborers. But the wage, five yen per day, was an enormous help to Toshié's family.

As a young adult, Toshié was in great demand for war-related service. She was a member of both the village youth association and the Women's Defense Association. In her limited free time, she attended send-offs for departing village soldiers; she helped out at funerals; she served as an air-raid warden; she attended lectures on health, nutrition, and emigration; and she made thousand-stitch belts and comfort packages. She also did her bit to entertain the hard-pressed villagers. Once a year, she took part in a village entertainment, where she dressed up and acted male roles. Toshié had a hard life by any measure. But she always felt grateful for the closeness, the friendship, and the mutual support of her hamlet community. Perhaps this is one reason why she, and others like her, did her utmost to fulfill her obligations to the community, and so to the village, prefecture, and nation.

Among the lectures that Toshié and other villagers attended were those encouraging them to emigrate to Manchuria. From the middle of the 1930s, momentum developed for a major national effort to export up to a million (mainly rural) emigrant families to Manchuria. The Manchurian emigration program led to the creation of a huge bureaucracy to handle the settling of the territory. It involved propaganda, lectures, and floods of writing aimed at persuading the rural Japanese that Manchuria offered them a golden future. And it involved countless village authorities in planning to send their poor to Manchuria and thereby eliminate the bitter social rifts that had opened up throughout rural Japan.

According to government plans, each emigrating family would be allotted 20 hectares of land (purchased from existing Chinese or Korean settlers at government-established prices or reclaimed from swamp or forest) as well as receiving financial assistance up to 1,000 yen per family. Villages that wished to participate would determine the ratio of surplus villagers based on a formula of the minimum amount of land for self-sufficiency and target a specific number of families for emigration. The village would then send a mission to Manchuria, to scout a suitable location for settlement and to report back to the villagers. On its return, the mission would mount an exhibition for the villagers to see the materials they had brought back.

There followed a long process of exhortation and persuasion. Not only the mission members, but also local and national emigration bureaus from the Manchurian Emigration Council, Colonial Ministry, and Ministry of Agriculture and Forestry as well as regional representatives of women's groups, youth groups, and farm cooperatives would visit to lead meetings. Once volunteers came forward, the village (with national subsidies) provided financing for the emigration and purchased emigrants' land from them (often, this purchase was used to cancel outstanding debts).

For those who decided to go, the Manchurian project brought heart-rending disillusion, despair, and ultimately, death or the separation of families. Of the total of some 223,000 emigrants, an estimated 78,500 died at the hands of Russians or Chinese or by starvation, disease, or suicide.

WELFARE

In spite of all the hardships endured by Japanese people during eight years of war, in some ways, Japan in 1945 was a more equitable, more caring, and more supportive society than it had been in 1937.

From the outset of the war the government was concerned about the health of Japanese civilians. In the difficult circumstances of labor and food shortage, rates of tuberculosis and child mortality began to increase. The health problems had a direct effect on the war effort since the nation depended on the labor of women, children, and the elderly. The government had been disturbed for years about the poor condition of conscripts taking their medical exams. In times of peace the army had had to reject over 40 percent of its candidates due to weak lungs, poor eyesight, trachoma, and tuberculosis. Now, the quality of conscripts declined even further, just as the army needed Japan's fittest men.

These concerns led to unprecedented efforts by the government to improve health conditions. For example, the 1938 National Health Insurance Law called for the creation of insurance associations throughout the country. Membership was optional, but the state subsidized premiums. By 1945, there were 10,432 associations and 41 million members—substantially the entire working population. From 1938, the newly created Welfare Ministry began offering financial assistance for health care facilities and the creation of health centers as well as for the prevention of parasitic diseases and tuberculosis. The scheme relied less on financial subsidies for treatment than on prevention activities. In the postwar period, Japan's population recovered rapidly and even exceeded the prewar levels of health and longevity. Clearly part of the explanation for this lies in the many reforms undertaken by the Japanese government during the war.

The war also saw an increase in the communalization of women's activities, such as cooking and childcare. Critics had been calling for such communal efforts for years, but the labor shortage of the war finally persuaded communities to act. By 1941, there were more than 18,000 communal cooking groups in Japanese villages. Many of them received financial support from the Imperial Agricultural Association or their local farm cooperatives. Food was normally provided by each of the roughly 30 households that made up a typical group, in addition to some purchases made with collected funds. A difficult issue was who to appoint as cook for the group. Different groups handled this issue differently, with some appointing the least busy women on an unpaid basis and others appointing the most skilled cooks and paying them.

The war also led to improvements in the lot of tenant farmers. Concerned that tenants would not be motivated to put in the extra labor needed to maintain or increase production if they had to give a large share of the proceeds to their landlord as rent, the government, in 1939, introduced farm rent control regulations and, when it introduced a system of compulsory purchase the following year, created a two-tiered pricing system that paid tenants more for their crops than landlords. By the end of the war, landlords were only receiving a fraction of the rent that they had before, and the profitability of landlordism had been almost erased—an important preliminary step to the postwar land reform.

The war is also credited with the reform of Japan's management system. Because of the severe shortage of labor and the mobility of workers, companies made extraordinary efforts during the war to offer their workers security of employment, regular pay increases, and various facilities, such as housing and meals. The government played an unprecedented role in managing the wartime economy, and this role, together with the reformed management system, survived into the postwar years to become the key-stones of Japan's "high-growth system."

It is one of the great ironies of World War II that the two defeated nations, Japan and Germany, recovered to become formidable economic competitors to the victors. Part of this was due to the destruction of the war, which allowed them to rebuild their industries based on the most modern methods. Part of it was due to American economic support. But a good deal was also attributable to the welfare policies and economic changes that took place during the war itself—a war that, as noted earlier, has been aptly described as "useful" to the people of Japan, however destructive it may have been to the millions of civilians who lost their lives, relatives, homes, and property as well as any illusions they may have had about war and the military.

NOTES

1. Quoted from Niigata-shi Gappei Chōsonshi Henshūshitsu, ed., *Ishiyama Sonpō ni miru Senjika no Nōson,* Niigata City, Japan: Niigata-shi Gappei Chōsonshi Henshūshitsu, 1984 (p. 112).

2. Matsumoto Sugizō writing in *Ie no Hikari,* September 1937 (p. 37).

3. Barak Kushner, *The Thought War: Japanese Imperial Propaganda,* Honolulu: University of Hawai'i Press, 2006 (p. 113).

4. E. Taylor Atkins, *Blue Nippon: Authenticating Jazz in Japan,* Durham, NC: Duke University Press, 2001 (p. 127).

5. See "Japanese Cinema Goes to War," in John W. Dower, *Japan in War and Peace: Selected Essays,* New York: The New Press, 1993.

6. Masaomi Yui, *Sensō to Kokumin,* Tokyo: Shūeisha, 1980 (p. 65).

7. For a detailed discussion of the wartime activities of women's associations, see Sandra Wilson, "Family or State? Nation, War, and Gender in Japan 1937–45," *Critical Asian Studies* 38 (2006): 209–37.

8. Thomas R. H. Havens, *Valley of Darkness: The Japanese People and World War Two,* New York: W. W. Norton, 1978 (pp. 135–38).

9. Details in "Sensational Rumors, Seditious Graffiti and the Nightmares of the Thought Police," in Dower 1993.

10. For the story of Toshié's life and society in rural Japan over the twentieth century, see Simon Partner, *Toshie: A Story of Village Life in Twentieth-Century Japan,* Berkeley: University of California Press, 2004.

SELECTED BIBLIOGRAPHY

Atkins, E. Taylor. *Blue Nippon: Authenticating Jazz in Japan.* Durham, NC: Duke University Press, 2001.
　　Chapter 4, "Jazz for the Country's Sake: Toward a New Cultural Order in Wartime Japan," explains the attempts by the authorities to purge Japan of "the enemy's music" and the ways in which musicians and music lovers circumvented the rules.
Cook, Theodore, and Haruko Taya. *Japan at War: An Oral History.* New York: The New Press, 1992.
　　Part 3 of these interviews focuses on the home front and includes memories of childhood and civil and war work as well as media and the intelligentsia.

Daniels, Gordon. "Japanese Domestic Radio and Cinema Propaganda, 1937–1945: An Overview." In *Film and Radio Propaganda in World War II,* edited by K.R.M. Short. Knoxville: University of Tennessee Press, 1983.
   A short introduction to the system, content, and public reaction to wartime broadcast media.
Dower, John W. *Japan in War and Peace: Selected Essays.* New York: The New Press, 1993.
   One of the leading scholars of wartime Japanese society, Dower's work contains extended articles on mutual images of the Japanese and Americans, the role of cinema, the "usefulness" of the war to Japan, and, especially relevant to this chapter, "Sensational Rumors, Seditious Graffiti and the Nightmares of the Thought Police" (pp. 101–54).
Havens, Thomas R. H. *Valley of Darkness: The Japanese People and World War Two.* New York: W. W. Norton, 1978.
   The single best wide-ranging social history of wartime Japan.
Kushner, Barak. *The Thought War: Japanese Imperial Propaganda.* Honolulu: University of Hawai'i Press, 2006.
   Chapter 4 describes the roles and routines of comic performers in wartime Japan.
Marshall, Byron K. *Learning to Be Modern: Japanese Political Discourse on Education.* Boulder, CO: Westview, 1994.
   Chapter 5, "Mobilizing the Spirit of the Nation, 1931–1945," details wartime educational policies and the impact of war on such things as freedom of thought and student associations.
Miyake, Yoshiko. "Doubling Expectations: Motherhood and Women's Factory Work under State Management in Japan in the 1930s and 1940s." In *Recreating Japanese Women, 1600–1945,* edited by Gail Bernstein. Berkeley: University of California Press, 1991.
   An analysis of the Japanese state's population-increase policy.
Partner, Simon. *Toshie: A Story of Village Life in Twentieth-Century Japan.* Berkeley: University of California Press, 2004.
   Chapter 3, "The Village Goes to War," expands on the section here on rural society.
Richie, Donald. *A Hundred Years of Japanese Film: A Concise History.* Tokyo: Kodansha International, 2001.
   The author is the premier historian and critic of Japanese film writing in the English language. He summarizes cinema during the war years (pp. 96–106).
Saga, Jun'ichi. *Memories of Silk and Straw: A Self-Portrait of Small-Town Japan.* Translated by Garry O. Evans. Tokyo: Kodansha International, 1987.
   A superb collection of oral histories covering all aspects of daily life and work in the first decades of the twentieth century. Essential reading for anyone wanting to understand the realities of daily life during this period.
Wilson, Sandra. "Family or State? Nation, War, and Gender in Japan 1937–45." *Critical Asian Studies* 38 (2006): 209–37.
   A lively and engaging discussion of the ideological confusion in wartime Japan between the woman as protector of the family and as active worker for the war effort.

SIX

Daily Life in Wartime Indonesia, 1939–1949

Shigeru Satō

In the historiography of Indonesia, World War II is normally equated with the period of Japanese occupation from March 9, 1942 (following two months of fighting against the Dutch colonial army) until August 15, 1945. Before the Japanese invasion, however, the daily lives of Indonesians had already been gravely affected by warfare. When Japan attacked and occupied the southern coastal cities of China in 1937–1938, trading between China and Indonesia plummeted. When war broke out in Europe late in 1939, the Dutch authorities in Jakarta also began preparing to be attacked. The Japanese surrender in 1945, moreover, was merely the prelude to even greater violence. On August 17, 1945, Indonesia declared its independence, and as the Dutch returned to reinstate their control, a brutal war erupted which was to last until the end of 1949. Thus while this chapter focuses primarily on Indonesian society under Japanese occupation, it is necessary to place events in their historical context by going beyond the usual time frame and looking at trends from around the outbreak of World War II in Europe to the end of Indonesia's war of independence.

In understanding something as broad as a society at war, it is also necessary to consider various perspectives. Modern Indonesian history often depicts the Japanese occupation as one of its darkest periods: Before 1942, daily life for many was a struggle for survival; during the occupation, many lost that struggle. Observing Jakarta in 1944, a Dutch Eurasian woman commented that

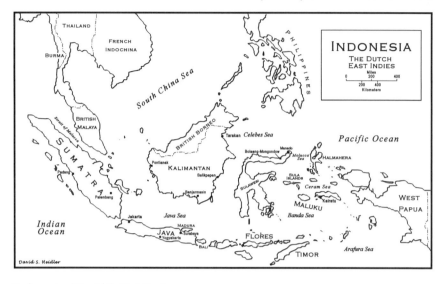

Indonesia. (David S. Heidler.)

the misery outside was a sight not to be borne. Beggars draped in burlap sacks or entirely naked with the most hideous wounds were lying by the side of the road. Their faces were like a full moon and their stomachs incredibly swollen. Downtown I saw several bodies being loaded onto a garbage truck; with his booted foot a Jap kicked many other poor wretches who, if they showed a sign of life, were allowed to remain lying there. . . . Poverty, poverty and misery everywhere! No medicine and no clothing, no food. My God, I thought, how long must this go on?[1]

Soon after Japan's surrender, one of Indonesia's greatest writers, Pramoedya Ananta Toer, wrote a novel describing central Java in mid-1945 in a similar vein:

When you go to the city you see children sprawled lifeless at the side of the road. In front of the market and the stores, down beneath the bridge, on top of garbage heaps and in the gutters there are corpses. Nothing but corpses. The place is filled with the dead—children and the old people. And you know what they do? If they are going to die, before they take their final breath, they first gather a pile of teak-wood or banana leaves that have been used to wrap food in. And they cover their bodies with these leaves and they die. It's like they know that in two hours they're going to die and that after they are dead no one is going to prepare them for burial. These are crazy times we're going through. And I don't know why it is. In all my life this is the first time I've seen anything like it. Corpses. Wherever you go, unattended corpses.[2]

Yet despite these scenes, there were others living very different lives. In sharp contrast to Burma or the Philippines, Indonesia was relatively free from warfare and bloodshed during most of the occupation period. The main Allied forces, in their counterattack, brushed past the eastern fringe of the Indonesian archipelago, pushing northward along a line connecting New Guinea, the Philippines, Okinawa, and Tokyo. In Java, where 70 percent of the 70 million Indonesians lived, there was no Allied bombardment or landing. Only Surabaya and a few other places experienced sporadic air raids from late July 1943. There was no significant underground resistance movement. The local people were generally cooperative with the occupation forces, and anti-Japanese riots were few and far apart. Among the Japanese in wartime Indonesia, the expression "Java is heaven, Burma is hell" was commonplace. The Japanese took over luxurious Dutch residences with servants for their own use, while the clubs for Japanese officers were well stocked with imported quality liquors served by young and attractive local women. A high level of goodwill between Japanese and Indonesians survived even in the later occupation years, when the local economy markedly deteriorated. The Japanese view was that the abject poverty they witnessed was the fault of centuries of Dutch colonial exploitation. When it was obvious that the war and the Japanese occupation worsened the standard of living in Indonesia, they often likened this to a challenge that the Indonesians must overcome if they were to be truly free and emerge as a New Indonesia. In these adverse conditions, many Japanese still cultivated friendship with the local people. Indeed, many Japanese and Indonesians remained in touch after the war, both as individuals and as groups, and a number of friendship associations existed decades after the war's end.

A further point to bear in mind is that historical records usually favor literate urbanites. In Indonesia at this time the vast majority resided in the countryside and were illiterate; their voices are scarcely heard in the histories. Yet there are gaps even for the literate minority. For instance, most Dutch citizens in prewar Indonesia were actually Eurasians born in Indonesia. Numbering some 150,000, Eurasian civilians were forced by the Japanese to choose between identifying themselves as Asian and joining the liberation movement or as European and being placed in internment camps. Naturally, most of them chose freedom, but after the war, they kept silent about their experiences, unlike the many internees who published memoirs.

These disparities are compounded with the varieties of life in the different regions of Indonesia. Day-to-day lives in crowded, squalid streets in Jakarta bore few similarities to those in the coconut-growing islands of Maluku, the plantation belt of east Sumatra, or farming villages in Java. In the inland of Kalimantan or highland of West Papua, there were many communities who remained completely unaware of the war until decades later, when outsiders, such as European missionaries, visited and talked about it.

It was not only in remote areas where people's exposure to the war was limited. In the most heavily populated island of Java the Japanese mobilized millions of people as forced laborers, known as *rōmusha* in Japanese. The well-established image of *rōmusha* is suffering and death due to exceedingly harsh work conditions and maltreatment. Fifty years after the event, however, an Indonesian historian interviewed 300 former *rōmusha* from the principality of Yogyakarta in central Java.[3] His interviews revealed that on some work sites, Japanese seldom appeared. Others have stated that they never saw a single Japanese during the entire occupation.

A variety of experiences can be observed within each small community as well. Large-scale oral history projects have been conducted in Indonesia, the Netherlands, and Japan. These projects have interviewed mainly articulate people who assumed important positions during the war or thereafter. Although these interviewees often state that they saw wartime poverty, they admit, if asked, that they themselves never experienced any comparable hardships. Some even managed to accumulate considerable personal wealth in this dark era.

The Japanese occupation had a profound impact on Indonesia in a whole range of fields, including politics, local administration, industry, social organization, military, education, language, ideology, arts, religion, and entertainment. The changes in these fields looked so fundamental and irreversible that among historians, the so-called transformation thesis emerged soon after the war; this swayed the historiography of modern Indonesia for

Indonesian *rōmusha* labor on Japanese work projects. (*Djawa Baroe*, no. 23, 1 December 1943.)

decades. The most notable transformation was in the field of politics, where the Dutch colony metamorphosed into the Republic of Indonesia, and the former political prisoners Sukarno and Hatta transformed themselves into president and vice president of the newborn republic. Being mesmerized with these transformations, historians have tended to overlook the fundamental continuity behind the revolutionary changes. Political scenes changed kaleidoscopically, but socioeconomic realities were slower to change. Thus while historians have scrutinized the political changes, they have tended to ignore the lives of ordinary people. The aim of this chapter is to go some way toward rectifying this by examining the impact of the war on the socioeconomic and cultural aspects of everyday life.

BEGGARS, PROSTITUTES, AND LABORERS

Marginalized groups like beggars, prostitutes, and the homeless had existed in Indonesia well before the war. They still exist today in large numbers, and some of them die without being cared for. The question to be asked is why and how those marginalized people increased during the war.

Unemployment and underemployment increased twice within the decade or so before Japan's invasion. The first instance was during the world depression in the 1930s, when export industries were devastated and workers were dismissed in large numbers. The second was in response to the outbreak of the European war, when the Dutch colonial government immediately sought to establish self-sufficiency in food and, as a result, restricted food imports. For a few months from September 1939, Indonesia's export industries experienced a boom, owing to increased international demand and stockpiling by the government and the military. This boom came to an end, however, when the Germans occupied the Netherlands on May 10, 1940. Not only did this undermine the Dutch authorities in Jakarta, it also meant the final loss of European markets, which remained crucial for Indonesian exporters.

These changes in international trading affected most Indonesians because their economy had become an integral part of the global economy. Many Indonesians worked for European big business in the colony, such as plantations and mining companies, which recruited more workers during the short-lived boom, but when the volume of world trade contracted, they shed workers en masse. Many also lived by growing crops for export, such as rubber, coconut (the long coastlines of the archipelago were rimmed with coconut trees), coffee, and sugar, or collecting for export forest products such as rattan, damar, and bird nest, a delicacy in Chinese cooking. For the indigenous communities, copra (dried kernel of the coconut used for a wide range of purposes, such as extracting oil or making soap) was the most important export item: Its annual production was over one million tons, about half of which was sold to Europe. By mid-1940, however, copra exports had dropped to about a quarter of the prewar level. Signs of economic distress became obvious and widespread. Medical investigations in Java showed a rapid increase in cases of malnutrition, and the death rate started rising in certain areas, even surpassing the birthrate, which declined. Thus well before 1942, beggars, prostitutes, and homeless people were pouring into the towns of Indonesia.

When the Japanese occupied Indonesia in early 1942, the number of registered job seekers increased rapidly in the cities. Many of these were former personnel of the colonial army and the navy, plus the staff of companies whose business came to a standstill as the world went to war rather than to trade. One company in Surabaya called Marine, for instance, originally had 25,000 employees, but the number dropped to 3,000 soon after the Japanese invasion. Municipal governments faced a hopeless task in trying to help the unemployed; the most they could do

Emergency provision of food, east Java, 1942. (*Wereldniews en Sport en Beeld*, 28 February 1942.)

was provide registered job seekers with 250 grams of rice and five cents per person per day.

Registered job seekers in the cities were the privileged ones. In the countryside, there was no such registration system nor comparable welfare services. Many villagers also lost their livelihood around this time: The collapse of tea exports alone led to nearly 200,000 lost jobs in west Java. Those unable to make a living in the countryside left their villages and walked to the cities. The population of Jakarta increased from about 600,000 to 850,000 during the Japanese occupation. Some of those who migrated to the cities found lucrative occupations, such as black marketeering, but many others became homeless and starved. The records of the Central Hospital of Semarang show an exponential increase in the number of starvation patients admitted over several months from late 1943.[4] Hospitals and other facilities soon became overcrowded with terminally malnourished people who died soon after being admitted.

For those who walked out of their villages, the options for survival were begging, scavenging, prostitution, and, if luck was with them, occasional casual employment. The number of people engaged in these activities increased heavily after 1940 in areas like east Java, where plantation products, such as sugar, coffee, and tobacco, lost their European customers. Early in the Japanese occupation, Muslim intellectuals in Java expressed their concern that poverty and misery were leading to moral depravity and yet further increases in sexual diseases. In July 1943, an Indonesian doctor testified that of those people who had married once, 5 percent had syphilis; of those who had married four times, the rate was 25 percent. When the Japanese carried out medical checkups of urban prostitutes throughout Java early in 1943 to select "clean" women for their military brothels, they found that between 60 and 80 percent, depending on their region, had venereal diseases, including syphilis. Military commanders knew that in modern international warfare, venereal diseases demoralize and sometimes kill more soldiers than enemy weapons. The Japanese therefore recruited relatively inexperienced young women for their brothels, employing deceit and coercion, although there were exceedingly large numbers of women already in the sex industry. For the so-called comfort stations of the officer class, Japanese recruited mostly Eurasian women. Of the Eurasians who stayed free, about 2,000 women became Japanese mistresses, according to one estimate. These people had few other means of survival.

In the first half of the occupation period, there was unprecedented unemployment in the densely populated island of Java. From late 1943, the Japanese launched a campaign for a "total mobilization" of manpower. This not only eliminated the problem of unemployment, but actually created labor shortages throughout Java. Although the infamous forced mobilization of workers is usually attributed to Japan's need to construct military facilities, the existing evidence suggests that about 90 percent of this forced labor was used in civil projects. That was because the serious disruption of international and interisland trading, particularly from around mid-1943, forced the occupation authorities to try and create economic self-sufficiency in each of the relatively small territorial units. Establishing self-sufficiency in a heavily populated island like Java was impossible, but the war made the occupation authorities confront many impossible tasks.

A whole range of import substitutes had to be locally produced, often by using intensive labor. This required a thorough economic restructuring and labor relocation. This, in turn, led, at the outset, to a decline in production efficiency, with ordinary people working harder but obtaining fewer resources. The Japanese started numerous projects with strict completion dates and drove the mobilized Indonesians extremely hard. Irrigation extension projects, for instance, had to be completed before the onset of the rainy season. When the target completion date approached, the supervisors often made the draftees work around the clock by employing a three-shift system.

The Japanese newspaper published in Java, *Jawashinbun*, reported on February 6, 1945, that the average working life of a forced Javanese laborer was just two months before physical exhaustion took over. The assigned period of work for those who were sent to west Java from central and east Java, however, was usually three months. By the time they completed their assigned jobs, many were utterly exhausted through hard work, undernourishment, and exposure to unhygienic conditions. Indeed, many construction works, such as draining swamps and clearing forests, were in areas infested with malarial mosquitoes. Men who lived in malaria-free villages had little immunity to the disease. Many of them soon contracted malaria and other diseases, such as dysentery and yaws; upon being sent back to their villages, they merely spread these diseases into new territories.

Many of the forced laborers escaped from work sites, often after contracting disease. They attempted to return home, but many perished on their way, from hunger, exhaustion, and illness. Thus the sight of people dying on the roadside became more common from late 1943, not only in the cities, but also along country roads and in other areas.

Those who completed their periods of work were sent back by train. This also created problems. The distance from the railway station to the village was sometimes a few days' walk. Many workers found themselves too weak to cover the distance on foot. At the time of Japan's surrender the number of such wandering former *rōmusha* suddenly increased because most people left the project sites almost simultaneously and attempted to return home on their own accord. Outside Java, Sumatra was the largest recipient of Javanese *rōmusha*. Some 120,000 Javanese workers were sent there during the occupation. Soon after the Japanese surrender, the Dutch reestablished their colonial authority in Sumatra. Their inspectors reported that tens of thousands of dislocated, disoriented, and undernourished Javanese were roaming around in many parts of the island.

The Japanese reworking of Indonesia's economy led to such an insatiable demand for labor that on February 6, 1945, *Jawashinbun* reported that even the urban homeless were to be mobilized as laborers. The police in the city of Jakarta began to hunt for the homeless at 3:00 A.M. on February 5 and by dawn had rounded up 931 people, consisting of 792 men and 139 women. Physical checkups revealed that 387 men (49 percent) and 90 women (65 percent) were unfit for work due to malnourishment and illness. Those who were fit would be put to work immediately, and those who were unfit would be provided with food and medicine until they were able. The newspaper remains silent about the children who accompanied the homeless adults.

CHILDREN AND SCHOOLING

A relatively small number of children received schooling in prewar Indonesia. In Java, in 1940, about 20 percent of children from 6 to 10 years of age were enrolled in primary schools offering three- or five-year courses. The enrollment rate in the first year was generally higher as many left before completing the first three years. In Bali the enrollment rate was just 12 percent, but in most other areas it was even lower. In certain areas, schools turned away some applicants due to shortages of facilities and teachers. Some areas had no school at all.

Literacy among the local population was low. Reading and writing were not important in most people's daily lives, so many of those who received even the basic skills soon lost their literacy after leaving school. Some Islamic teachers, moreover, discouraged people from learning the Roman alphabet. That was because some Christian missionaries, under the pretext of promoting literacy, attempted to spread Christianity in the predominantly Muslim communities. Some Muslim teachers feared that the spread of Western-style education would undermine the foundation of their faith.

At their first encounter with Indonesians the Japanese were apparently not so surprised at the low literacy rate among adult Indonesians, but they were surprised at the low level of numeracy. Few Indonesians knew their own age, for instance. This could be attributed to the custom of being unconcerned about precise ages, but other instances showed that they were indeed weak with numbers. For example, many found it difficult to work out the total cost of six items if each item cost 20 cents. A Japanese military officer who trained local youths to create indigenous defense forces also noticed this. He ordered the trainees to make sure at the end of each military drill that no weapons were missing. The youths apparently had difficulty in counting, so everyone lined up, each holding one rifle, and if everyone had one, they concluded that all the rifles were there.

The Japanese considered education to be the foundation of their "Greater East Asia." They therefore aimed at doubling the school enrollment in

Indonesia, dispatched teachers from Japan, recruited local people with teaching qualifications, and reformed the education system and the curricula. To overcome the shortage of school buildings, they introduced a two-session system (one group studying from 8:30 A.M. until around 1:30 P.M., and the second group from 1:30 P.M. until 6:30 P.M.). They also abolished schooling fees. During the Dutch era, the children of the most impoverished households with a monthly income of 2.5 guilders or less were exempted from paying fees, but the other children had to pay about one percent of the household income; this was a considerable burden for parents.

The outcome of these reforms was, initially at least, remarkable. In Bali the number of pupils in public primary schools increased from 23,859 before the Japanese invasion to 50,987 in April 1944 (the enrollment rate rising from 12 to 25 percent). The increase of enrollment in grade one was particularly large because many older children, who had never been to school, now enrolled in that grade. The number of high school students overall remained very small, but the relative increase, from 170 to 705 in the same period, was enormous.

A Japanese educator, Suzuki Masahei, worked as the school superintendent in Bali during the occupation and wrote reports regularly to his colleagues in Japan. One day, he proctored an oral examination for the applicants for a newly established sailor training school. He lamented that most applicants, who had completed at least three years of primary education, knew little about Asia or the significance of what Japan termed the Greater East Asia War. In response to the question of why the Japanese had come to Indonesia, most applicants could only guess. Instead of the required answer—to liberate Asia from Western colonialism—one applicant suggested, *Cari tanah!* (looking for land); another offered, *Cari makanan!* (looking for food). Yet another added that the Japanese came to Indonesia to practice their Malay (Indonesian) language with the local people.[5]

In terms of public information and understanding of the war, radio had only a limited reach. Ownership of radio receivers in Indonesia was confined to a small number of wealthy urban dwellers, that is, the Dutch, Chinese, Arabs, and upper-class Indonesians. Battery-operated transistor radios became available only after the war, so before 1945, people needed an electricity supply to listen to the radio. However, at that time, there was no electricity in most of Indonesia's countryside. The mass of ordinary civilians were therefore never exposed directly to Japanese radio broadcasting.

What was more influential than Japanese propaganda in reconciling Indonesians to the occupation was the so-called Joyoboyo prophecy. This prophecy, attributed to King Joyoboyo of the Hindu kingdom of Kediri in east Java, was originally vague but was gradually modified before the Japanese invasion to suit the contemporary situation. In this form it suggested that soon, yellow monkeys would arrive from the north and drive away the white rulers. These monkeys would stay only for the time it took for the maize to mature (three and half months). Thereafter they would be replaced by the indigenous *Ratu Adil* (Righteous King).

Seeing the Dutch Army retreat prior to the Japanese landing, Indonesians felt that Joyoboyo's prophecy was being materialized. This led some to hinder the Dutch retreat by cutting down large roadside trees and leaving them lying across the main roads. When the Japanese arrived, what the Indonesians witnessed were scruffy bunches of bandy-legged boys trudging along, covered in dust, sweat, and flies, many wearing spectacles with round frames on their unshaven faces. Yet many Indonesians enthusiastically welcomed these smelly troops and offered them food and drink. Some even removed roadblocks made by the Dutch or the Indonesians to help the Japanese advance.

Soon after their arrival, the occupiers opened Japanese language schools for the local people at many places. The first was established in Menado in northern Sulawesi on March 5, 1942, four days before the Dutch surrender. The language schools were usually filled on the first day of registration, and students' progress was remarkably fast. The main reason was that local people knew that mastery of the new ruler's language was a key to social success. The Japanese also offered monetary incentives in the form of additional monthly allowances for those who passed the language tests: 1 guilder for grade one, rising to 15 guilders for grade five. These were substantial amounts at that time.

The Japanese criticized the education system in the Dutch era for aiming merely to impart technical skills such as basic literacy and numeracy, while suppressing national awakening and the sense of self-reliance. It also neglected moral and physical education; most village schools had no sports ground. Instead of Malay, which Indonesian nationalists chose as their national language, indigenous primary schools used vernacular languages. This prevented children from developing any sense of belonging to the wider community. In the villages, there were no high schools. Secondary and tertiary education was conducted in the cities using Dutch as the medium of education, but Dutch was not taught at the village primary schools. The vast majority of Indonesians were therefore barred from postprimary education. Only a small number of privileged Indonesian children were admitted to the Dutch primary schools that led to higher levels of schooling. Ability to speak Dutch was the key to prominence and social success, but the Dutch provided the opportunities to learn their language only to a privileged few.

In sharp contrast to the Dutch the Japanese enthusiastically taught their language. Making Japanese the common language of Greater East Asia was Japanese official policy. As of December 1943, in Java alone, there were 2,211 Japanese language schools with 122,198 students. They also made the Japanese language a compulsory subject at all levels of formal education and quickly produced Japanese language textbooks for Indonesian pupils. In August 1943, they established a teachers' college in Jakarta and obliged the future teachers in the humanities stream to take 13 hours per week of Japanese language and those in the science stream to take 12 hours per week. In addition, they set aside two hours per week for Japanese culture. At the Medical College in Jakarta, too, Japanese was compulsory and combined with lectures on *Dai Nippon* (Great Japan); the medical students had to spend more hours learning Japanese and about Japan than any other subject.

Apart from the schools recognized by the Department of Education, there were numerous Muslim schools, large and small, throughout Indonesia. Some large ones were equipped with their own buildings and dormitories. Some individuals also ran small schools using their own homes or mosques to teach Islamic texts to local children. The Japanese gave increased financial support to some of these schools to secure Muslim teachers' cooperation. They also distributed Japanese language textbooks to them so that pupils could teach themselves.

The Japanese also confiscated Dutch-owned radios and redistributed them to central points, such as 1,000 schools and about 1,500 public places; a radio stuck on top of a little tower in a public place came to be called a "singing tower." There is a story that some old ladies in one city were so astonished to hear human voices and music come out of a little box on top of the tower that they prostrated themselves in front of it and worshipped it as the voice of God. The state-controlled radio carried news in simple Japanese for the local people to practice their listening comprehension. For reading practice they also published a newspaper, *Kana Jawashinbun,* and some other publications that were written just in the simpler Japanese script known as kana.

Turning Japanese into the common language or the medium of education within a short period was impossible. The occupation authorities recognized this, and even though children's knowledge of Malay was limited at best and primary school was normally taught in the vernacular, they also encouraged the use of Malay for later years in primary schooling. In secondary and tertiary education, Malay replaced Dutch, making postprimary education far more accessible to the local population. That is one of the reasons why enrollment in high school in Bali quadrupled during the occupation.

The Japanese also made moral and physical education compulsory. They introduced many group activities, such as sports carnivals, excursions, cultural exhibitions, regular morning exercises, marching in columns, singing in chorus, and dancing together. These activities, designed to foster esprit de corps among the children, were very popular. Children and parents alike also were keenly interested in the various styles of fitness exercises conducted to music—these included radio exercises, navy exercises, and girls' exercises—and they often asked for more of

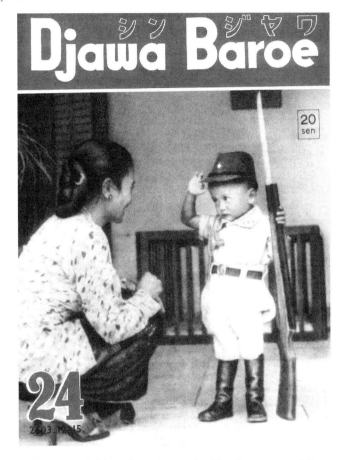

Indonesian children learning to be like Japanese soldiers.
(*Djawa Baroe*, no. 24, 15 December 1943.)

these. Many boys also loved to play soldiers. It became trendy among them to crop their hair short like Japanese soldiers and wear hats made of palm leaves. Some would not remove the hats, even in the classroom. When asked why, they answered that with hats on, they could salute like soldiers.

On September 7, 1944, the Japanese prime minister, Koiso Kuniaki, made a parliamentary speech promising independence for the East Indies in the near future. The Japanese in Indonesia used this news to whip up Indonesian nationalism. The exultant atmosphere of the time is well captured in Benedict Anderson's classic study, *Java in a Time of Revolution* (1972). Many of the Indonesians who were high school students, for instance, would testify even now that this was the most exciting time in their lives and that some of the Japanese teachers who encouraged them to adopt can-do attitudes were the most admirable people they ever met.

As part of this effort, the Japanese created the "Oath of the Students." It was made compulsory every morning at school to read this in the original Japanese before classes started. In Java, the text was as follows:

> *Warera wa Shin Jawa no gakuto nari.*
> *Warera wa Dai Nippon no shidō no moto,*
> *Daitōa kensetsu no tameni manabi,*
> *Daitōa kensetsu no tameni shinshin o tanrenshi,*
> *Daitōa kensetsu no tameni yū no jinzai tarankoto o chikau.*

> We are students of New Java.
> We swear that, under the guidance of Great Japan,
> We shall study for the construction of Greater East Asia,
> Train for the construction of Greater East Asia,
> And become useful resources for the construction of Greater East Asia.

In Bali and other areas also under the Japanese Navy's rule the students were required to recite similar oaths.

As the war continued and the economy deteriorated, the Japanese authorities, in Japan as well as in the occupied areas, began to mobilize students. In Japan, many female students were sent to ammunition factories, and male university students were sent to the battlefields. In Indonesia, most pupils were too young to be so directly involved in the war. Instead, they were mobilized for agriculture and handicraft production, most of which was only marginally related to the actual warfare. In fact, some Indonesian intellectuals who acted as advisors for the Japanese occupation suggested that practical knowledge in the fields of agriculture and handicrafts was more relevant and more important for village children. The Japanese educators did not necessarily agree in principle, but the demands of war forced them increasingly to rely on the pupils' work potential.

In wartime Japan the authorities ordered all schools to convert their playgrounds into vegetable fields and construct air-raid shelters. Indonesian schools had no playgrounds, but they mobilized pupils for similar purposes, such as sowing unused plots of land with castor oil plants (from which the lubricant for airplane engines was extracted), working in cotton fields (which the Japanese expanded greatly throughout southeast Asia), and replanting trees on mountain slopes after timber was harvested for various war-related projects. High school girls were mobilized for spinning, weaving, and making gloves and socks for the soldiers. They also mobilized pupils for their notorious "forced delivery of rice," explained later.

The deteriorating wartime economy began to take a toll on schooling. In Java the enrollment in the first three years of primary school in 1941 was 1,286,082; this rose to 1,842,804 in 1943 but dropped to 1,697,358 in 1944. The main reason, according to contemporary investigators, was actually a lack of clothes to wear to school. Imports of clothes (which used to come mostly from Japan) stopped before the outbreak of the Pacific war, when the Allied countries placed an economic blockade on Japan. Even before the occupation, therefore, there were serious shortages of clothing, and before long, many people's clothes were reduced to tatters. By about 1944, many children had no decent clothes for school. In Bali the children kept turning up to school naked. In Java, enrollment dropped, and absentee-ism among those who were enrolled rapidly increased. According to a survey in 1944, the average absenteeism rate ranged from 20 percent to 53 percent, depending on the school. Lack of food and lack of stamina were other reasons for this decline in schooling.

THE BASICS OF LIFE: SHORTAGES OF FOOD AND CLOTHING

Existing histories usually explain the severe food shortages in wartime Indonesia in terms of Japanese exploitation. This is not entirely accurate. It is true that the Japanese exploited food in the lands they invaded. At the end of the war, six million Japanese were outside of Japan proper, living off local food. Most of them, however, were in China. In the areas called the "Southern Regions," which included all of southeast Asia, the south-western Pacific islands, and the Andaman-Nicobar islands, the Japanese population was no more than 750,000. In Java it fluctuated around 50,000, which was 0.1 percent of the local population. Most of the Japanese com-batants who invaded Java soon shifted to the eastern battlefront. This left no more than 15,000 troops in Java, and thus the majority of the 50,000 Japanese in Java were civilians.

The average Japanese consumed about three times the amount of food of the average Indonesian. Nonetheless, Japanese consumption cannot explain the serious food shortages created by the occupation. The Japanese shifted rice from southeast Asia to Japan, but not from Indonesia. That was because southeast Asia had three major rice surplus areas in Burma, Thailand, and French Indochina.

The Japanese in Java consisted of a wide range of people, such as government officials, railway engineers, ship builders, language teachers, doctors, nurses, and staff of the companies assigned to administer eco-nomic projects; artists, such as writers, musicians, painters, cartoonists, and propaganda filmmakers; and academics who carried out research in various fields.

Three researchers who were specialists in rural sociology and agricul-tural economy conducted detailed studies into socioeconomic realities in three selected rice-growing villages in west, central, and east Java. Their findings provide a social context for examining the food issue. On the basis of their door-to-door surveys with regard to landholdings, incomes, expenditures, and so on, they classified households according to the size of the land held by each household. From this they obtained a pyramidal structure. The broad base consisted of landless peasant households, then households with minute patches of farmland. As the size of landholding increased, the number of households decreased, and the pyramid was completed with the small triangular pinnacle consisting of large land-holders.

The largest landholders in each village included the village chief and his staff. That was because the best tracts of land in the villages were put aside for the village officials instead of salaries. The landless peasants, who constituted the majority in many villages in Java, were employed by landholding villagers as agricultural laborers. Some were engaged in a variety of cottage industries or petty trading, full-time or part-time. Each village included a few Chinese shops, whose incomes were incomparably larger than the local peasant households.

One striking feature of rice-growing villages in Java was that the vast majority of the villagers were rice purchasers. Landless peasants, ped-dlers, and artisans were cash earners and bought rice from the local market. Landed farmers, too, sold most of the harvested stalk paddy to earn cash. Most villagers bought cleaned rice from market according to their daily needs. Only a small number of large landholders put aside a sufficient portion of their harvested rice for their own consumption. This meant that unlike in rice-growing villages in Japan and some other countries, rice was primarily a commercial crop, even when consumed by Javanese villagers.

The best part of the incomes of landless peasants and smallholders, often over 90 percent after taxes, was spent on food for family consumption. Employment opportunities for landless peasants were meager, and poor households that could not afford sufficient amounts of rice had to rely on cheaper and less nutritious food like cassava. In fact, the vast majority of villagers in Java were undernourished, even after spending almost all of their disposable income on food.

Any disruption of the rice market would jeopardize the survival of rural Indonesians, who led a precarious existence. Indonesia experienced two major disturbances in the two decades before the outbreak of the European war. The first came in the wake of World War I. The combina-tion of economic blockade, bad weather, and the influenza pandemic that killed 50 million people worldwide quadrupled the market price of rice. The second major disturbance occurred during the world depression. When world trade contracted, the price of rice from Thailand, Burma, and French Indochina also dropped. The resulting influx of cheap rice undermined the economic foundation of the rice farming communities in Indonesia. The Dutch colonial authorities therefore began to take a series of protectionist measures from 1933 and restricted imports of rice, while also making efforts to increase food production within the colony.

When news of the German invasion of Poland in 1939 reached Jakarta, the Dutch moved swiftly to strengthen Indonesia's ability to feed itself;

they further restricted rice imports, enacted the so-called forced cultivation ordinance, and launched a campaign to increase food production in the Outer Islands (that is, Indonesian islands other than Java). This campaign involved extending irrigation canals, converting plantation land into food crop fields, propagating high-yield varieties of rice, and introducing more labor-intensive cultivation methods. To replace imported rice, Indonesia had to increase its production by 260,000 tons annually.

This meant changes to the pattern of rice distribution in Indonesia. Until the global depression, urban citizens and those in areas with large export industries, such as plantations and mining sites, consumed imported rice, while people in rice-growing villages consumed locally produced rice. With imports restricted, Indonesia's rice started to flow from the countryside to the cities and plantation and mining areas. This stimulated the proliferation of motorized rice mills. Ethnic Chinese, who had virtually monopolized the rice-importing business, now moved into the rice-milling industry and quickly established a virtual monopoly. In the 1930s, Java's milling capacity tripled, and rice milling became Indonesia's fourth largest industry in 1939 in terms of total wages paid to workers.[6]

The colonial government promoted the building of rice mills after late 1939 and obliged all millers to sell processed rice to new rice distribution centers. This gravely disturbed social relations in farming communities. Previously, rice was manually harvested, dried, sold, and pounded by villagers. Harvesting and pounding were important sources of income, particularly for women of landless households. With the growth of rice mills, brokers funded by the mill owners began appearing in the villages and bought crops from large farmers while rice was still in the ground. They later brought in their own gangs of harvesters. This deprived many local women of income. The purchase of rice by outsiders also caused a price rise. Large farmers profited, but the vast majority of rural people suffered from the combined effect of decreased employment, decreased availability of rice, and increased prices. When the Japanese Army invaded, this popular anger exploded, and Indonesians in many places destroyed rice mills and ransacked Chinese shops.

The Japanese invaded Indonesia just before the main rice-harvesting season. Destruction of mills and shops by local people, and the scorched-earth tactics of the Dutch, including the demolition of transport infrastructure, all combined to block rice distribution, resulting in shortages and high prices in the cities, plus stagnation of harvested rice and a drop in its price in the villages. The Japanese occupiers spent their first year taking emergency measures, buying rice in the countryside with a special budget and releasing it in the cities. From April 1943, they largely reinstated the system created by the Dutch.

When the main harvesting season of 1943 was over, the amount delivered to the government was still substantially below its target. One explanation for this was that farmers avoided delivering rice to the mills, and the mills avoided delivering rice to the government. This was because the recovering market price was higher than the official purchase price set at the pre-invasion level. In late 1943, and again from April 1944, the Japanese tried to force large farmers to deliver their produce to the mills. This sparked a series of peasant riots in one of the major rice-producing regencies in Java, Indramayu. The riots lasted for months and were ended only by bloody suppression in July. When they were over, an Indonesian advisor to the government inspected the area and reported the following:

Last year, when the government bought paddy in a similar manner, many children and adults starved to death because there was little rice left in the villages. The villagers had to feed their children with things like banana leaves and leaves of other trees that are unsuitable as food for animals, let alone for people. This was simply to fill their stomachs. Very often the parents had to go without food for two or three days. They were unable to seek employment because, afflicted by under-nourishment, they had no energy to work. The upshot was that numbers of people, particularly children, died.

At the gathering in Kapelongan, the people therefore decided to oppose the government collection of paddy. If they were shot dead by the police, their fate would still be better than if they died of hunger, in which the suffering grows increasingly unbearable as the days pass. Moreover, if they were shot dead, they would not have to witness the sufferings of their children or their parents as they die of starvation. Because neither the local bureaucrats, nor government, nor anyone else heeded their requests, the villagers' anger reached its climax and exploded, and they were overcome with fury.[7]

The Japanese allocated production quotas to each residency (the largest administrative subdivision within Java), and each residency subdivided the quota and sent it down to the villages through bureaucratic channels. Village officials, who occupied the best rice fields, chose not to sell their own produce to the mills but, instead, allocated the quotas to the smaller farmers. Thus began the infamous forced delivery of rice. Small farmers, who had never sold their paddy to the mills, were now compelled to carry their produce to the mills or to the designated collection centers.

In their campaign to deliver rice to the government, the Japanese mobilized a wide range of new social organizations, such as youth corps, vigilance corps, women's associations, and even schoolchildren. To make the campaign merry and festive, they added musical instruments, such as gamelan gongs, and gave the people flags to wave. What may have been a typical scene was observed by a Japanese in Bali on September 2, 1944. The excerpt is lengthy, but it is highly evocative and says a great deal about the campaign:

The number of schools mobilised today was nine, with 1,693 pupils and twenty teachers, which was almost all of them. Over some five kilometres to the rice purchase centre in front of the district office of Punuguru, pupils walked from all directions, boys carrying bunches of paddy on their shoulders and girls on their heads, marching to the military songs, forming two regular columns. The labor service corps that filled the roads with endless lines of people would have been an ideal scene for filming.

The amount each pupil carried ranged from five to thirty kilograms, and the total was reportedly seventeen tonnes. This itself is not a small amount but what mattered more was the impact this selfless service had on society. The district authorities said that rice delivery in general had improved since the mobilisation of school children a while ago. They discussed the political significance of this campaign, and observers from other districts and regencies also appeared profoundly interested in it.

There were many unforgettable scenes such as small children of seven or eight, either on their own or with another pupil, carrying paddy with their rather unsteady steps, or each service corps, after laying the paddy at the purchase centre, acting in an orderly manner, really using the training they got in the Shonendan [Junior Youth Corps]. The closing ceremony, with speeches expressing gratitude and encouragement, was particularly impressive.

It began with distribution of sweets to each pupil by Mitsui Industries, the Japanese company in charge of rice purchasing, followed by speeches from the local chiefs and the schools' representatives, and it concluded with the song "Umi Yukaba" [Over the Seas]. This was one of the most profoundly touching scenes that I have witnessed since I came to the Southern Regions.[8]

Campaign to increase rice deliveries, 1944. (*Djawa Baroe*, no. 22, 15 November 1944.)

In fact, despite this scene and the increasing pressure from above, the actual delivery of rice to the government constantly decreased. To improve matters, village officials often sent men to search farmers' houses and barns; if they found concealed rice, they confiscated it in the name of the occupying government. There was also a ban on shifting foodstuffs from one region to another. To impose this, local authorities employed social organizations such as the economic police and the Vigilance Corps (Keibōdan), created throughout Java and elsewhere by the Japanese. These local groups, often consisting of youths with questionable reputations, were given the role of cracking down on food smuggling. They often waited near the border of a village or a district like a gang of bandits in olden days, and when they spotted anyone carrying foodstuffs over the administrative boundaries, they seized him. The food confiscated by these vigilantes sometimes went beyond the officially banned items and included such things as onions and other vegetables.

Despite this upsurge in local policing, clandestine economic operations continued. Adding to the gravity of the declining food supply was a 40 percent fall in the actual production of food in Java. Behind this was a drought in 1944, excessive mobilization of labor from farming communities to other projects, also poor maintenance of infrastructure, such as irrigation canals, and, crucially, the low official price of rice, which acted only as a disincentive to farmers.

Before the war, Indonesia had relied partially on food imports, but its clothing came almost entirely from Europe until World War I and, thereafter, mainly from Japan. During the Great Depression of the 1930s, the Dutch authorities began to take protectionist measures and promoted construction of weaving mills in Java. Indonesia's weaving capacity rose exponentially in the decade preceding the Japanese invasion, but the industry still relied on yarn imported from Japan, and by the end of Dutch rule, the production of textiles in Indonesia remained less than 10 percent of local demand. In late colonial Indonesia, therefore, clothing materials (yarn, cloth, garments) constituted the largest group of imported items.

Japan was then the world's largest textile exporter, and textiles constituted more than half the total value of all of its exports. The raw materials, however, came mostly from outside Greater East Asia; cotton was bought from the United States and British India, and wool came from Australia.

To reduce this dependence, the Japanese tried to expand cotton production within Greater East Asia. Soon after occupying southeast Asia, they implemented a five-year cotton cultivation plan. This aimed at planting cotton in over 1.3 million hectares of land, with 180,000 hectares in Java, 140,000 hectares in Sumatra, and 339,600 hectares in the rest of Indonesia. Cotton, castor oil plant, and other nonedible stuffs were to compete with food crops within the limited farmland. To produce these supplies without damaging food output, the Japanese relied on labor mobilization. Thus as well as introducing a high-yielding variety of rice, they began campaigns for more labor-intensive cultivation methods and constructed irrigation and drainage canals across Indonesia (at 62 places in Java and Madura alone). While the campaign for total mobilization of labor is usually interpreted by historians in terms of Japan's need for military facilities, in Java, nearly 90 percent of the drafted laborers were used in this way to increase agricultural production and in other civilian projects.

A major error on the part of the Japanese, and one with serious consequences for ordinary Indonesians, was the determination to mobilize what appeared to be the nonessential workforce, such as landless peasants. This overlooked the fact that this apparently superfluous workforce did much of the agricultural labor for landed farmers in the busy seasons. Their removal made farming difficult or impossible in many villages. Moreover, the occupation authorities planned to shift 85,000 oxen from east Java to central and west Java in order to improve transport of harvested rice from village to mill. This would only deprive farmers of draft animals needed for plowing. Already suffering from the drought, neglect of infrastructure, and low prices, these added burdens meant that in the second half of the occupation period, many fields were left uncultivated, and chances for work in the village disappeared.

In the first half of the occupation period, when local people desperately needed jobs, many volunteered to work for the Japanese. They were attracted by the wages, particularly when they saw former *rōmusha* return loaded with cash. From late 1943, however, few were willing to volunteer for the increasingly harsh labor. Instead, the Japanese implemented a quota system for each village, just as with the delivery of rice. In this the village official selected the draftees and sometimes sent them away without even telling them their destination or how long they were to work.

In these later years the Japanese overworked the labor force and provided only a starvation diet. Where laborers were billeted in a local community, they had to buy food from their wages. When the work site was in a remote area, they were put in temporary barracks and given raw foodstuffs, which they cooked for themselves. As the amount of rice delivered by farmers to the government declined, so workers were left with lesser rations. There were also reports that foodstuffs sent by rail to work sites disappeared along the way. On the work site, foremen misappropriated the food meant for the workers. Even trying to buy food from local merchants became more difficult as wages quickly depreciated and the availability of daily essentials dwindled.

The level of bitterness and frustration with the Japanese occupiers extended to all areas of food and drink. When the author of this chapter was a student, an Indonesian professor, a young man during the occupation, recalled in his lecture that the Japanese were cruel because they provided the people with enough tea but no sugar. This meant the tea was undrinkable (unlike the Japanese or Chinese, the Indonesian people put heaps of sugar in their tea). Indonesia had many plantations of tea and sugar. During the occupation, it also had large stocks of tea and sugar that could not find external markets. While the Japanese claimed that they had released more sugar domestically, this was not the feeling among ordinary people, and so each time they rested for a drink of tea, it was, in fact, their anger that was refreshed.

The interrelationship in wartime life between food, clothing, and labor is clearly illustrated in a report on the Sula islands. Before the war, these islands exported copra and imported rice and clothes. This pattern of exchange stopped as Japan invaded. Shortages of clothes soon became serious. If a stranger came to visit a family and that family had only one sarong left, the children and younger women would hide and give the sarong to their mother, who would show herself. This was, of course, no laughing matter because women would have to go out if they were to obtain food. The Japanese, however, took away 1,500 men from Sanana Island to Kairatu as *rōmusha*. The resulting manpower shortage locally led to a 10 percent reduction in cultivated land in 1944. The remaining women worked the fields, but they could not till the land and mend the fences at the same time. The fences suffered from disrepair, and wild pigs ruined the crops. Food prices consequently increased nearly fourfold by mid-1944. Meanwhile, the price of an old gunnysack (from which local people made clothes to cover their nakedness) rose 12-fold.[9] If the pillars of daily life are food and clothes, then the women of the Sula islands increasingly were having those pillars removed from them by the war. Indeed, they could not live without both.

In north Sulawesi after the Japanese surrender, some Chinese traders began to shift rice from Bolaang-Mongondow to Minahasa and to bring in clothes in return. Soon the Dutch reestablished their authority in Bolaang-Mongondow and imposed a ban on export of rice, which was scarce. Both the Chinese traders and the local authority criticized the Dutch measure. The local raja explained that while the nationalists were shouting *"Merdeka atau Mati"* (Freedom or Death) and waging a war of independence, the choice for the population in this region was between *Malu atau Mati* (Embarrassment or Death). Exporting rice and importing clothes would relieve some from being *malu*, even though others might have to face *mati* from lack of food.[10]

RECREATION AND CULTURE

Schoolchildren were hungry and nearly naked, but they had some excitements in outdoor activities. Drafted laborers suffered from hunger, overwork, and diseases, but they, too, had moments of pleasure. When draftees gathered at collection points and had a few days to wait before being sent away by train or ship, the local officials usually treated them reasonably well by providing food and medical care (including inoculation) or organizing entertainment like *wayang* (traditional shadow puppet theater) and other theatrical performances.

At the gathering points and work sites they were also shown movies. Before the Japanese invasion, there were about 300 commercial cinemas in some 80 urban centers and nine movie studios in Java; these were mostly owned by Chinese businessmen. In rural Indonesia, there were no cinemas, and most villagers had never seen a movie. During the occupation, Japanese propaganda corps formed movie-projecting teams. Each team carried a movie projector, a screen, an electricity generator, and reels of propaganda films on a truck and visited villages, work sites, and the *rōmusha* waiting for departure. Each team was accompanied by well-known Indonesian figures, who presented speeches to the crowd before showing the films. The speakers were not always warmly received (some audiences jeered, "You speak well, sir, but we are hungry and have no clothes to wear"), but the films were always popular. Rural Indonesians were fascinated, appreciating them as a form of entertainment rather than as propaganda. In early 1944, there were 15 such teams in Java, showing films to 126,000 *rōmusha* in two weeks.

Most cinemas in Java before the Japanese invasion were designed for wealthy urbanites (mostly Dutch and Chinese), with just a few seats in each cinema set aside for not so wealthy Indonesians (a first-class seat cost two guilders, while the cheapest bench seat cost six cents). To cater to the local population, the Japanese modified the system and increased the number of the cheap seats by 50 percent in each cinema. However, they had few films to show. Before the war, about three-quarters of the films shown in Indonesia were American-made, with Dutch subtitles, and about half of the rest were Chinese films.

As the Japanese had no alternative movies to distribute, they did not immediately ban American films. Instead, they censored them to remove "inappropriate" themes. This created some confusion. For instance, *Romeo and Juliet* was shown, but the kissing scene was cut. This cut was done in such a clumsy manner that the spectators started laughing instead of sympathizing with the tragedy of the romance. From April 1, 1943, the authorities banned all films made by the enemy. With fewer movies to show, the number of commercial cinemas decreased by about two-thirds to just 117. The Japanese realized, to their great embarrassment, that most of their domestic films would not impress an international audience. Hollywood movies, from *Gone with the Wind* (released in 1939) to Walt Disney productions, were designed to entertain. The Japanese movie industry had nothing comparable: Many of its films dealt with hardship, like domestic conflicts in an impoverished fishing village, and showed peasant women in work clothes living in a dilapidated thatched hut. The occupation wanted to present Japan as a glorious, advanced country and raise the spirits of filmgoers. However, they did not dare reveal the truth of Japan's countryside or the lifestyles of the struggling urban poor. Instead, they used newsreel that showed only the Westernized aspects of Japan, such as the part of Tokyo's cityscape with tall buildings, the military's powerful warships and tanks, and traditional high culture, such as beautiful kimono.

Such newsreels and documentaries, however, were scarce, so the authorities made films in Indonesia specifically to disseminate propaganda to local people. Those made in Java were obviously more about Indonesia than about Japan. Their two main themes were defense and production. They were designed to show people how to increase production of food, clothing, and other essentials. It is not known exactly how many films were produced in wartime Java. The men in the film units testified that they burned most of the reels after the surrender, but the returning Dutch managed to capture just over 150 such films (these can still be viewed on videotape and DVD at various institutions in the Netherlands).

Apart from banning Western movies and music, the Japanese monopolized radio broadcasting and sealed all the dials of radio receivers to make it impossible to receive shortwave broadcasts from overseas. They also forced commercial newspapers and journals to merge, in part to conserve supplies of paper and ink, but primarily so that they might be controlled more effectively.

One of the side effects of this systematization and rationalization of media was a great increase in the use of Malay (Indonesian) as the common language. With a ban on the use of Dutch, and Japanese understood by only a few, Malay was the only choice of language in the majority of films, broadcasting, journalism, postprimary education, and law. The occupation government issued numerous decrees in Malay. Recognizing that most of the people were illiterate, they then broadcast these decrees over the radio. Many urbanites understood basic conversational Malay but found it difficult to understand the formal Malay used in the occupation media. Rural Indonesians usually did not understand Malay, except in certain areas where the vernacular language was similar. For that reason, Indonesian intellectuals were hesitant to use Malay as the means of education, even though they had decided at the Youth Congress in 1928 to adopt it as their national language but to call it Indonesian. The Japanese insistence on using it as the language of government extended to setting up a Committee for Improving the Indonesian Language. This committee created an extensive list of technical terms to make the language usable in higher education, governance, and other areas where Dutch formerly had dominated. Thus the occupation years serve as a turning point in the written and spoken language of the Indonesian people.

Having banned American movies, music, and other kinds of entertainment, the Japanese were hard-pressed to find alternative ways of relieving the pressures of war on the ordinary people. As with film from Japan, so the traditional forms of Japanese popular entertainment, such as theater, narrative folk songs, and comic dialogues, were too insular to be exported. One of the few things the Japanese were happy to spread was singing. Both Japanese and Indonesians loved singing, and they instantly came to embrace each other's songs. The romantic and sentimental melody of the Indonesian song *Bungawan Solo* (The Solo River), composed in September 1940, captured the hearts of Japanese soldiers and civilians alike. In return, Japanese songs such as *Shina no Yoru* (China Night), composed in 1935 and even more sentimental and romantic than *Bungawan Solo,* was so popular that older generations of Indonesians even 60 years later were still able to remember its lyrics.

The wartime exclusion of Western entertainment also led to a revival of indigenous forms. These included what came to be called *sandiwara* in Malay. *Sandiwara* was a kind of vaudeville or music hall show that took drama, music, dance, and fashion parades as well as farcical interludes and mixed them all together in a revue. The number of *sandiwara* companies increased to over 300 in Java alone. They traveled around using empty cinemas, school buildings, and other facilities, entertaining local people as well as Japanese soldiers and civilians. Some performances were fairly sophisticated, while some were rather crude. Some were propaganda for the Japanese (who supported the resurgence of *sandiwara*), while some were sociopolitical satires. Criticizing the government was a risky act, but performers no doubt thrived on the excitement of being daring. In one satirical sketch a man appears on stage almost naked and complains that since the Japanese came, he has nothing to wear, and the rats are trying to nibble his private parts. The straight man reminds him that this is not a game they are playing but a war to liberate themselves from the Dutch, so they must be prepared to sacrifice not only clothes, but anything and everything. The comic lead quickly cups his genitals and runs off screaming, "Oh, no!" The spectators got the joke and roared with laughter.

The Japanese authorities were highly sensitive to any form of criticism, and, indeed, they imprisoned some performers. They employed many spies, but their censorship, as we have seen, was clumsy, and many Indonesians managed to express criticisms or make sarcastic comments by insinuation and other means. About 10 percent of any *sandiwara* performance was government propaganda, a similar proportion was criticism of the Japanese, and the rest was pure entertainment.

The removal of Western cultural influence and Japanese encouragement of nationalism also invigorated other forms of cultural activity. These included literature, fine arts, and music. The Japanese attempted to use these media for their propaganda and frequently held art exhibitions as well as short-story and song-writing competitions. Indonesian authors who previously had used the Dutch language now switched to writing in Indonesian. One of Indonesia's renowned poets, Chairil Anwar, emerged during these years, although his poetry was largely unconnected to the aims of Japan. As a general statement, it would be fair to say that the occupation, just as it was a turning point in Indonesian political history, was also a turning point in its cultural history.

A final point about the cultural life of Indonesians during the war concerns religion. The Japanese military regime was fanatical at home and within its own ranks about emperor worship. However, this was one more area of Japanese life that clearly was never going to export well. While some attempt was made to generate respect for, and worship of, the Japanese emperor in some parts of Greater East Asia, in Indonesia it was more common for existing religious activities to be respected. This was particularly the case with Islam, which shared the experience of being subjugated by Western colonialism and its values. Thus in the predominantly Muslim areas of Indonesia, the Japanese not only promised to respect Islamic beliefs and customs, they also sought cooperation from Muslim leaders. In fact, some Muslim clerics took advantage of this cooperative relationship and forced those civilians who were only nominally Muslim to attend services at the local mosque. If Japanese native religions were too parochial to win converts overseas, there is, however, at least one instance of a senior Japanese in Indonesia being won over by Indonesians. This was on the island of Flores, where the people were devout Catholics. The island was under the administrative control of the Japanese Navy. As the commanding officer, Satō Tasuku, explained in his idyllic postwar memoir of his time there, *I Remember Flores,* he was so touched by the piety of the lifestyle he witnessed that he, too, converted to Catholicism. This is a reminder that in any form of war, occupation, or colonialism, there is always a measure of mutual exchange between the new rulers and the ruled.

RECONTEXTUALIZING THE IMPACT OF WAR

The war of 1939–1945, and its attendant conflicts both before and after, altered the world economy and affected virtually the entire human population. We therefore need to examine its impact on people's lives in a global, local, and historical context. Until now, however, the impact of the Japanese occupation on Indonesian daily life has been interpreted more or less out of context. Civilian suffering has been attributed to direct actions, such as brutality and exploitation. It is true that the Japanese mobilized great numbers of Indonesians as laborers and maltreated them; as a consequence, many lost their lives. Many others were indirect victims of the war and Japan's reckless attempt to construct a "Coprosperity Sphere." Yet, as we have seen, some draftees never came into direct contact with any Japanese. That was because local people, such as government officials and labor foremen, carried out the plans of the occupation, and the Japanese themselves appeared on work sites only rarely. For that reason, merely blaming individuals as war criminals would not provide a mature understanding of the war's impact.

The forced mobilization of labor and forced delivery of food were the two most infamous occupation policies affecting the Indonesian people.

We have seen, however, that the occupation authorities never achieved the annual purchase target of food, which they set at about the same amount as the earlier Dutch colonial government. Their attempts and failures created chaos in the food distribution system and shortages of food in the occupied lands. This issue, too, needs to be examined in a broad international and regional context.

The Dutch had been well aware that once Indonesia became isolated due to war, it would face serious economic problems, particularly in terms of providing food and clothing to the local population. Consequently, they began moving to improve Indonesian self-sufficiency in these areas as soon as war commenced in Europe. The Japanese economic policies were broadly a continuation of these moves. When Japan surrendered, the newly formed Indonesian government took over. Indonesian political leaders naturally were aware of public resentment over Japan's failures in food and clothing, but unable to think of any alternative, they basically maintained the same policies in such matters as the rice delivery system. Their achievement also was far below their procurement target so that for many civilians, there was some level of unsatisfactory continuity in their economic lives over the period of the three regimes.

The essentials of daily life in Indonesia did not improve much after Japan surrendered. Food and clothing remained in short supply, although imports of small amounts of clothes resumed. A year after the proclamation of independence, Javanese villagers under the republican government were furious. The cause of their anger was a system that discriminated against the poor. In this system, relatively wealthy farmers who were "less than 95 percent naked" received a ration of cloth for delivering 50 kilograms or more rice to the government; those who could not deliver the same amount of rice received no clothing ration at all.[11]

Both the Indonesian Republican government and the Dutch who came to retake their colony distributed clothing to some people. However, the immediate postwar years was a time when global production of food and textiles declined, and even former major textile exporting countries struggled to meet their domestic needs. This adversity provided business opportunities. Some traders in Indonesia apparently collected old gunnysack clothes from those who had now obtained proper clothing, shifted them to the poorer areas of the country, and made profits by selling them to those who could not afford, or could not find, new garments. Thus many poorer Indonesians wore secondhand gunnysack clothes long after the Japanese had left. In certain areas in east Java in 1947, 80 percent of the villagers were still wearing makeshift clothes of old gunnysacks.[12]

As with the traders of secondhand clothing, war, while it tended to destroy existing economic systems, also opened up new arenas for profit. Indeed, the war created many official and unofficial business opportunities, such as interisland trading. Large ships that operated in the region in the prewar years generally belonged to Britain and the Netherlands; local people usually owned smaller boats. However, most large ships left the region prior to the Japanese invasion so as to avoid capture. Initially, the Japanese hoped to exert a monopolistic control over interisland shipping. For that purpose they attempted to commandeer all remaining ships, but many of these small vessels also disappeared before the Japanese came— not out of the region, but to the bottom of the sea. The owners scuttled their boats to prevent them from being impounded, but once the owners felt the coast was clear, the vessels were refloated.

The Japanese, being aware that complete control of interisland transportation was neither possible nor desirable, connived at much of the unofficial trading operated by small boat owners. There was therefore a good deal of clandestine trading going on across the Java Sea, the Strait of Malacca, or from one port to another along the coast of the same island. Before the occupation, clothes were imported from Japan to Java and reexported to the Outer Islands. The occupation disrupted this pattern and created desperate shortages of clothing in the Outer Islands. On the west coast of Borneo, a sarong smuggled from Java cost 150 guilders in August 1943; it would have cost 2.50 guilders before the war. Prices were much higher in south Borneo. By smuggling clothes from Java to Pontianak, and then to Banjarmasin, traders could make handsome profits. Much of the smuggling was, in fact, unofficial maintenance of prewar trading patterns.

The war also presented official opportunities to businessmen. Like the Dutch before them, the Japanese attempted to control the economy, and for that purpose they made use of the existing system. In particular, they relied on local government officials and the ethnic Chinese business networks. The forced delivery of rice, for instance, was implemented by local officials, and the delivered rice was handled by Chinese rice millers. Indigenous officials and Chinese rice dealers often colluded and embezzled substantial parts of the profits, and also put much of the delivered rice on the black market just at the time when many people were starving. The ordinary people took their revenge when the Japanese rule ended. They ransacked Chinese shops, raped Chinese women, and assaulted government officials. As the study by Anton Lucas explains, the amount of public suffering during the occupation, and the vacuum of power in the revolutionary period, is reflected in the fact that this violence was more destructive, widespread, and lasted longer after the Japanese surrender than during their invasion.

The variety of experience in war for Indonesians is further illustrated by the farming community. Some wealthy farmers fared relatively well. That was because many poor farmers, in desperate need to obtain cash to buy daily essentials or pay taxes, sold their land or livestock. Being in no position to bargain, this meant they had to accept whatever price was offered to them. In this way the richer farmers could easily improve their wealth and, with it, their authority within the village and the region.

The economic and political turmoil of war was accompanied by cultural change, both positive and negative, depending on one's viewpoint. When imports of foreign media ended, local artists began using their own media, albeit under continuing foreign domination. Many actors who became popular during the Japanese occupation, for instance, became movie stars when Indonesia gained independence and movie production resumed. Similar phenomena can be observed in fields such as literature, music, and the fine arts. We should not, however, be too quick to attribute these changes to the Japanese occupation. As in the economy and politics, signs of early cultural change emerged before the Japanese invasion. These included some Indonesian writers and public speakers who started their career using Dutch but independently made the switch to Malay before 1942. The Indonesian politician Mohammad Husni Thamrin, for example, began to make speeches in the colonial assembly in Indonesian; this was in defiance of the Dutch members, who had difficulty understanding his comments.

This chapter has suggested that the Japanese occupation was a catalyst rather than a cause of change in many fields and that for a fuller understanding of the complex ways in which the war affected Indonesian life in the occupied territories, we need to examine the event in a broad historical and global context. The complexity of the war's impact reflected both the complexity of Indonesian society and the way in which Indonesia constituted a part of the global community.

NOTES

1. L. de Jong, *The Collapse of a Colonial Society: The Dutch in Indonesia during the Second World War* (Leiden, Netherlands: KITLV Press, 2002), 279.

2. Pramoedya Ananta Toer, *The Fugitive,* trans. Willem Samuel (Harmondsworth, England: Penguin Books, 1990), 33.

3. P. J. Suwarno, *Romusa Daerah Istimewa Yogyakarta* [*Romusha* in the Special Region of Yogyakarta], Yogyakarta, Indonesia: Penerbitan Universitas Sanata Dharma, 1999.

4. Boentaran Martoatmodjo, "Pemandangan Singkat Perihal Kesehatan dan Makanan Rakjat dll [Brief Overview of the People's Health and Food etc.]," *Berita Ketabitan: Madjalah dari Djawa Izi Hoko Kai* [Medical News: Journal of the Java Medical Service Association] 4–6 (1944): 43–52.

5. Masahei Suzuki, *Nippon Senryōka Bari-tō karano Hōkoku: Tōnan Ajia deno Kyōiku Seisaku* [Reports from Bali under the Japanese Occupation: Education Policies in Southeast Asia] (Tokyo: Soshisha, 1999), 91.

6. *Economisch Weekblad voor Nederlandsch-Indë* [Economic Weekly for the Netherlands Indies] November (1940): 2065–67, December (1941): 87. In 1941, there were about 1,000 rice mills in Indonesia, half in Java and half in the Outer Islands. Many of the mills in Java were large, and most of those in the Outer Islands, built after 1939, were small.

7. Prawoto Semodilogo, "Menindjaoe Keadaan di Indramajoe [Inspection of the Situation in Indramayu]," Collection of C. O. van der Plas, 2.21.266, no. 160, The National Archive, The Hague.

8. Suzuki 1999: 187–88.

9. "Compilation of NEFIS Interrogation Report, nos 351–364," Indonesian Collection 061024, The Netherlands Institute for War Documentation, Amsterdam.

10. "Rapport inzake de Algeneene Situatie in de Onderafd. Bolaan-Mongondow [Report on the General Situation in the Subdistrict of Bolaan-Mongondow]," 17 June 1946, NEFIS/CMI collection, part one, no. 1769, held in the Ministry of Foreign Affairs, The Hague.

11. Tuong Vu, "Of Rice and Revolution: The Politics of Provisioning and State-Society Relations on Java, 1945–49," *South East Asia Research* 11 (2003): 256.

12. William H. Frederick, "The Appearance of the Revolution: Cloth, Uniforms, and the Pemuda Style in East Java, 1945–1949," in *Outward Appearance: Dressing State and Society in Indonesia,* ed. Henk Schulte Nordholt (Leiden, Netherlands: KITLV Press, 1997), 207.

SELECTED BIBLIOGRAPHY

Alisjahbana, Sutan Takdir. *Kalah dan Menang* [Defeat and Victory]. N.p.: Dian Rakyat, 1978.
    This novel, written by the writer who worked in the Committee for Improving the Indonesian Language, captures the sociocultural atmosphere in Java during the Japanese occupation.
Anderson, Benedict R. O. *Java in a Time of Revolution: Occupation and Resistance, 1944–1946.* Ithaca, NY: Cornell University Press, 1972.
    An outstanding scholarly work that analyzes young Indonesian revolutionaries in Java in the period from the late occupation to the early revolution.
de Jong, L. *The Collapse of a Colonial Society: The Dutch in Indonesia during the Second World War.* Leiden, Netherlands: KITLV Press, 2002.
    The focus of this work is mainly on Dutch and Dutch Eurasians, but it also pays attention to Indonesian daily life.
Frederick, William H. *Visions and Heat: The Making of the Indonesian Revolution.* Athens: Ohio University Press, 1989.
    This traces political and social changes as well as continuities in Surabaya over the Dutch, Japanese, and Indonesia eras.
Kratoska, Paul, ed. *Asian Labor in the Wartime Japanese Empire: Unknown Histories.* New York: M. E. Sharpe, 2005.
    This book contains five chapters on the Japanese manpower mobilization in Indonesia and its consequences.
Lucas, Anton. *One Soul One Struggle: Region and Revolution in Indonesia.* St. Leonards, Australia: Allen and Unwin, 1991.
    This is a pioneering, detailed case study of the revolutionary movement by peasants in central Java after the Japanese occupation.
Malaka, Tan Malaka. *From Prison to Prison.* Translated by Helen Jarvis. Athens: Ohio University Center for International Studies, 1991.
    An autobiography of the Indonesian communist leader who worked as a caretaker of the *rōmusha* mobilized for coal mining in west Java during the Japanese occupation.

Pakpahan, G. *1261 Hari di bawah Sinar Matahari Terbit, 6 Maret 2602–17 Agustus 2605* [1261 Days under the Rising Run, 6 March 1942–17 August 1945]. 2nd ed. Jakarta: Marintah Djaya, 1979.
  A detailed account of daily life in Indonesia as observed by an Indonesian who lived in Japanese-occupied Jakarta.
Satō, Shigeru. *War, Nationalism, and Peasants: Java under the Japanese Occupation, 1942–1945.* New York: M. E. Sharpe, 1994.
  This book analyzes the economic impact of the Japanese military administration on Java's peasantry.
Satō, Shigeru. "Emperor Worship and Language Teaching in Java under the Japanese Occupation." In *Coloniality, Postcoloniality and Modernity in Japan,* ed. Vera Mackie et al. Melbourne: Monash Asia Institute, 2000.
  A survey of wartime Japanese ideology and education policy in Java.
Satō, Shigeru. "Indonesia 1939–1942: Prelude to Japanese Occupation." *Journal of Southeast Asian Studies,* 37, no. 2 (2006): 225–48.
  This article analyzes the economic impact of the European war on Indonesian society and the colonial government's response to it.
Satō, Tasuku. *I Remember Flores.* New York: Farrer, Straus, 1957.
  An account of daily life in the predominantly Catholic island of Flores by the Japanese military commander who was so moved by the people that he converted to Catholicism.
Toer, Pramoedya Ananta. *The Fugitive.* Translated by Willem Samuel. Harmondsworth, England: Penguin Books, 1990.
  The first major novel by this renowned author, depicting a young Indonesian revolutionary's struggle at the end of the Japanese occupation.
Vu, Tuong. "Of Rice and Revolution: The Politics of Provisioning and State-Society Relations on Java, 1945–49." *South East Asia Research* 11 (2003): 237–67.
  This article points out the similarities between the Japanese and the Indonesian policies with regard to food distribution.

SEVEN

Korean Civilians North and South, 1950–1953

Andrei Lankov

On August 15, 1945, Korea was freed from 35 years of colonialism by the surrender of Japan. There had been at least three main reasons in 1910 why the Korean monarchy and its government had been unable to prevent the loss of independence. First, Korea had resisted industrialization in the late nineteenth century because of the social chaos it might bring; this made the country both relatively poor and difficult to mobilize. Second, the Korean elite was educated in orthodox Confucian beliefs, and so the military was generally despised as an occupation; this made the country's defenses inadequate. Finally, the traditional protector of Korean interests was China, but at that point, it was in rapid geopolitical decline, and there was no other power willing to prevent a Japanese takeover of the Korean peninsula.

After liberation in 1945, there were two competing nationalist regimes: the communists, led by Kim Il-sung, who had come to prominence as a guerrilla leader fighting Japanese interests in Manchuria; and the conservatives of Syngman Rhee, whose support base was among elites formerly in exile. What both regimes shared was a commitment never to allow Korea once again to be weak in the face of external threats and an absolute belief in their respective ideologies as the best defense for the country. Their refusal to accept any form of power sharing led, in 1948, to the creation of the Republic of Korea (R.O.K.) in the south and the Democratic People's Republic of Korea (D.P.R.K.) in the north. Ironically, both regimes looked to outside aid in order to strengthen their positions against each

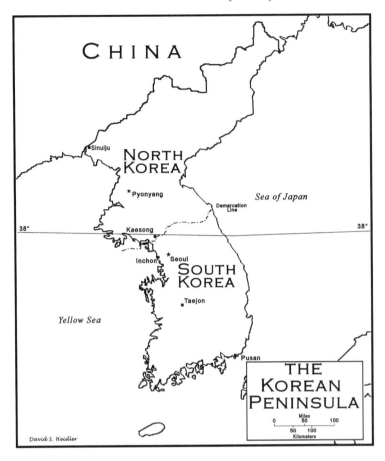

The Korean peninsula. (David S. Heidler.)

other. By 1950, however, the United States had pulled back from its support for Rhee and was consolidating its position in Japan. At this point, Kim Il-sung managed to convince his supporters in the two major communist powers, Stalin in Moscow and Mao Zedong in Beijing, that Korea could be reunited by a short civil war. Thus, early on the Sunday morning of June 25, 1950, the North Korean army launched a surprise attack across the 38th parallel, the ad hoc line of separation created at the end of World War II by the United States and the Union of Soviet Socialist Republics (U.S.S.R.). The military planners in Pyŏngyang and their Soviet advisers both assumed that the war would be over at most within three months. However, it was to rage for three years and simmer for at least another half century; during the so-called hot war, it was to leave approximately three million Koreans dead and turn the great cities, such as Seoul and Pyŏngyang, either into ghost towns or wastelands.

Initially, things developed as intended by the communist generals. The North Korean divisions were well trained (many soldiers had recent experience fighting alongside the victorious communist armies in China) and well armed; they easily cut through the demoralized South Korean units on the 38th parallel and began their advance on Seoul, just 50 kilometers farther south. In 1950, Seoul was the largest city of the country, with a population of one and a half million. A capital for over 600 years, the city enjoyed tremendous political prestige and was home to the nation's elite. It was also the major goal of the attack.

To many observers, the war did not come as a surprise since tension between the two Korean regimes had been mounting since 1945, and more especially from the late 1940s, as each side probed for the other's weakness. In Seoul, Kim Song-ch'il, arguably the most eminent diarist of the era, noted in 1950 that "the threat of a civil war which has been hanging over our heads for five years has finally became a reality." Chang To-yong, then head of South Korea's military intelligence, was more laconic: "What should have happened, has happened."

Nonetheless, in the first hours of the campaign the average civilian in Seoul hardly understood the significance of what was happening along the 38th parallel. People had grown accustomed to clashes at the border. Hence many dismissed this as yet another tussle which would pass and leave their lives basically unchanged. Indeed, for a while, Seoul's inhabitants did not even know about the speed or scale of the North Koreans' advance. They may have noticed some emergency measures taken in the city. For example, the radio ordered all soldiers to report back to their units, the nationwide student sports competition was stopped, and at least one theater halted its performance. In some cinemas the show was interrupted to notify people about recent events, and the term *war* was actually used. However, these were the exceptions, and even here, the warnings were regarded as symbolic, used merely to keep people alert.

In fact, for the people of Seoul, the Korean war started with a demonstration of the old adage that the first casualty in war is truth. In this case they were the victims of their own technology as the radio, only increasing in ownership in recent years, was used by the government to persuade listeners to continue life as normal. Thus even while South Korean defenses disintegrated, news bulletins reassured the public that the initial North Korean advance had been halted and even reversed. Although the distant sound of artillery fire could be heard in central Seoul by the morning of the 27th, still the people were told by their leaders that all would be well. Only those in the northern suburbs, for whom the sound of battle was disturbingly close, chose to leave their houses and begin to move to what they hoped was the safety of the downtown area.

The public's false impression of normality was reinforced when, later on June 27, 1950, Seoul radio stations broadcast a speech by President Rhee. In this, he exhorted all residents to do everything to protect Seoul from the enemy. Most Seoulites assumed this was a live broadcast—they were not yet accustomed to prerecorded programs—and so they believed the president was standing by their side. Actually, by the time Rhee's voice was in the air, the man himself had already fled south. Soon he was to be followed by the R.O.K.'s major institutions.

While many people, such as businessmen, the educated, and those who had prospered in any degree under Japanese colonialism, had reason to be afraid of the advancing communist armies, many others seem to have felt that politics was something distant from their daily lives; that is, many ordinary Koreans in the south were broadly indifferent to the warring parties. Rhee's administration was unpopular (even if the man himself commanded some respect for his years campaigning for Korean independence). The expectation in 1950 was that any change of government could only be an improvement on the recent corruption, cronyism, and assassinations of political rivals. Thus most people in Seoul or other parts of the R.O.K. did not worry unduly about the coming communists. Moreover, ordinary people may have noted how popular the Chinese communist soldiers had seemed at the time of their victory in late 1949; events in China may also have made people more emotionally prepared for the triumph of communism elsewhere in Asia, including in Korea.

Recently declassified papers from the Russian archives confirm what had been long suspected by scholars: The North Korean strategists were sincere when they assumed that their invasion would ignite a massive communist uprising among repressed people in the south. They were wrong. Most South Korean civilians were ready to fight neither for the communist north nor the republican south. Most simply wanted to muddle through dangerous times, more so since the war was essentially an internal struggle between rival regimes, not a great patriotic campaign against some invading foreign army. There were also those who were completely disillusioned by the sight of Koreans fighting Koreans a mere five years after liberation from Japanese rule. The general attitude of many ordinary people, therefore, may best be described by a Korean proverb: "Even if the heavens fall down, there must be some escape holes." Thus the common citizens began their search for these proverbial holes.

THE WAR: PENDULUM OF DESTRUCTION

For all Korea's civilians, the pace and nature of the war fell broadly into two sections. At the outset, there was a flurry of dizzying movement backward and forward of differing armies and changing flags. Thereafter there were years in which the movement of forces on the ground virtually disappeared. In its place, there was, for North Koreans, the constant threat of bombing and, for South Koreans, a period of waiting and enduring for the end of hostilities.

On June 28, 1950, Seoul was taken over by the northern forces, and by early August, the communists controlled at least 90 percent of the Korean peninsula. It appeared as if North Korea had won the civil war as easily and bloodlessly as Kim Il-sung had predicted. However, at that point the U.S. government under President Truman decided to salvage the R.O.K. in order to shore up his policy of containing global communism. This decision was taken with the backing of a U.N. mandate which thus made military intervention justified in the new international legal order. For all practical purposes, however, the U.N. forces consisted of American and South Korean troops, plus some British and Turkish units as well as token contributions from several other countries. On September 15, the U.N. forces, led by General Douglas MacArthur, landed at Inch'ŏn, the port closest to Seoul on Korea's west coast. In late September they took over Seoul and then began their own rapid advance to the north. Just as the R.O.K. forces in mid-1950 had crumbled, so the North Korean units now disintegrated under the heavy blows of the better-armed and supported U.N. assault. On October 19, MacArthur's troops entered Pyŏngyang. The North Korean government fled to the Chinese border, while the North Korean army ceased to exist as a fighting force. By late November, it was the U.N. forces which controlled at least 90 percent of all Korea—a complete reversal of the situation in August.

At that stage, another great power decided to join the war and force another swing of the pendulum. The recently installed communist government in Beijing saw the advance of U.N. forces to its border with Korea as a direct threat and, through diplomatic channels, warned MacArthur that for its own security, it would be compelled to act unless he came to a halt. The United States took no notice of the warning. With this the Chinese army (officially described as "the Chinese People's Volunteers" to maintain the diplomatic fiction of Chinese neutrality) moved south from Manchuria into Korea. The Chinese offensive began in late November and, as with all the previous engagements in what had started as a civil war but now was a war of nations, developed with breathtaking speed: Pyŏngyang was retaken in early December, and on January 4, 1951, Chinese tanks rolled into Seoul. In one last twist the U.N. forces regrouped and soon retook the southern capital. Thereafter a prolonged period of trench warfare ensued; this was to last until the formal end of hostilities in July 1953. During these years, the north was subjected to intense bombing by the U.S. Air Force, but on the ground the frontline remained generally stable. On July 27, 1953, an armistice was finally signed, and the hot war was over. Despite this, a state of war between the two Korean regimes was to continue for many more decades and ensure that militarization and preparation for war became a fundamental part of civilian daily life on both sides of the 38th parallel.

SEOUL: THE CHANGING FACE OF THE OCCUPIERS

At 11:30 A.M., on June 28, 1950, people in downtown Seoul saw a North Korean banner being raised atop the massive central government building known to foreigners as the Seoul Capitol. The building had originally been constructed as the office of the Japanese colonial administration deliberately to tower over the mostly one- or two-story structures of the downtown district (it was demolished in the 1990s in a belated act of nationalism). After merely three days of fighting, both the building and the whole of the capital of South Korea were now in the hands of the North Korean armies. The northern rule was to last three months, until late September.

Seoul was then, and still is, a primate city; that is, in 1950, it was far and away the biggest city in the country and contained a majority of South Korea's population. Among this mass of people, even those who wished to run away from the communist advance were deceived by their government's propaganda and surprised by the speed of the north's success. Consequently, they, too, found themselves under occupation. They included 60 out of the total 200 members of the South Korean parliament. It is estimated that out of a population of 1.45 million, no more than 400,000 (some 27 percent) left Seoul before the collapse of the South Korean defenses.[1] A large part, perhaps even a majority, of those who managed to flee were actually recent arrivals from the north, people who had both firsthand knowledge of life under the North Korean regime and no established home in Seoul to protect. They also believed (generally with good reason) that their initial flight from the north to the south would make them targets if the communists came to power. Others who managed to escape were prominent politicians and top bureaucrats, men who were better and more accurately informed about the reality of the war. They sent their families farther south over the course of June 26–27, so, on those days, the southbound roads, largely narrow and often unpaved, were jammed with the cars of the Seoul elite. However, most Koreans in 1950 had no access to private cars: In the late 1940s, there were only 10,000 cars and trucks in the entire country, that is, roughly one vehicle per 2,000 people. Instead, the waves of ordinary refugees either boarded an overcrowded train or walked.

A major role in imprisoning the population in Seoul was played by the R.O.K.'s own forces. Following false reports about enemy tanks in the area, South Korean commanding officers at dawn on June 28 ordered the two bridges that crossed the great Han River to be blown up; these bridges provided the only escape route for both refugees fleeing Seoul and for troops retreating to it. The explosions killed several hundred people who had the misfortune to be on or around the bridges at the very moment the charges were detonated. Now unable to cross the river, the citizens of Seoul were given no choice but to deal with the victorious communist army.

During their time in control of Seoul, however, the North Koreans did not think or act as conquerors. Even the 1948 North Korean Constitution stated that the capital of North Korea's Democratic People's Republic of Korea should be located in Seoul, the political center of united Korea since the late fourteenth century; Pyŏngyang was considered merely a provisional headquarters of the government. According to their own official viewpoint, the North Korean forces were defenders of all Koreans and had served the entire nation by driving away the puppet administration imposed on the south by the so-called U.S. imperialists. Thus Kim Il-sung issued an address in which he congratulated the "people's masses of Seoul" on being liberated by the soldiers of the north. Moreover, the discipline of North Korean troops in the early days was high, and this won them favor with local residents; only in September, as the nature of the war altered, did cases of marauding and theft by northern troops become relatively common.

The communists worked hard to restore normal life in the city. As early as June 27, well before they had secured their authority, an interim Seoul People's Committee was established to act as the metropolitan government. This committee was headed by Yi Sŭng-yŏp, a prominent communist who had been politically active in Seoul until his defection to the north (later on, he was to become a victim of the political purges in the north). Recognizing the public's general indifference to politics but its very real concerns about basic needs, one of his first acts was to try and limit any damage to jobs, wages, and supplies. On the evening of June 29 he took to the radio and urged the civilian population to "be in peace and continue your work and business at factories, farms and shops."[2]

A typical scene of Korean women in the street, 1950. (Russian state archives of photo and cinematic documents, 0-211755.)

Other major aspects of restored normality included education and mobility. Seoul primary schools resumed classes in mid-July. The school curriculum was hastily changed to fit the new political situation, but most lessons for children in simple reading or writing were too basic to merit major alterations. The ability of adults to write to each other was also guaranteed by the communists with the post offices continuing to accept mail; in a major symbolic gesture of national unity, this included, for the first time in years, mail to and from the north (normal postal exchanges between the two parts of Korea had continued for a while after the division in 1945 but soon fell victim to the north-south standoff). One irritant in daily life, however, was the question of postage: The communists banned the use of stamps previously issued under Rhee, and since new stamps took time to arrive, the public had to pay in cash for every letter or package. Within Seoul the tram service resumed its operations after only two days of hiatus: This was also of major symbolic and practical importance as the trams were the principal means of public transportation within the city limits. By early August 1950, some 120 carriages traversed the Seoul streets—not much below the prewar total.

Along with communication and movement, there was also the restoration of media, although now with a very different look and sound. From early July the cinemas reopened their doors to the public. Instead of the bourgeois and decadent Western movies, however, Seoulites were soon offered the somewhat more puritanical, if inspiring, works of Soviet cinema. These ranged from a fairy tale titled *Stone Flower* to *Young Guard*, a heroic saga of patriotic Soviet resistance to Nazi brutality in World War II. The works of Lenin and treatises on communist theory also went on sale in Seoul bookshops.

From early July the North Korean authorities began to publish two newspapers in Seoul itself. Soon they also started selling copies of *Nodong Sinmun* (Workers News), the major official daily from Pyongyang of the ruling Korean Workers Party (KWP). However, in the ongoing conditions of war, it proved difficult to transport a sufficient number of copies from the north. Thus most of the information made available through the media to the people of Seoul was provided by the local communists.

In this way, daily life in communist-controlled Seoul appeared in the beginning to be recognizably normal. However, in a matter of weeks, things began to unravel. One of the greatest difficulties for the new metropolitan government was how to counter the increasingly frequent U.S. armed forces air raids. As defense measures against air attack, the movement of vehicles was forbidden between 9:00 P.M. and 5:00 A.M., and civilians were ordered to build simple air-raid shelters. The task was eased because they could repair shelters which had been dug in 1944–1945 when the Japanese colonizers expected U.S. air raids (which never came—the United States, at the time, may well have acknowledged that Koreans were the victims of Japanese imperialism rather than its supporters). The raids, however, demonstrated to the people of Seoul the fact that the war was far from ended.

Also undermining the authority of the communist government in Seoul was the difficulty of controlling such an enormous urban population. In this sense, the North Koreans might actually have benefited if more refugees had managed to leave the capital in June. On the changing mood of the people, the diary of Kim Song-ch'il, often cited in Korean works of history, is both remarkably telling and remarkably even-handed.[3] A young professor of history in a major university, Kim stayed in Seoul throughout the three months of North Korean occupation. Like so many others, he did not start with feelings of hostility toward the communist administration, but he also was no supporter of Syngman Rhee. When the North Korean tanks first rolled into the city, Kim wrote that he could not possibly view these fellow Koreans as the enemy, and his diary frequently applauds the discipline and good training of the North Korean soldiers. By late September 1950, however, he and many others were eagerly awaiting the U.N. troops. He still harbored no illusion about Syngman Rhee and his regime, and he was somewhat understanding of those Koreans who threw in their lot with the communists. Yet he had now come to realize that under duress, both of the rival regimes treated the ordinary people with brutality, but on balance, he believed the communists were the worst.

One of the problems was in the nature of contemporary communist politics. Like other Stalinist regimes, the North Korean government felt it essential to use techniques of mass indoctrination and mobilization. This meant that commoners in Seoul were required constantly to demonstrate their enthusiasm for the new regime. North Korean officials never tired of reminding the people of the so-called liberated areas that their individual happiness and collective strength rested on being "cleansed" of decadent bourgeois thoughts and habits and being remodeled into exemplary socialist citizens through ideological reeducation.

As a result, political meetings and obligatory indoctrination sessions became a constant part of life. Ordinary workers spent days and days listening, with varying degrees of interest and understanding, to political speeches. Among other subjects, they were lectured on the evils of U.S. imperialism (even though the United States had taken the major role in defeating Japan in 1945), the glory of the Soviet Union (which, in repelling and destroying Nazi Germany, was true enough), the virtues of Stalin and Kim Il-sung (as yet unproven to the people of Seoul), and the wickedness of Syngman Rhee (arguably demonstrated in his recent abandonment of Seoul).

In addition, household owners were ordered to fly the flag of the Democratic People's Republic of Korea. This caused some concern; in a regime where every action was now politicized, a simple mistake could be construed as an act of resistance. As Kim Song-ch'il wrote in his diary on July 7, "Bought some blue and red ink and began to paint a flag of the DPRK. . . . To make sure that the shape is not wrong, went to a ward office to compare."[4]

Wherever the communists were in power in Korea, they ordered householders to write slogans. This also was a feature of other communist regimes, most obviously in China. The typical slogans were "Long live the Democratic People's Republic of Korea!," "Long live General Kim Il-sung, our beloved leader!," and "Long live Comrade Stalin, the wise protector of the oppressed nations of the world!" Banners displaying these slogans were to be fixed to one's house gates. The amount of visual propaganda in wartime Seoul was, as it was meant to be, simply overwhelming and, for many, also exhausting.

For all its intrusiveness in the lives of civilians, political indoctrination soon came to be seen only as a minor nuisance. From late July the far more pressing and immediate problem was food. During the first weeks of the occupation, the North Korean administration declared repeatedly that food supplies would arrive "soon" and that, before long, a comprehensive food rationing system would be introduced. However, this never happened. By mid-July, Kim Song-ch'il wrote in his diary, "Whatever they say, food is the greatest problem."[5] He also noted that in some cases, young men volunteered for military service in the belief that they at least would have enough to eat (as we know, this was not necessarily the case; the food supply in the army units was also inadequate). Being unable to feed a city whose population exceeded one million, the new authorities now decided the only solution was to force people to move. Although many of Seoul's residents were ordered to relocate to the countryside, this plan was never carried out on the intended scale and thus did not solve the problem.

Recognizing the failure of their new rulers, the common people of Seoul began, from July 1950, to set up an alternative economy, selling or bartering household items for food. Urban residents began making regular expeditions to the countryside, walking to surrounding villages in search of anything edible that might be exchanged for household goods. A radio set or a sewing machine was almost worth its weight in gold as either could be bartered for a week's supply of food. Already by mid-August, however, all of the villages within walking distance of the capital were running short of food as well. This forced people to travel farther and farther, often loaded like beasts of burden with heavy goods for barter.

The first communist rule lasted for three months only. The end came in mid-September 1950 as the U.N. forces landed at Inch'on and began to fight their way to Seoul. Of all four takeovers experienced by the city between June 1950 and March 1951, this was by far the bloodiest. The North Korean headquarters decided to fight to the death, on the (generally correct) assumption that the loss of Seoul would deliver a mortal blow to their entire regime. Between September 20 and 30, 1950, Seoul and its vicinity was turned into a battleground. Parts of the downtown area were wiped out by artillery fire, and in many districts, any building of size or substance was destroyed or damaged.

The scale of the fighting unavoidably led to casualties among the civilian population. Although some communist sympathizers quietly left the city, there was no effort by the communist government in the days after the U.N. landing to stage a mass evacuation. Instead, it acted much in the same way as the Rhee administration in June, aiming to prevent chaos or protest by hiding the news of the U.N. troops' advance. Again as with Rhee, it was the approaching sound of gunfire outside the city that exposed the truth to ordinary citizens. By this point, there was no safe avenue of escape. Thus many people remained in the city and spent the days of the decisive battle hiding in air-raid shelters, basements, or cellars.

The victory of the U.N. forces in Seoul was welcomed by most city residents. It meant the end of the constant and intrusive mobilization of people's daily lives in support of communism and Kim Il-sung. More importantly, the United Nations arrived with large quantities of food aid. Thus the desperate routine of trekking, bartering, and loss of all possessions in order just to eat was broken. However, the U.N. victory also brought a large-scale witch hunt against real and alleged communist collaborators, of whom there were many. This meant that anyone could be denounced, even those who had simply flown the North Korean flag or posted communist slogans outside their homes. In such a heightened and even hysterical political climate the failure to resist an occupier could easily be turned into evidence of collaboration.

In early October, some South Korean refugees and most government offices began returning from Pusan on the far south coast. For a while it seemed that life in Seoul was heading back to its prewar normality. However, within just another three months, communist forces were to be back at the city gates, and this time, the North Koreans were to be joined by the Chinese.

On this occasion, however, the U.N. Command ensured that nearly the entire population of Seoul moved away before the city was surrendered to the communists. Those civilians who had stayed under the earlier North Korean administration were also better prepared this time and more determined to avoid any repeat of their experience. As a result of this mass exodus, only 130,000 people, that is, less than 10 percent of the original population, remained in the capital throughout the second communist occupation. Many of these were old people, unafraid of the military draft and often with no other place to go. Also, this time, the communist authorities viewed Seoul first and foremost as a base for military operations and did not try to reestablish even a semblance of normal civilian life in what had so quickly become a virtual ghost town.

In March 1951, Seoul was retaken by the U.N. forces, thus changing hands for the fourth time in eight months—fortunately, without much bloodshed on this occasion. However, for the rest of the war it remained a wreck, partially ruined and abandoned by most of its one-time dwellers. Fighting continued in its vicinity; the frontline was barely an hour's drive north. This meant that all government institutions and most refugees preferred to stay in and around Pusan. When, in February 1952, the municipal administration of Seoul issued so-called citizens' certificates to its inhabitants (largely as a way to confirm the bearers' political reliability), the resident population was only 321,626—about a quarter of the prewar total.[6] Only with the official cessation of hostilities in August 1953 did the central government of the R.O.K. declare that it was returning to Seoul. Yet with only a partial settlement of the war, and faced with the enormous task of rebuilding the city, most refugees waited for another one to two years before they began returning to their homes or to the spot where once their homes had stood.

PUSAN: THE REFUGEES

Immense crowds of refugees was one of the recurring images of the Korean War in the contemporary Western media. Photographs and newsreels depicted badly dressed, visibly exhausted people, overloaded with personal belongings, walking for days in the thousands. The war was a time of large-scale human movement, but this had actually begun well before the outbreak of hostilities, indeed, right after the division of the Korean peninsula in 1945. The land reform in the north and persecution of alleged pro-Japanese elements meant that many well-to-do northerners fled to the south. Later, the violent antireligious campaigns of the communist regime alienated many Christians of all social classes, not merely the elites (in fact, Christianity had been prominent in the anti-Japanese nationalist movement, especially in the early years of colonialism, and Kim Il-sung himself came from a Christian family). The total number of prewar refugees from North Korea is unknown, but a reasonable estimate is approximately one million, or roughly 10 percent of the entire North Korean population. With the fluctuations of war, inevitably, the number of people either forced or choosing to abandon their homes increased dramatically. In March 1951, when the number of the displaced in South Korea reached its height, it was suggested that 5.8 million people, or one out of every five Koreans, was a refugee. Thus both before and during the early war years, moving in search of security was simply a fact of civilian life.

Evacuation of civilians from Seoul and its surroundings had been a chaotic free-for-all at the outbreak of war, but through late December 1950 and early January 1951, nearly all the local population was moved by the United Nations away from the advancing communist armies. This was one of the largest waves of refugees in the history of the war—but also one of the best organized. Yet, during this evacuation, the refugees relied on the train network. These were not comfortable passenger cars but cargo vans, heavily overcrowded and with people often riding on the roof. Those who failed to find a toehold on the trains had to walk, carrying only as much as they could bear. Before the war, the average birthrate was six children per woman. This meant that many Korean women had to carry their small children instead of any kind of household item. In the

Refugees: Taedong River bridge, Pyŏngyang. (U.S. National Archives, 111-SC-355225.)

first year of war it was not unusual for a family to walk the entire length of the Korean peninsula, from Sinŭiju, close to the Chinese border in the north, all the way down to Korea's southernmost city, Pusan, a distance of over 1,000 kilometers. Refugees often collapsed from exhaustion, hunger, and fear, and a corpse on the roadside was a normal sight in the summer and autumn of 1950.

From mid-1950, Pusan acted as the provisional capital of the R.O.K. and took over from Seoul as the center of political, social, and economic life for almost the entire length of the Korean War. On July 27, 1950, the R.O.K. parliament met there, holding its first session in a makeshift tent. Soon it was followed by other national institutions. Excepting the brief return of government to Seoul during the initial U.N. occupation, Pusan was to remain the working center of administration until the cessation of hostilities. The cabinet took over the building of the provincial government, while the parliament (with presumably unintended irony about the nature of modern politics) occupied the city's largest movie theater. President Syngman Rhee and his family resided in the mansion of the local governor (another vestige of Japanese colonialism, the mansion was originally built for the Japanese governor of South Kyongsang province in 1926).

A survey conducted in February 1951 showed that Pusan was now a crowded home to approximately half a million refugees.[7] Many of them had just arrived following the second occupation of Seoul by the communist forces (smaller cities along the southern coast of Korea took many other refugees at this time). Its southerly position means that Pusan is a relatively warm city; in winter the air temperature seldom goes below the freezing point. However, the refugees still needed to be housed in some kind of solid structure. This meant that all public buildings, including churches, schools, and factories, were emptied to serve as temporary shelters. Despite this, there were a few refugees who, having believed they had finally found safety, froze to death in the winter months of 1950–1951.

One of the major challenges was supplying the refugees with drinkable water. The city's water supply had been built in the 1930s to provide for just 300,000 inhabitants (one-fifth of the actual total in 1951–1953), and by 1950, the system had not been repaired for over a decade. Some of the able-bodied male refugees saw this as an employment opportunity and began to deliver water from distant pumps and wells to the better-off houses, eateries, and other places. A water vendor, equipped with two large buckets, usually made of used oil drums, was a typical figure on the narrow alleys of wartime Pusan. A term that is still vividly remembered in Korea is *Pukch'ong mul changsu* (a water vendor from Pukch'ong). This city in North Korea produced an unusually large number of the water vendors in Pusan, who, according to a popular (and partially correct) myth, were working mainly to earn money for their children's education. The shortage of water for many people, however, also led to other dangers: Epidemics in crowded quarters were an ever-present threat, and fires, which might otherwise have been extinguished, regularly devastated the refugee camps. To combat the various threats to public health and safety, the authorities relied on large-scale information campaigns: Posters on the walls reminded people of the danger of epidemics, exhorted everyone to take care over personal hygiene, and asked them to take all necessary precautions against outbreaks of fire. The disinfectant known as DDT was also widely used in public places, such as schools.

Refugees who initially lived in tents and dugouts eventually began to establish more permanent shelters for themselves. They used any kind of material that was available. By the end of the war, there were some 40,000 makeshift dwellings in Pusan stitched together from corrugated iron, discarded planks, and plywood. The boxes for U.S. Army rations provided one of the most common types of building material. These houses were crowded to the extreme: Typically, a family of five to seven members lived in a dwelling of 10 square meters, and greater densities were not unknown.

The refugees made their living by small commerce or through casual work, sometimes of a very unconventional nature. Among other things, people gathered floating wood from the sea, dried it, and then sold it as firewood; collected old cans or drums and made them into pieces of metal for use in constructing makeshift houses; or gathered edible waste discarded near the military bases and used it for cooking. These dishes served in the refugee canteens were sometimes called "U.N. stew" but more frequently were known as *kkulkkul-i chuk,* or "pigs' soup."

There were more conventional activities as well. Refugees worked as porters and manual laborers, ran food stalls, or looked for jobs in still-functioning industries. Many of these people were skilled workers and technicians, but there was often no demand for their expertise. Instead, South Korean industry was hindered by the fact that colonial Japan in the 1930s had industrialized the north and kept the south for agriculture. Thus during the war, what little there was of industry in South Korea generally came to a complete standstill. Jobs were scarce, so every morning, queues grew in front of places where there might be some chance of casual work. Any job at the U.N. military base was a dream for many but a reality for very few. In the midst of this dislocation and distress, it was inevitable that some men turned to violent crime or joined gangs, but these did not constitute a serious problem in wartime cities. Small theft, however, remained a common nuisance (a popular saying in Seoul after the war was "if you close your eyes, someone will steal your nose!").

With the loss of jobs, homes, and possessions as well as relatives killed in this massively destructive war, many ordinary people had to rely on humanitarian aid. Much of this was coming from overseas, but the inefficiency of the government bureaucracy as well as rampant corruption made orderly and fair distribution difficult. As an alternative and more reliable source, those without contacts in government or business looked to the Christian churches of all denominations. Although Christian believers were to expand massively in number after the war and, in 1950, only about one percent of the people were practicing Christians, many Korean church groups had long-established connections with congregations in the United States and thus were able both to appeal directly for aid and to take a prominent role in ensuring this reached the people who needed it most. Among the general chaos and social disruption of four years of war, the Christian groups retained a remarkable degree of cohesion based, no doubt, on the strength of their religious faith and the sense that keeping together in war was the highest test of an individual and a community. It would appear that to be a member of one of the Christian churches was an enormous advantage for refugees in surviving the war.

The Confucian tradition of social duty, however, also helped to ease the trauma of dislocation. Thus local village communities naturally turned to their wealthier members to shoulder greater responsibility for those displaced by war. As a result, refugees often took over larger houses in the southern regions, frequently with the approval of the house owners.

The war greatly damaged family life. Men often had to leave their families behind, either because they were drafted to one of the fighting armies or because they were fleeing political persecution. Women were left alone to take care both of their children and, following an old Confucian custom, their elder in-laws (in many cases, women lived with their parents-in-law if the latter were still alive). Survival was hard enough for men, but it was even tougher for women. To get food every day, they first sold or bartered their cloth and all nonessential family belongings and then looked for some job. Few of the women had any marketable skills, so most jobs available to them were as unskilled workers or household servants.

The pressures of war and the presence of foreign troops also encouraged prostitution. The U.N. army barracks soon were surrounded by shantytowns inhabited by all kinds of uprooted people. They housed many young women who survived through prostitution but also through doing chores for the soldiers, like laundering, pressing, or mending clothes. These campside shantytowns also attracted pimps and small entrepreneurs, who opened bars, dance halls, and shops catering to the soldiers and prostitutes. One byproduct of camp prostitution was the spread of biracial children, who were rejected by the monoethnic Korean society and who, in the immediate postwar years, were mostly adopted by overseas foster parents.

Prostitution was not limited to serving the foreign troops (although this was where the earnings were greatest). The barracks of the South Korean forces and the major centers of refugee camps attracted prostitutes as well. This was the case also in wartime Seoul; the neighborhood of Chongryangli railway station became a marketplace for commercial sex around 1952. This was when the station began to serve as the terminal for all trains heading east along the frontline. Most of these trains were carrying soldiers to their positions. Faced with the prospect of coming under fire, these men were willing customers, and many girls from villages hit by starvation flocked to Chŏngryangli to earn enough money to survive.

The heavy death toll of males on the frontlines produced a new society of widows and orphans. According to data from 1957, there were 550,000 war widows in South Korea at that time, mostly wives of soldiers and policemen killed in action between 1950 and 1953. Of these women, only a fraction, that is, 34,000, were living by themselves; all the others were forced to take care of relatives—not only their own children, but also elderly parents or parents-in-law as well as younger siblings. This meant that over 900,000 people were members of households headed by widows. In getting through the war and the postwar years, these women had to be exceptionally strong; their prospects were bleak in that Korea, like so many largely agrarian societies, had not valued education for women, and of all these war widows, no more than 640 (or 0.1 percent of the total) had college tuition, while approximately half of them had never regularly attended any school.[8]

Having said that, one of the undeniable achievements of South Korean society in the war years was its ability to sustain and even develop education. Among children of school age, nearly 70 percent attended primary school, even in 1951, the most difficult of the war years, and the level increased to nearly three-quarters in 1953. Indeed, one of the most common memories of ordinary people from the war is the provisional school, often operated under the open sky or inside a large army tent (when such a luxury was available). In 1950–1951, a school was usually nothing but a fenced-off yard. Students sat on the ground, while the teacher stood or sat in front of them. Several classes were held on the yard simultaneously. The number of students in a classroom could be 100, with only one textbook for every five children. Learning was also hindered by severe shortages of pencils and paper. Still, classes continued, and in most cases, one constant and insistent theme in the wartime lives of children was being told by their parents to study hard.

University education was a relatively new phenomenon for Korea: Prior to 1945, there was only one university in the entire country (originally created by the Japanese authorities in the 1920s). Throughout the late 1940s, several new universities were opened, although largely by means of upgrading existing junior colleges and even high schools. In early 1951, the South Korean universities established four joint wartime campuses, and from September 1951, the major tertiary institutions were sufficiently confident to operate their own provisional campuses. Class numbers increased greatly, not least because male students were exempted from the draft. Women remained a small minority: Of 27,542 students enrolled in 1952, only 3,958 were female. This proportion for women, however, did not differ greatly from the pre-1950 level and was not to improve significantly until the late 1960s.

In contrast to the radical student movement in South Korea of later decades, most of those studying at college in 1950–1953 were right-wing and anticommunist. Under Rhee, various youth organizations were established, and membership was, in effect, obligatory. These organizations were responsible for ideological indoctrination and also provided noisy support during progovernment rallies. Photographs of teenage girls insisting on the need to fight to the death against communism were regular features of propaganda and often appeared in the overseas media. Yet it would be inaccurate to say that the students were merely being manipulated. In the context of the north's invasion and the subsequent destructiveness of the war, their anticommunist convictions were undoubtedly genuine.

One thing to note about wartime South Korea is that once the active hostilities moved north in the spring of 1951, life became routine as people waited for the war to end. The threat of famine and shortages of basic supplies were never far away, but unlike Koreans in the north, the chance of a violent death for civilians was minimal. This sense of a sphere of peace within the war allowed for the return of some forms of leisure. Cabaret shows catered for the better-off; the less affluent could go to the movies, where the films were overwhelmingly American. Mass forms of entertainment were obviously more affordable for the ordinary people. Very few had the money to dine in restaurants, but individuals could relax in the teahouses (actually, though they were called "teahouses," they generally served instant coffee diverted through the black market from U.N. bases or from Japan). In wartime Pusan, there were teahouses patronized by small-time businessmen, others frequented by journalists, and still others popular with writers and artists. In this way, civilians were able to create havens and use socializing and relaxation to deal with the stresses of war.

NORTH AND SOUTH: THE ROUTINIZATION OF VIOLENCE

Politicized violence was common in wartime Seoul and other major cities. As early as July 1950, the more important of the suspected class enemies of communism were placed before open show trials; this was in accordance with the contemporary Chinese model. In Seoul, these trials were staged in the downtown area, usually in the square near the city's cultural center and not far from the city hall. Most of the defendants were people who had played some role in Rhee's government. Proceedings consisted of heavy doses of Stalinist-Maoist rhetoric and ended with a death sentence, which was greeted by loud cries from the crowd. In some cases the victim was shot on the spot. In the case of Kim Ki-jin, however, formerly a prominent leftist writer and tried in 1950 as a traitor, the executioners failed to do their job properly; although he was shot, he survived, and later, regaining consciousness, was able to crawl away. Overall, however, this brutalization of the city street produced a lasting impression on many witnesses.

Yet it was in the countryside where political persecution could, on occasion, take its most violent and indiscriminate form. Broadly speaking, the overall impact of war on civilian life in the countryside was less pronounced than on the cities. Most Korean farmers were self-sufficient and had little need for interaction with the strategically important population centers. Contacts between urbanites and villagers increased in 1950 through bartering, but after 1950, such exchanges became rare as international food aid began to arrive. Being dispersed rather than concentrated in a town or city also gave villagers some hope of avoiding hostilities. However, when there was fighting in the countryside, murder and terror were commonplace. Both armies employed guerrilla tactics and encouraged the use of terror against their opponents. Dramatic changes of the military situation also created favorable conditions for settling political and personal scores. Thus those identified as suspicious persons were often summarily executed. Local militias, both of the left and right, ran amok, and the official forces of both rival governments ignored the legal niceties. Murders committed by one side led to a desire for revenge by the other, and in this way the cycle of violence became entrenched. An independent South Korean commission early in the twenty-first century investigated some wartime massacres. It concluded that about 200,000 civilians were killed between 1946 and 1953 as a result of insurgencies and arbitrary executions; in its report, most of these were described as victims of the South Korean government forces.[9] In the countryside, therefore, the way to survive was to learn swiftly which way the wind was blowing. As one South Korean officer wrote of villagers in his memoirs, "Through hard experience, they learned that it is wise to be on the victorious side."[10]

One of the groups in society least able to defend themselves were those already under arrest. The first months of the war were marked by large-scale slaughters of prisoners by both retreating armies. In South Korea the most infamous massacre of this kind took place early in July at Tae-jon prison. This held many political prisoners. As the communist army approached the city, R.O.K. police trucks arrived at the prison every evening, loaded up with prisoners, and drove to the mountain forests. There trenches were prepared, the prisoners were shot, and their bodies were pushed into the trenches. Within just a few days the police murdered at least 1,800 men.[11]

Taejŏn massacre was far from unique. In July and August 1950, political prisoners were killed in many places across South Korea at the first signs of the communist advance. Many, or perhaps even most of those executed were not active enemies of the R.O.K. regime. Their crime might simply have been participation in a communist-led industrial strike or nothing more than a few badly chosen words addressed to a local policeman. One thing the executioners clearly did not do was discriminate.

While, numerically, many of the murdered civilians were victims of the South Korean official and unofficial forces, the North Korean authorities, in essence, acted no differently. As the U.N. army advanced rapidly on Pyŏngyang in October 1950, so the North Korean government summarily executed all of its political prisoners in the city's jails. These included people who were innocent even by the extremely dubious standards of Stalinist justice. The victims were dragged to nearby air defense shelters and shot or were machine-gunned in the vicinity of the prisons. About 2,000 people were killed in Pyŏngyang between October 10 and 15. Similar killings took place in other major North Korean cities.

In addition to outright violence, another feature of wartime life was the presence of political terror. During their occupation of the south, the North Korean armies attempted to impose a full-fledged Stalinist regime of surveillance and exposure. The local authorities followed the Stalinist tradition of setting quotas for the number of class enemies to be unmasked in any particular district. Everybody who collaborated with

Rhee's government (that is, anyone who worked at any government institution), or had even a small business, could be branded a "reactionary element." In order to show one's loyalty to the regime, it became necessary to inform on others; it also served as a form of self-defense, that is, denounce others before they denounced you. As in the countryside, this climate of fear gave free rein to personal animosities.

Government persecution often appeared to be random. This was a deliberate technique to keep everyone living in a climate of uncertainty. Thus the local communist authorities might arrest an old farmer who had been a village elder under Rhee's government, or a local herbal healer who happened to be affluent by village standards, or just an ordinary worker from Seoul whose only crime was to be a stranger in the area (these examples are real, and these arrests took place in a village with a population of less than 100 families). An arrested class enemy was generally never again seen alive.

When R.O.K. forces retook control of an area, they did not differ much in their willingness to exterminate the enemy. The spirit of the times is expressed by a former right-wing militiaman who recently said in a TV interview, "We had to kill the Reds, had to kill! Why? If [we] did not kill one bastard, he would kill 10 of us later. Thus, we'll lose 10 or 20 of our people by leaving just one [of them] alive. So we had to kill. If the person was Red, we had to kill."[12] No doubt this attitude was shared by the communist forces, and neither side tried overly hard to determine their victim's real politics.

One of the areas in which townspeople and villagers alike lived with a sense of trepidation was in forced mobilizations to the army. These were widely practiced by both sides, but it seems that the communists, less corrupt and better organized, were more efficient in rounding up men and putting them in uniform. The first of these mobilizations during the war years took place on July 1, 1950: The North Korean government decreed that all men aged between 18 and 36 could be called to arms at any time. Since the existence of South Korea as a separate entity was not recognized (it was considered "a territory illegally occupied by the U.S."), this general mobilization law applied to North and South Koreans alike.

A large-scale mobilization was then launched in August 1950. To distinguish between the regular North Korean army and new forces hastily drafted in the south, the latter were called *ŭiyŏnggun*, or "Army of Righteous Heroes." Despite the rhetoric, and apart from a minority of left-wing volunteers, in most cases these men were very reluctant heroes. The mobilization was modeled after the Soviet pattern, much harsher than its American or West European counterparts. In Sihŭng county, for example, the quota required of the authorities was 3,050 draftees. Since the total male population of the county, young and old, was only 6,591, this meant that virtually every man between 18 and 36 years of age would have to fight and risk death or injury.[13] Sihŭng county was not an exception, and thus the composition of villages in South Korea as well as in the north was fundamentally altered by the manpower demands of war.

One of the inevitable consequences of forced mobilizations was that men in uniform looked for ways of escape. By early August, many North Korean units included a large number of South Korean draftees. Unlike the skilled and well-trained North Korean troops, these fresh recruits often did not know how to shoot a rifle, panicked under fire, and hence were killed in droves. Those who survived were also the first to desert when the North Korean armed forces began to disintegrate in the last days of September. So, for many of those so-called volunteers, their military service lasted for just a few weeks, after which they became civilians again—often doing their best to avoid being drafted to the R.O.K. forces. Indeed, facing a permanent shortage of military recruits, the R.O.K. authorities created police teams whose task was to hunt down adult males. Thus for the young and middle-aged civilian males across Korea's towns and villages, fear remained a part of everyday existence throughout the war years.

PYŎNGYANG: LIFE IN THE WASTELAND

As with South Korea, moving was a part of prewar and wartime life in North Korea. This movement included an influx of differing peoples from the south. Before 1950, some communist sympathizers in the south of the peninsula fled from Rhee's far right government. In mid-September 1950, after the U.N. landing at Inch'on, many South Koreans who had worked with the communist administration also decided to flee to the north. Some of them were driven by a sincere political commitment: They hoped to continue the fight for a cause in which they passionately believed. However, most were people who were afraid of being vilified as collaborators and punished.

Among the arrivals from the south were those either opposed to communism or generally indifferent to politics. Thus from August 1950, the communist government in Seoul began sending a large number of South Koreans northward. In some cases these were prominent members of the old elite, such as politicians and journalists who were being isolated from their supporters; in others they were skilled workers or soldiers who were drafted into Kim Il-sung's army and then moved to the north with their units. It is impossible to distinguish between voluntary and forced migration, and all available statistics must be treated with caution. However, the claim of the South Korean government in the 1950s was that about 88,000 people were sent to the north around this time.

Compared to the south, North Korea, by 1950, had become a better organized society, but the level of social control was also much tighter there. Indeed, the presence of Soviet advisers meant that the control system of what might be called mature Stalinism was implanted in Korea, and a sort of quasi-Stalinist state emerged. Yet in recovering from the humiliation of colonization by Japan, strict policies and tight regulations were often supported by many Koreans. The KWP—the local incarnation of the typical Leninist party—was the only political force that mattered, but it was also respected as a disciplined, structured, and cohesive body, completely subordinate to the will of its leadership. Its ranks were swelled with young and ambitious people who were driven by a mixture of ambition and idealism and who accepted the party's nationalist and socialist goals more or less unconditionally. Youth such as these ensured that the North Korean army possessed high morale; their ideological faith made them fierce soldiers. The mix of ideology and war also made them able to treat their enemies with remarkable brutality; equally, it meant that they often became the primary targets of terror or violence from the South Korean and U.N. forces seeking to eliminate the north's most committed fighters.

Of course, not all North Korean officials were ideologically committed to communism. For some, communism was simply the government around them, and so they tried to find the best place for themselves within the existing system. In fact, when the North Korean state fell apart in October 1950, most KWP members got rid of their party ID cards. This was in defiance of one of the important myths of Stalinist communism: A good party member was supposed to protect the ID card at all times. Nonetheless, an investigation in 1951 showed that in some northern counties, more than 80 percent of all KWP members were unable to produce their cards following the brief period of South Korean occupation: Those who had discarded their IDs knew that being identified as a party member by the R.O.K. forces was equivalent to a death sentence.

For those civilians of North Korea who were not heavily involved with the communist regime, the arrival of the southerners was a mixed blessing. Their cities were no longer targeted by U.S. bombing, and they could count on some much-needed food being distributed. The members of persecuted groups, including Christians, naturally welcomed the southerners as liberators. However, it is also clear that there was little support among northerners for Syngman Rhee, and the use of terror by incoming R.O.K. troops simply alienated many ordinary people.

On October 30, 1950, the people of Pyŏngyang got their first direct look at Syngman Rhee when he visited their city. He delivered a speech to a crowd that gathered in front of the city hall and even briefly mixed with the people. This was a brave act since the war was not over, and there remained the chance of assassination. What the visit was meant to symbolize, however, was that the North Korean state had ceased to exist, and its territory was now under the control of the republican government in Seoul.

Despite Rhee's bravado, the South Korean occupation did not last long. In a sense the new system was never established since most parts of the north were under South Korean control for less than two months. This was long enough, however, to spawn local right-wing militia groups, which began hastily to execute alleged communist collaborators. In just a few weeks' time, however, it was the turn of the militiamen to run away or face certain death at the hands of the returning communists. The large-scale Chinese offense ended the short northern rule of Rhee's administration by December 1950.

Soon afterward, the frontline stabilized, more or less along the same line where the war had begun. A prolonged period of trench warfare ensued, and this meant that there was relative stability for ordinary people in the rear of both parts of the country. By late 1951, the North Korean bureaucracy had recovered, and even strengthened, its control over society. North Korea emerged from the war as a classical Stalinist state. Closely following on the experience of Stalin's Soviet Union, the regime created an extensive network of supposedly voluntary wartime organizations for mobilization. At the top was the KWP, which, by the end of the war, included nearly 10 percent of the entire population. The Democratic Youth Union was another major association; its members included most North Koreans aged 15–25. This network reached every household, and in the course of time the state's control over daily life increased enormously, despite the widespread destruction of the urban landscape.

As a result, civilian life in North Korea became more orderly and predictable than in the south. At the same time, individuals had less chance to defy official orders. Unlike the south, where draft dodging remained common until the end of the hostilities, in North Korea it soon became impossible for any able-bodied male to avoid military service. The demands of war reached all levels of the people: Those who stayed behind—largely women, children, and old men—were frequently subjected to labor mobilization campaigns. Indeed, in 1953, foreign diplomats in the north were shocked to see girls aged 13 operating sophisticated and dangerous machinery in the factories.

While in the south the switch to trench warfare meant that civilians were generally out of immediate danger, the situation in the north was very different: A large proportion of its civilian population was killed in 1951–1953. For the north this was a time of intense and relentless bombing. In this regard, South Koreans were lucky since the U.N. air superiority spared them from any serious threat of aerial attack. The U.S. command hoped that large-scale bombing raids would undermine the war-making capabilities of North Korea. However, this strategy was entirely misconceived as the North Korean and Chinese forces employed Soviet and Chinese weapons; the North Koreans were responsible only for transportation. The number of victims of these bombing campaigns will never be known. The estimated losses for the north vary greatly; the best available estimate is 1.3 million North Koreans dead after three years of bloodshed. These figures include some 300,000–500,000 military casualties, but most of the victims were civilians, largely victims of bombing. This meant that one out of seven North Koreans was killed during the war.

North Korean civilians after U.N. bombing: Sinŭiju, 1951. (Russian state archives of photo and cinematic documents, 1-7677.)

As a result of intense bombing, most North Korean cities were transformed into piles of rubble. In Pyŏngyang, virtually no prewar building survived intact, and most structures were destroyed completely. All major industrial towns and railway stations were flattened as well. Those people who stayed in the city had to live in trenches, dugouts, or, less securely, in tents. Often a family had to survive in a shelter that they dug in the backyard of their home. However, the majority of urban dwellers were relocated to the countryside. Most important state institutions were also scattered across the country for safety. These included the north's major institute of learning, Kim Il Sung University, which was moved to a mountain area and continued its classes; the academically most gifted of students were even recalled from the trenches in order to further their education. Thus in the north as in the south, education both continued and even advanced during the war years. However, for those serving in government institutions, relocation could mean the division of the family, with only the necessary personnel going along and being housed in dorms or dugouts with a strict routine modeled on that of an army barracks. Thus the movement of the population and facilities added to the separation of family members in wartime.

The North Korean answer to the bombing was a large-scale program of underground fortifications. This program was made possible by the government's ability to organize civilians into labor teams; it was this manual labor that did most of the work, working long shifts and equipped with no more than the most basic tools. Young people were worked especially hard. The North Koreans built elaborate underground facilities, which included military installations, munitions plants, and barracks The North Korean government headquarters were housed in the system of underground tunnels and shelters deep under the Morangbong Hill in Pyŏngyang. In these subterranean cities, there were also cultural centers, like the underground theater in Pyŏngyang, which provided entertainment and also served as a venue for official events. The government strove to provide entertainment for its people, but this always had to be "healthy" and ideologically sound. Many of the movies were brought from the Soviet Union and dealt with stories of patriotic sacrifice, but there were also musicals and fairy tales. Around the country, the films were shown in tent theaters, easily assembled and then dismantled.

In addition to constructing underground worlds, North Korean civilians were also routinely used as nighttime workers above ground. One of the key jobs in keeping the north in the war was the constant repair of transportation facilities, above all, the railway tracks. The U.S. air forces specially targeted the railways in order to disrupt supply lines. During the daytime, U.S. pilots had no trouble destroying the tracks. However, every night, the North Korean authorities were able to send out civilian work teams and repair the damage. Where gaps in the transport network existed, civilians were also often drafted to work as porters, moving heavy loads on their backs where no train or truck could be used.

The relative efficiency of the restored North Korean bureaucracy also made possible a comprehensive distribution system, which has remained a part of North Korean life ever since. More or less all urban residents during the war were receiving rations of grain and basic foodstuffs; this, after all, was essential if they were to meet the labor demands of the government. Farmers were supposed to survive on whatever was left to them after obligatory purchases of their produce by the state. However, a high-level official in the north estimated in the spring of 1953 that over one-quarter of the rural population was starving.[14] As in the south, there was no real class equality in wartime: Officials received far more generous rations than the commoners. For the average man or woman, rations were meager, but the authorities at least guaranteed subsistence for the majority. Still, the lack of medicine and basic necessities remained a major problem. Wartime mortality was high, not only because of air raids, but also because of the disintegration of sanitary services. Throughout the war, one needed special contacts as a civilian to be admitted to a hospital, which were intended for the military only. The best medicines were also reserved for the army, and so such things as antibiotics were difficult to obtain. Tuberculosis (TB) was a major killer of civilians and soldiers alike; some 250,000 soldiers were believed to be infected with this disease in 1953 (there were only five military specialists in the treatment of TB at the time and probably fewer among the civilian population). In late 1953, a North Korean physician told a foreign diplomat that more people had died of TB in the past half year than on the battlefront.[15]

Thus for North Korean civilians the proverbial holes of escape were only temporary and partial shelters. The war rained down on their heads through the daytime, and they worked through the night to repair what had been destroyed. They lived in the ground to avoid the immediate threat from the air, and they struggled with hunger and disease. They were separated from their families, either by distance, following some kind of relocation, or forever, following the enormous death toll. Throughout they were under the increasingly powerful direction of a state that made enormous political capital, then and for decades after, out of its genuine ability to survive all that the forces of capitalism could throw against it.

EPILOGUE

On July 27, 1953, the Chinese, North Korean, and American generals signed an armistice treaty; this was not a declaration of peace but merely a cessation of conflict. It meant that Koreans on both sides of the 38th parallel were to live with the threat of renewed war thereafter, and thus civilian life was never again to be fully separated from war.

Until the early 1990s, politics and administration in both North and South Korea were dominated by people who had experienced the war, often as civilians, and still harbored wartime bitterness. Most of the people who died during the war were civilians. Many of these in the south were killed by acts of terror and, in the north, by air raids. The memory of the war's brutality, often revived and manipulated for political purposes, has not disappeared to this day. This bitterness is one of the factors obstructing reconciliation between the two states.

The refugees have long adapted to their new homes. However, the mass exodus of the politically restive population actually helped the enduring stability of both regimes. Without the large-scale refugee movements of 1945–1951, the North Korean state would not have been so devoid of internal opposition. In the south the arrival of desperate refugees contributed to the rigid conservatism of politics (even though the man at the top might be replaced, as with Rhee in 1960). After the mass killings on both sides, opposition was either eliminated or terrorized into silence. Thus the impact of the war on civilians in Korea, north and south, reached deep and long into their political, cultural, and daily lives.

NOTES

1. Kim Tong-ch'un, "Hankuk chonchaeng-ŭi misichŏk punsok. Sŏul simin-kwa hankuk chŏnchaeng: Chanliu, tokang, p'inan [Microanalysis of the Korean War. Seoul Population and the Korean War: Staying at Place, Crossing a River, Fleeing]," *Yŏksa pip'yŏng* (summer, 2000): 45–46.

2. Chŏn Sang-in, "6.25 chŏnchaeng-ŭi sahoesa: Sŏul simin-ŭi 6.25 chŏnchaeng [Social History of the Korean War: Seoul Population and the Korean War]," in *Hankuk-kwa 6.25 chŏnchaeng* (Seoul: Yonsei University Press, 2000), 187–88.

3. The most recent publication of this document is Kim Sŏng-ch'il, *Yŏksa ap'esŏ* (Seoul: Ch'a-pi, 2005).

4. Kim 2005: 92.

5. Kim 2005: 95.

6. Son Chŏng-mok, *Hankuk tosi 60 nyŏn-ŭi iyaki* [The 60-Year Story of Korean Cities], vol. 1 (Seoul: Hanul, 2005), 70.

7. *Chung-gu chi* [Description of the Pusan Central District] (Pusan, Korea: Pusan Chung-gu office, 1990), 264.

8. *20 seki yŏsŏng sakŏn sa* [The History of Female-Related Incidents in the 20th Century] (Seoul: Yŏsŏng sa, 2001), 124.

9. *Korea Times*, 11 January 2005.

10. Paek Sŏn-yŏp, *Kun-kwa na: 6.25 chŏnchaeng-ŭi kirok* [Army and Me: A Memoir of the Korean War] (Seoul: Taeryuk yŏnguso, 1989), 233.

11. For the most recent research of the Taegu massacre and other similar events, see Pak Myŏng-rim, *Hankuk 1950: Chŏnchaeng-kwa pyŏnghwa* [Korea 1950: War and Peace] (Seoul: Nanam, 2002), 320–27.

12. Interview for the MBS TV company, cited in Yi Sin-sh'ŏl, "6.25 nampuk chŏnchaeng sigi ipuk chiyŏk-esŏ-ŭi minganin haksal [The Massacres of Civilians in the Northern Part of the Country during the North-South War from June 25]," *Yŏksa-wa hyŏnsil* 4 (2004): 154.

13. Pak Myŏng-rim 2002: 211.

14. Balazs Szalontaii, *Kim Il Sung in the Khrushchev Era* (Stanford, CA: Stanford University Press, 2006), 44.

15. Szalontaii 2006: 44.

SELECTED BIBLIOGRAPHY

Cumings, Bruce. *Korea's Place in the Sun: A Modern History.* Rev. ed. New York: W. W. Norton, 2005.
    Cumings is one of the major historians of modern Korea. In this book, written for a general audience, he offers an excellent summary of the events that led to the Korean War and its impact on the subsequent history of the country.
Goldstein, Donald M., and Harry J. Maihafer. *The Korean War: The Story and Photographs.* Washington, DC: Brassey's, 2000.

A collection of wartime photos. It covers both military operations and civilian life.

Lee, Ho-chul. *Southerners, Northerners.* Translated by Andrew Killick and Cho Sukyeon. Norwalk, CT: EastBridge, 2004.

Based on true events, this is a fictionalized account of life in Korea before and during the war.

Ottoboni, Fred. *Korea between the Wars: A Soldier's Story.* Sparks, NV: Vincente Books, 1997.

An eyewitness account of life in Korea in the late 1940s.

Peters, Richard, and Xiaobing Li. *Voices from the Korean War: Personal Stories of American, Korean, and Chinese Soldiers.* Lexington: University Press of Kentucky, 2005.

A collection of memoirs from soldiers of all the major armies, with some references to the lives of the civilian population.

Riley, John W., Jr., Wilbur Schramm, and Frederick W. Williams. "Flight from Communism: A Report on Korean Refugees." *Public Opinion Quarterly* 15 (1951): 274–86.

An early field study of refugees in Korea, it provides a valuable contemporary understanding of the problems.

Stueck, William. *Rethinking the Korean War: A New Diplomatic and Strategic History.* Princeton, NJ: Princeton University Press, 2002.

Accounts of the Korean War are numerous. This is recommended as one of the most up-to-date and one that makes good use of newly available sources.

West, Philip, and Suh Ji-moon, eds. *Remembering the "Forgotten War": The Korean War through Literature and Art.* Armonk, NY: M. E. Sharpe, 2001.

Articles dealing with the perception and memory of the war, both by the military and by civilians.

IN KOREAN

Hanguk-kwa 6.25 Chonjaeng [Korea and the Korean War]. Seoul: Yonsei University Press, 2002.

A collection of articles dealing with the impact of the war on the society and daily life of South Korea.

FILMS (WITH ENGLISH SUBTITLES)

Spring in My Hometown. Directed by Yi Kwang-mo. South Korea, 1998.

A drama about life as experienced by a Korean teenage boy growing up in the early 1950s in a rural town.

Taegukgi [Korean Banner]. Directed by Kang Jegyu. South Korea, 2004.

A fair and unbiased view of the painful choices faced by Korean youth in wartime.

EIGHT

Remembering Life in Urban South Vietnam, circa 1965–1975

Stewart Lone

One of the things that stands out in memories of people from South Vietnam is that war was always a fact of daily life. World War II brought occupation of Vietnam by the Japanese forces; the end of that war saw the return of French colonialism and, with it, the war of independence between 1946 and 1954; and soon after that, the civil war erupted, fought largely in the rural areas of South Vietnam by the government forces and the communist guerrillas, or what came to be called the Vietcong. The civil war then expanded from 1965 with the influx of U.S. ground troops and a vastly greater scale of destruction of life, land, and property, especially within the south (where the U.S. military dropped six times as many bombs as on North Vietnam). By 1969, there were about one million South Vietnamese men in the Army of the Republic of Vietnam, with another half million largely very young and very inexperienced American forces in the country. In 1969, U.S. president Richard Nixon made a unilateral announcement that the U.S. military presence in Vietnam would be reduced and a greater responsibility for fighting this greatly inflated war would be handed over to the South Vietnamese government; this was part of a wider change in U.S. policy in Asia under what was known as the Nixon Doctrine. As American troops withdrew, the regular North Vietnamese military began to see an opportunity for victory; in March 1972, North Vietnamese units, with tanks and heavy artillery, launched an all-out offensive into South Vietnam. This was repelled, but an invasion in 1975, following the impeachment of Nixon and, with it, a radical

reduction in U.S. support for Saigon, was successful. Thus in total, South
Vietnam was either at war or on the edge of war for 35 years. During this
time, entire generations were born and matured into adulthood.

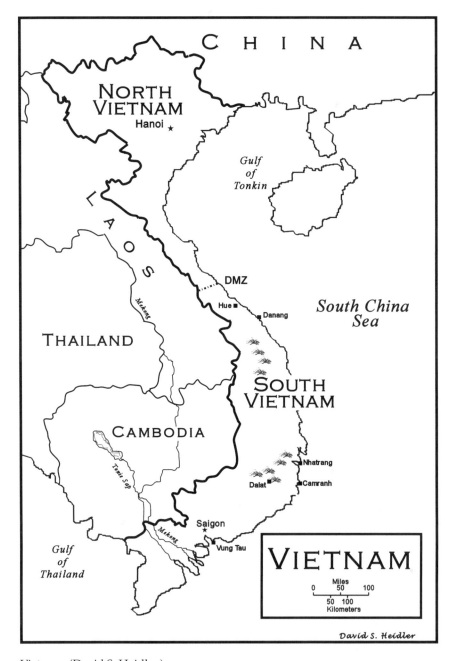

Vietnam. (David S. Heidler.)

The first thing one would notice upon waking in Saigon City in the 1960s was the noise. This was not the noise of war, of trucks moving or soldiers marching, nor of government rallies and propaganda. Instead, from about 5:00 A.M. onward, there would be the tumult of street vendors. These vendors were almost entirely women; they had risen much earlier to prepare the food that they carried in two baskets balanced on a pole across their shoulders. There were vendors, among other things, of noodles, of sticky rice (wrapped in a banana leaf to make it easier to eat), and of French breads. The vendors all headed toward the main marketplace, but customers, either on their way to work or those, such as street cleaners, returning home from a night shift, would stop them along the way and purchase breakfast. For the vendor the first sale was the most important; this was the sign of good luck for the rest of the day, so any customer who called over a vendor was then morally obligated to buy, whether or not he liked the look of what he saw. Such breakfasts might be consumed in the street, at home, or at the workplace. The noise was intense because of the number of people on the move, not because the women fought to be heard (they had no need to shout with so many customers around). Unless you lived among the quiet suburbs of the elite by the river, it was the sound track to which many city dwellers rose to greet the day. For many in the cities it was also the reassuring hum of modern life, compared with the unsettling stillness of the countryside.

Increasingly, from the 1960s, there was another noise also. This was the growl of machine-driven traffic. Changes in the sound of movement arose not so much because of the war, but rather because of the worldwide greater availability of small, inexpensive motor vehicles. Before the 1960s, urban traffic in Vietnam consisted mainly of bicycles. This was the most common form of transport, and the bicycle was an important family possession—there might only be one to a family. The prized makes were French, and French influence was still obvious in the popularity of cycling as a sport, not least in the national cycle race, the Tour d'Indochine, modeled on the Tour de France. The cheapest and best-used taxis, known as "cyclo," were also bicycles, with a carriage for perhaps two passengers; in the western provinces, where it was actually called *xe loi* rather than cyclo, the carriage was fitted to the back of the cycle, and so one sat behind the driver, but in Saigon, it was placed at the front, which made the passenger feel like he was in a dodgem car as he was hurried through the crowded streets.

In the 1960s, there were more taxicabs on the roads of the cities; these were almost entirely French-made Renault compacts, painted in the same two patriotic tones of blue and yellow. While the fares were relatively expensive, making the cabs largely the preserve of businessmen and officials, there were at least 700 professional cab drivers in Saigon by 1968. Private vehicles, by contrast, were still quite rare; the total number of imported cars registered between January and May 1967 was just 1,587.[1]

As with bicycles, the late 1960s saw a shift for those who could afford it from French makes to the larger and more imposing American vehicles. A photograph of a university parking lot in Saigon in 1972, however, suggests that the upper middle class of academic staff were still bound either by price or cultural prejudice to European compacts.

The dominant sound of the street in late 1960s Saigon and other towns and cities was that of the Honda. The rise of Japanese motorcycle production at this time meant that established names across the world, whether American, British, or Italian, were being replaced by Honda, Yamaha, and Suzuki. In South Vietnam, the 50 c.c. Honda was so popular that the brand name actually came to mean *motorcycle*. Men and women from their late teens into middle age used the Honda to accelerate through the city in daytime, go to the movies or coffee shops in the evening, or, from Saigon, make day trips to the popular nearby beach resort of Vung Tau. For women, there was the Honda *dâme*, smaller, more brightly colored, usually with a shopping basket on the front wheel and mudguards to protect clothing from mud or dust. Small engines were also attached to some of the cyclo, but an innovation from the 1960s was the Honda *ôm*; in Vietnamese, *ôm* is a hug or embrace, and for the more intrepid passenger, this new form of taxi involved riding pillion and holding tightly to the rider.

Workers commuting from the suburbs might use their own Honda; for those employed at a government office or large business, there would be attendants who would look after the vehicle during the day. For others the risk of motorcycle theft was also just a part of life in the cities. Owners of cars were actually better off; there were so few cars around the streets that any thief would instantly attract attention. The suburban train system was heavily used; tickets were cheap, and there were plenty of small stations around Saigon. The main market was just outside the central railway station, so the trains were particularly useful for market traders. According to the memories of Saigon residents, the central station was never attacked by the Vietcong, despite its importance to city life and the ease with which anyone could enter its doors.

The wider railway system, however, was less well used precisely because it was regularly bombed. The lines between the major cities were soft targets; according to a young visitor to Hue in 1968, the train station there was defunct because so many lines had been disrupted.[2] Also, the very fact of a railway timetable of regular services made life easier for the insurgents. Mines were a constant threat, and there were often trains that were either hit by explosion or derailed because of damage to the track. By contrast, travel on buses and thus in smaller groups at least gave the passengers some hope of avoiding the Vietcong's attention or of being able to drive around the spots of greatest danger. There was also the bus driver's assistant, who, throughout the trip, was constantly on alert and on the move, leaning out of doors and scrambling over the roof, in order to get the vehicle to its destination.

The one noise or sensation that was not common in the streets of 1960s Saigon, or in those of other smaller towns, was that of fear. This remained the case until 1975. To that point, so many people had lived with war for so long that they actually knew no other routine. As in other countries at war over a long time, people accepted the possibility of an explosion or an act of violence, and once it occurred, they overcame the shock quickly and moved on with their lives. Moreover, with the exception of the 1968 offensive at the lunar New Year or Tet, when the Vietcong launched an all-out assault on urban centers along the length of South Vietnam, actual face-to-face combat was confined to the countryside rather than the town. Indeed, for many urban residents, Tet 1968 was the first time they had ever seen a Vietcong fighter. One caveat to this is that in some small towns, government forces would occasionally display the corpse of a Vietcong in the marketplace as a warning to others.

At a more general level, there were parts of Saigon and, no doubt, other cities that civilians either avoided or moved swiftly through, especially at night. In Saigon the danger spots were around two of the city's bridges, Cau Muoi (Salt Bridge) and Cau Chu Y (Y Bridge). In these areas, or at the Bay Hien intersection, the danger at night might be from criminals throwing stones to knock motorcyclists to the ground, where they could more easily rob them. Another type of theft that was evident in the late 1960s and seemed only to increase after the fall of South Vietnam was of riders speeding past another motorcyclist and grabbing bags or jewelry, such as watches and bracelets. It was not uncommon for such mobile thieves to work in pairs. Their preferred targets were young women riding Honda *dâme* or older women walking along the street. Away from snatch-and-grab robbery, young men were more likely to be the victims of con artists; these worked the market squares, often using card tricks to get men to gamble on what seemed easy odds, only to find themselves quickly separated from their money.

In stark contrast to the bustle of early morning, the nights in South Vietnam were a mix of inner-urban quiet and external fury. The curfew from around midnight to 5:00 or 5:30 A.M. meant that anyone in the street was immediately suspected of being a communist. In practice, those breaking the curfew just before daybreak tended to be farmers, living in the city for protection against the Vietcong, who felt compelled to set off early to tend their plots beyond the city limits. The few men legitimately walking about the town over night were adults or older teenagers serving in civil defense teams. A youth of 19 in 1970 remembered that in the provincial town of Tuy Hanh, this kind of service was expected of all young men. The routine at Tuy Hanh was for a man to patrol once a week, working in pairs and rotating on one-hour shifts. The men carried guns, although the regulations stated that they were normally to keep gun and bullets separate. As he further recalled, however, he and other youths would sometimes remove the percussion cap from a bullet and bang the empty case into a tree; this would fill the bullet with slivers of wood, and they would amuse themselves occasionally on what usually were very dull nighttime patrols by shooting these blanks at wandering dogs.

The one constant sound of the night was the unnatural symphony of battle in the forest beyond the city. Here there was the rattle of gunfire and the percussion of bombs. There might also be the wailing of the dead; one of the tricks of the U.S. forces was to broadcast recordings of ghostly voices from helicopters as a way to scare the Vietcong. While there was also combat during the day, the noise was at least partially blunted by the competing sounds of the city; at night, this protective blanket was withdrawn. However, it seems that ordinary people also managed to adjust to this reminder of the proximity of war and find ways to sleep in peace. Indeed, one former university student in Saigon in 1972 recalled that she always woke with a sense of enthusiasm and energy for the day ahead.

This kind of adaptability may also have been present in the villages. One man recalled his boyhood in a village just across the border into Kampuchea. There his father ran a timber mill, employing a large number of migrant Vietnamese workers. Following the start of U.S. bombing in Kampuchea from 1969, he and his family, of necessity, fell into a routine of hearing the approach of U.S. spotter aircraft, knowing from experience how many minutes they had before the bombers would arrive and the bombs would begin to strike, and also knowing how close was the nearest available bunker either at home or at school. Once in the bunker, they had some small store of food and perhaps a candle for light, useful also for scaring away the spiders, which terrified some of the children almost as much as the bombs. They could also guess, however, roughly how long the bombardment would continue, and so in this way, civilians learned how to deal (as far as one could) with the intrusion of war. In this example the one thing the boy's father could not do was to continue his business; the trees of the forest proved to be so full of metal shards from the bombs that they could no longer be cut and used commercially.

Until the mid-1970s, children could walk to school, catch the bus, or take a cyclo or *lambretta* (a tricycle with a buggy seating up to eight on two benches). Small schools dotted the urban landscape, so children were rarely faced with an extended trek from their homes. Within primary schools the class might be as small as 20 children, meaning that there could be close contact between the teacher and the taught. At higher schools the classes were generally larger, with perhaps 50 pupils. Teachers were both male and female; teaching was, and is, an occupation of great social status in Vietnam, as across the rest of Asia, and so both boys and girls included being a teacher in their lists of career ambitions. However, there is also a saying among Vietnamese about the natural and unnatural forces of human torment: "first is the devil, second are ghosts, third are students." One of the tricks among high school pupils in 1960s South Vietnam was to take revenge against an unpopular teacher by waiting until he was writing on the blackboard and then surreptitiously coating his chair with a sticky kind of itching powder. Among boys, this could lead to competition over who could be the most daring, but such tricks were also not unknown among girls.

Classes at primary school ran five and a half days of the week, but in Saigon, in the hottest months, this might be only for half the day at a time. Thus at some schools, one group of children would use the classroom from 8:00 A.M. to 12:00 P.M., and another would take over from 2:00 to 6:00 P.M. As one former education official explained, the guiding principle of South Vietnamese education, which was not changed by war, was "morals first, culture second." This was in line with the traditional Confucian belief that the civilized man is the one who recognizes first the difference between right and wrong, rights and duties, and that without this strong moral foundation, neither the individual nor the society can progress to a higher culture. Thus both at primary and high schools, there were several hours given over to lessons in morality. Where young people were given alternatives at higher schools and universities, girls were often drawn toward the arts and boys toward the sciences. Everyone, however, felt the need to excel at mathematics; this was arguably the most important achievement for all schoolchildren. Sports for girls centered on track-and-field events such as running, while skipping was popular at home. Boys, influenced by the French, were addicted to soccer, playing this endlessly outside of school and taking a keen interest in competitions between regional soccer teams in Vietnam. Basketball was also popular among boys, as was table tennis and, at home, a game called *da cau,* a kind of badminton played with feet rather than a racquet. Even though baseball had long been popular in Japan, it was virtually unknown in Vietnam until the end of the war.

There were various groups set up for children to reinforce their education in morality. These included the so-called Buddha's Children, which actually included youth up to their teenage years. Members were distinguished by a sober gray uniform, shorts and shirt for boys and blouse and skirt for girls, plus a cap and a blue neckerchief. There were also Vietnamese branches of the international Boy Scout and Girl Guide associations. These, as in other countries, taught such survival skills as how to tie knots and how to explore the countryside. One difference with some other countries, however, was that there seemed to be very little wildlife left around Saigon's immediate region (and the zoo had so few animals that it was a major disappointment to children). Thus it was difficult to get any sense of native bird or animal life. For urban children the wider sense of nature generally came through visits to relatives in the countryside, especially at the Tet holiday.

Popular culture for children in the 1960s to early 1970s was not so very different in kind or content to that for children in other capitalist societies. Major preoccupations included playing with friends, cycling around the town or village, or perhaps going fishing. One of the games popular with

boys with little or no money was to form a circle and throw their shoes at a
can to test their marksmanship. One consequence of the war and the mass
militarization of adult males, however, was that there were many more
weapons in society. Thus children whose fathers were officers in the army
might secretly be able to gain access to real guns and bullets. Another dangerous game learned from military relatives was how to make grenades
using hot coals. Away from the war, however, much of the fascination
and enjoyment of life seemed to come from weekly magazines, such as
Thang bom, and from comics. In South Vietnam the two streams of comic
entertainment were, as in other spheres of life, French and American. Thus
South Vietnamese boys, and some girls, still remember clearly when looking back from late middle age the adventures of Asterix and Tintin from
France as well as Spiderman, and even Dracula, from the United States.
When television began to appear more widely late in the 1960s, children
also enjoyed cartoons, including *Astro Boy* from Japan, and live-action versions of comics, most notably *Batman,* the quintessential program of that
time with its mix of style, energy, and self-mockery.

There were, of course, many who were denied the life of school and
games. Indeed, the single most direct impact of the war on children was
the increasing number of orphans. While orphanages provided a home
for some, it was still commonplace to see children living off the streets of
South Vietnam late in the 1960s. For these children, one way to survive
was to work as shoeshine boys; another was to sell lottery tickets. More
dangerous methods included selling drugs, such as marijuana cigarettes,
to American soldiers. There were also scams, such as scattering nails in
the road to puncture bicycle tires and then turning up just at the right
moment with a repair kit. Some very young teenagers, whether orphans
or with parents, joined street gangs: In Saigon, in September 1968, there
was a report of two gangs of 13- to 14-year-olds fighting for supremacy in
the Thu Doc market.[3] Boys who were orphaned or who cut school could
find money or action in the street. For girls the alternatives tended to be
hidden from sight. There might be jobs in bars (even in British-controlled
Hong Kong in the mid-1960s, the legal age at which girls could work in a
bar was apparently just 14). There also clearly was prostitution involving
minors.

The goal of schoolchildren (or at least of their parents) was to pass the
exams in order to enter a state-run high school. Here education was free.
Those who failed in the exam would have to join a private school, maybe
run by a Buddhist or Catholic association, and pay heavy tuition fees. In
order to guarantee success, those who could afford the additional expense
would send their children for extra tuition to a teacher's house in the evenings or on weekends. At high school, mathematics again was one of the
most important subjects, taking up to six hours of the weekly curriculum.
The state school pupils were identified by their uniforms, usually a white
shirt or blouse and dark-colored trousers or skirt. At high school, also,

the imperative was to study. There was little time for recreation, although the wealthier parents encouraged their children to learn music, often the piano or violin, studying either with a home tutor or at a music school. During the long, three-month vacation over the southern hemisphere summer, primary school boys might help relatives with farmland or animals, play soccer or go fishing, but those in high school were expected to continue studying so as to ensure a place at university.

The exam at the end of one's high school life that provided for entry to university was held only in the larger towns and lasted three days. These days, and the months leading up to them, were described by one former student as "the time of nightmares." Teenagers would taunt each other with reminders of how many days remained before this moment of truth. It was the single most important event for young South Vietnamese, largely determining the rest of their lives. The added pressure from the war was the fact that university students and graduates of universities were exempted from military service. Consequently, those young men of 17–18 who failed the exam were virtually guaranteed to be drafted into the army before too long. In contrast to contemporaries in the United States who might cross the border into Canada, there was no real safe haven for those who refused to fight; some of the more militant Buddhist groups were accused of harboring draft dodgers, but there were few real hiding places in a country already at war. Thus apart from the extreme of physically harming oneself, entering university was the surest method of defending oneself from the brutality of the army and the likelihood of dying young.

Student fees for the state universities were low enough that most teenagers could hope to get a place if they passed the exam. At university, however, the regime of constant study actually increased in pace. Student dormitories were constructed like army barracks, with row after row of bunk beds in vast, open rooms and with only a kind of footlocker for young people both to stow their possessions and use as a desk. Those who had relatives in the city naturally chose to live with them. In return, however, this increased the familial obligation on the student to excel. A student association library might be open for all the hours of the day (until curfew), and instead of borrowing books, students would use carbon paper to copy an entire text (students in Japan in the 1980s did the same thing using photocopiers). An additional challenge for young Vietnamese was that textbooks in different disciplines were often written in different languages (such as French and English, even Russian for some technical works, and perhaps German for medicine). This meant that foreign language learning was also a normal part of student life.

University education only became a mass phenomenon in many societies, including the United States, Britain, and Japan, after World War II. Thus, especially in the 1950s–1960s, universities were constructed at a rapid pace. In Saigon, one of the major new institutions was the

Female business students in traditional dress: Van Hanh University, Saigon, 1972. (Courtesy of Ms. P. H. Lam and Ms. H. Nguyen.)

Buddhist-run Van Hanh University, built in 1964; a regional example was Hoa Hao, a college majoring in business studies, established in the western city of Long Xuyen late in the 1960s. The architectural style of the new universities was generally a kind of international modern, a mix of smooth, undecorated white concrete walls, perhaps on pillars, with vast sheets of glass windows. At the time, this was considered fresh and, in its minimalist way, beautiful rather than, as it may be from the perspective of later years, cold and unwelcoming. Along with new or expanding universities, young men and women traveled overseas for training—aspiring Vietnamese professors went to France and the United States—and there were new and modern topics being taught, such as social sciences and communications. It was the general goal of governments to educate as many of their youth as possible, seeing this as a national investment for the future of each country's economic and social progress. As a result, it became commonplace for young people to attend university but, equally, to find themselves studying among a great number of other young men and women. In many classes in Saigon the lecture theater was so over-crowded at the start of the 1970s that a TV screen and PA system had to be set up to broadcast the lecture to others sitting just outside. True to the saying about devil, ghost, and student, some of these "outsiders" amused themselves by shouting taunts at the lecturer, trying to provoke a reaction from him while on camera.

Student and youth demonstrations were a recurring fact of life in the war years, especially in Saigon. Among the most militant were Buddhist groups. This was a continuation of the leading role played by Buddhist priests in opposing Ngo Dinh Diem, the first president of South Vietnam from 1955 until his assassination by his own generals in 1963. The con-tinuing politicization of Buddhist students was indirectly encouraged by Ngo's successors. After 1966, when the Vietnam Unified Buddhist Church split into two factions—the radical An Quang and the moderate Vietnam Quoc Tu—the regime of President Thieu openly began to favor the moder-ates. This only intensified existing rivalries.

One of the peaks of youth protest came in May 1970. There had been growing tension since March, when a student leader in Saigon had been arrested on suspicion of being a communist agent. Further arrests of students soon followed, and the threat was that they would be tried by a military, rather than a civilian, court. Also, at the end of April, it was announced that U.S. and South Vietnamese forces had taken the ground war into neighboring Kampuchea. In the midst of these developments the competing sects entered into a miniwar of their own. This began on Sunday, May 3, when 200 An Quang monks and their disciples invaded the main temple of the Vietnam Quoc Tu, about a mile from their own headquarters. Two days later, the moderates attacked before dawn to retake the premises. The battle involved at least 1,300 people, and of these, it was reported that about 10 were killed and 18 seriously injured. Even as this was happening, 200 students of the Buddhist Van Hanh University on May 4 (the same day that four antiwar protestors at Ohio State University were gunned down by National Guardsmen) were defying the official ban on demonstrations by blocking downtown traffic and staging a sit-in for peace on the steps of the National Assembly. The usual response of the police was to disperse protestors with tear gas; on this occasion, half of the students were also arrested. Students assumed that once arrested, the police would use torture to make them confess to being supporters of the Vietcong. Immediately in the wake of the May 1970 protests the govern-ment also closed all schools in Saigon and instructed the police to stop and search youths, particularly those on motorcycles.[4] In fact, one of the strongest memories among students from the 1970s was the nervousness arising from frequent police roadblocks to check identity documents.

The student and youth radicalism of South Vietnam in the 1960s and 1970s was not directly linked to international student movements starting in Paris in 1968 and quickly spreading as far as Tokyo. These movements were against general trends, such as the rigidity of education systems, the power of big business and entrenched bureaucracies, and the absurdity of governments and militaries in the Cold War stalemate of what was known as M.A.D., the mutual assurance of destruction in the event of a nuclear war. For students overseas the Vietnam conflict was just one element in a deeply unsatisfactory world. For students in South Vietnam, however, war was the only reality they had known, and committed unconditionally to the ideal of freedom (although this was true in a more general sense of many politically aware youths across the world in the late 1960s), they were intrinsically opposed to what they saw as communist totalitarianism. Consequently, while they opposed expansion of the war and government repression at home, they were not seeking to overthrow the political system or in any way assist the Vietcong.

At the level of personal behavior rather than political radicalism, South Vietnamese youth did take part in the international trend in the late 1960s toward the hippie lifestyle. This centered on withdrawal from life in the urban, capitalist, and materialistic world. Instead, the "flower power" ideal of the hippies was about enjoyment of nature, the freeing of emotions, the rejection of human aggression and institutional uniformity, and a celebration of the virtues of peace. All of this was neatly encapsulated in the popular slogan "make love, not war." In many ways, their philosophy was similar to the utopian anarchists of the nineteenth century. Thus, influenced by imported magazines and movies, there were some young men in South Vietnam who began to wear long hair as a sign of resistance to conservative norms of gender behavior. In his autobiography, Nguyen Qui Duc, a student in Hue in the early 1970s, recalls being arrested for hair just long enough to touch his collar; this was seen as a crime because it showed disrespect to the military (where all men were given crew cuts).[5] Some youths also took to wearing peace signs or beads in line with the fashion for things Indian and spiritual. According to a former teacher, students in high school and university especially adored the fashion for sunglasses decorated with flower stickers and were reluctant to remove these even in class.

The act of generational resistance by some young, urban Vietnamese women late in the 1960s was to begin wearing miniskirts. The extent of this resistance, however, is apparent if one bears in mind that holding hands in public or going to a swimming pool, among other things, were regarded as inappropriate behavior for young women earlier in the decade. Indeed, in some towns, the only place for a teenage boy to approach a girl was at a local bridge on a hot summer night as a crowd of people gathered to cool by the water (the routine was for a boy to follow a girl homeward and make comments about her or shout out what can only be called sassy invitations; if she returned to the bridge the following night, the boy knew he stood a chance of getting to know her better).

The great Chinese writer and essayist of the mid-twentieth century, Lin Yutang, once noted that the purpose of Chinese (but, by extension, Asian) dress was to conceal, while that of Western dress was to reveal. While this was obviously true of the miniskirt, there were other forms of Western dress that also appealed to Vietnamese women. One fashion for brides in Saigon on their wedding day in the early 1970s was to wear the Western veil along with the traditional *ao dai* (a close-fitting dress over trousers, which, for a bride, was preferably of red material as a symbol of good luck). In the more conservative city of Hue, by contrast, brides retained the *ao dai* and more usual, turban-like headdresses.

In the early 1970s, young men adopted the current Western fashion of enormous collars patterned on the stage suits of Elvis Presley, plus trousers with flared legs but skin-tight waists (as one former student recalled, these had to be so tight that one had no chance even of sliding a wallet into the pocket). The trousers of women also became increasingly flared, while the *ao dai* dress became slightly shorter. Thus, late in the war, both male and female Vietnamese youth in Saigon and other cities were altering the way they presented themselves and perceived each other.

When young people left university, the high achievers aimed to become government officials, engineers, or teachers. Perhaps inevitably in war, politics was heavily dominated by military figures, and for women especially, a political career was a rarity: In 1968, a 45-year-old widow named Tran Kim Thoa became only the third female elected to the 136-member South Vietnamese Lower House (she was the owner of a printing office and had several years of experience on the Saigon Chamber of Commerce; the other two members of parliament were a newspaperwoman and the widow of an army general).[6] The legal profession was less popular among youth; the saying among university students was that it was easy to get into a law course but virtually impossible to graduate because the work was so demanding.

For those willing to spend longer years in study, medicine was a popular choice. Women also increasingly began to hope for medical careers in the 1960s. One impact of the war was to increase the need for nurses. In addition, one of the fastest-growing sectors of business at the time was in Western-style pharmacies (French pharmaceutical companies were well established in Vietnam and dominated the market for prescription drugs). Cosmetic surgery for women, in South Vietnam as elsewhere in capitalist Asia, was also growing in popularity and often centered on changing the shape of the eyelid to give a rounder, more "Western" look. However, practitioners of medicine had a mixed reputation. In 1968, there was a proposal to employ about 1,000 doctors from South Korea; this was as part of South Korea's broader commitment, along with the dispatch of ground troops to Vietnam, to prevent communism making further gains in Asia.

The prospect of this foreign competition, however, intimidated those Vietnamese doctors known popularly, or unpopularly, as "guillotines." In other words, they were seen as rapacious, almost as if they were cutting the wallets from their patients by charging excessive fees. Indeed, it was normal among South Vietnamese civilians to avoid seeing a doctor unless one was seriously ill and, for all other ailments, to turn to the pharmacies or traditional cures.

For young men and women in the 1960s, the opportunities for leisure were still relatively limited. At university, first-year students might be taken in hand by their peers and taught one of the essential social skills: ballroom dancing. Actually, one student, arriving in Saigon from the provincial city of Long Xuyen in 1971, recalled being told that the reason he was expected to study the cha-cha-cha, the rumba, and even the tango was so that during his college years, he could avoid boredom and loneliness, which might lead him into drink or other social ills.

Teenagers and students usually congregated at shops selling soft drinks rather than at cafes (these were regarded as places for older, more mature patrons). Especially in the summer months, groups of friends would gather to drink *che,* a concoction of sweet-tasting red bean, coconut milk, and ice. These shops were often open until about 10:00 P.M., and some of them had background music. Ice cream parlors were also popular; to keep the ice cream from melting, it might be served in a glass or in a bread roll cut like a cone. The great favorite among ice cream was the "four seasons," mixing the flavors of chocolate, vanilla, pineapple, and strawberry.

For those in love, or simply lovers of music, the place to go was a tearoom (actually, it was normal for such establishments to use the French term *salon de thé*). This was a small club where one could drink beer or the increasingly popular Coca Cola, dance, again usually in the more formal ballroom style, and listen to a singer or a combo. Two of the most famous tearooms in Saigon were Au Baccara and Queen Bee.

Au Baccara had been opened after the Second World War for the pleasure of French servicemen, and so it could claim a sense of French authenticity. It was popular in the 1960s and early 1970s with young Vietnamese couples because it was located off the main streets and had an intimate, romantic ambience. Its advertising for the month of May 1970 reveals that patrons could listen to the popular group of young women singers known as the Cat's Trio, also a performance from the Pink Clouds, and a group with an obvious sense of self-mocking humor, the Nincompoop (its members were My Hang, Kim Phung, and Prosper Thang). The nightly show ran from 7:30 until 11:30 P.M.

The Queen Bee opened in the mid-1960s in a second floor venue in the heart of Saigon. It was the place to hear one of the great voices of South Vietnamese popular song in these years, Khanh Ly; she organized the bill, while a Franco-Vietnamese man, Jo Marcel, handled the business side. The Queen Bee advertised itself as the place to hear the "young sound," with "stirring vocals for swingers." This phrase, the *young sound*, was common in the late 1960s and early 1970s; it was a deliberate assertion of a new generation defined by its music. The house band at Queen Bee was called Shotguns. Major performers included Elvis Phuong, famous for the beauty of his voice, especially when singing in French, and for a passing facial resemblance to Elvis Presley. The Pink Clouds performed here as well as at Au Baccara.

One of the changes in Saigon's nightlife and leisure industry in the 1960s was the rise of foreign tastes and sounds. Whereas the French cultural influence remained profound in language, literature, film, and music, from the mid-1960s, there was a growing presence, at least in Saigon, of Japanese and Koreans. At the upper end of commerce and entertainment, these were mostly restaurants and cabaret performers. For example, in January 1970, it was announced that Miss G. G. Song, "direct from Korea,"

Pop music and modern graphics: Newspaper advertisement. (*The Saigon Post*, May 1970.)

was appearing at the Tour d'Ivoire cabaret (noted for its French-Chinese cuisine). The Japanese influence was both because the Japanese economy was booming and expanding across southeast Asia (Japanese-made TVs, radios, cameras, and, of course, motorcycles became commonplace in the 1960s) and also because many American troops serving in Vietnam were becoming familiar on their rest and recreation leave with things Japanese. The Korean influence resulted largely from the presence of South Korean troops in Vietnam. One of the taste changes identified with the arrival of these troops was what Vietnamese knew as "Korean noodles," the name given to the first instant noodles to be marketed locally. These were advertised on billboards across the country and were regarded as modern and convenient, but also, somewhat surprisingly, as a breakfast delicacy.

Radio was the place where most people received their news and their entertainment; the capital station, Radio Saigon, broadcast around the clock. Radio sets, often the large cabinet-style, European-made receivers such as Philips and Telefunken, were a prominent feature of the main room in homes. One of the popular broadcasts was of soccer matches. A former footballer named Huyen Vu was such a rousing commentator that people felt that just by listening to him, they could actually hear the ball being kicked. There were soccer teams for regions and also for occupations, such as the army, police, and, stronger than most, the customs inspectors. For those unable to get into Saigon's main city stadium, Cong Hoa (or climb one of the trees outside the stand so as to snatch a view), the radio commentary on the weekends was something to look forward to. Moreover, it appears that matches continued throughout the war years, and stadiums were never bombed, despite the crowds of perhaps 20,000 at the biggest games. This also gave people a sense of escape from the war.

One of the big stars of South Vietnamese radio and popular entertainment was Tran Van Trach, a larger-than-life character with his stocky frame, his shoulder-length hair, and his endless energy. He was an entertainer of many gifts. He wrote his own songs but was best known for his ability to imitate virtually any sound in nature and for his comic monologues, in which he would find humor in the simplest of acts, whether it was getting a train, listening to a dog bark, or watching one's house burn down while waiting for the fire truck to arrive. His humor revolved around the normal misadventures of ordinary people, but one reason for his popularity was that he always found a moral point to these comic observations.

Tran was also the voice of the radio program announcing the result of the weekly national lottery. Each Tuesday at 3:00 P.M., many of the South Vietnamese people would listen in to the broadcast of the state-run National Reconstruction Lottery, with its dual appeal of contributing to rebuilding the country and, for one person at least, the promise of becoming an instant millionaire (by 1973, the first prize was VN$5 million). That was, at least, if one had bought a legitimate ticket rather than one of the many forgeries and if one could convince the authorities to accept it as legitimate. The routine every week of buying tickets, waiting for Tran's lottery song *Xo So Kien Thiet Quoc Gia*, and listening to the result (usually followed by the inevitable disappointment) was an important part of life, regardless of the war. In the regional town of Tuy Hanh, ticket buyers would wait impatiently for the afternoon airplane carrying the newspapers from Saigon simply to get the fortune-teller's column giving advice on that week's lucky numbers.

As in many societies in the 1960s–1970s, recorded music came to play an increasing role in the daily lives of civilians with the increasing ownership of radios and record players. Young adults would choose their favorite cafes according to the décor and the comfort, but also according to the kind of music that was played. The range of styles available in the record shops went from Chinese-style opera, through traditional folk songs, to modern Vietnamese and Western pop. One of the most famous singers in the more traditional style was Thái Thanh, a woman in her twenties who sang songs of longing and loss. Late in the war, however, Trinh Cong Son became famous. With his acoustic guitar he sang his own compositions, often with a motif of sadness about the devastation of war. His song titles included "Cannon Fire Lulls the Night," "A Song Dedicated to All the Corpses," and "Ballad of a Woman Who Has Lost Her Mind." These were particularly moving when interpreted by the husky voice—distilled from too much alcohol and too many cigarettes—of Khanh Ly from the Queen Bee tearoom (where she advertised herself as "the soul of Trinh Cong Son"). Trinh was described by someone who certainly knew what she was talking about, Joan Baez (one of the great activist folk singers in 1960s America), as "the Vietnamese Bob Dylan." His concern for the victims of war, however, gave him a reputation as an antiwar protestor, and this made him a target of police repression and censorship. Yet he was clearly not a supporter of the North Vietnamese (he had been born in the central highland province of Dakluk and grew up in the former imperial capital, Hue) nor of any group advocating violence. He elected to stay in Vietnam even as the communists seized total control in 1975 and was to spend a decade imprisoned in communist reeducation camps.

Until the late 1960s, television sets were the exception in people's homes. They were mainly to be seen in government and military offices. Anyone in a residential neighborhood who had a TV would usually find a crowd of neighbors peering endlessly through the window in the evenings. The broadcast on the South Vietnamese channel in the early 1970s began at 6:00 P.M. and went through until about midnight. The typical schedule was for a children's show at 6:10 P.M., followed by news and government programs for much of the evening, and then later, depending on the day of the week, serial drama or variety entertainment involving such people as Tran Van Trach. One consequence of the war was that more civilians were able to buy a secondhand TV from U.S. or other forces returning home. Also, by the beginning of the 1970s, color TVs were starting to rival the earlier black and white sets.

Where the Vietnamese people most often got their images of America and the outside world was from TV shows and the movies. There were few films made in, or for, South Vietnam in these years, and any that did reach the screen, such as *We Want to Live* (circa 1960), a story of northerners fleeing repression, were usually overloaded with anticommunist propaganda. In 1973, there were 13 cinemas in Saigon, including the Rex. This dated from the mid-1960s and was typical of the last era of cinema as a "dream palace." It stood right in the city center, housed an audience of several hundred, who were guided to their seats by uniformed male and female usherettes, and, for the pleasure of children and adults alike, had sellers in the aisles of *Esquimo* (that is, Eskimo), one of the most popular of ice creams. One memory of those who visited the Rex is that as soon as the sign "Do Not Smoke" was lit, all the men would reach for a cigarette! Indicative of the global trend in the 1970s toward the much smaller, less impressive multiplex, however, there was also, by 1973, the Mini Rex A and Mini Rex B.

Young people in particular adopted the cinema as a place of respite from society; students would buy an all-day ticket and spend several hours at a time watching the same program being replayed. Most of the films were made in Chinese and carried subtitles in Vietnamese as well as English or French. Films from the West, including those of the archetypal cowboy hero John Wayne, were usually dubbed into French. The most popular genre among young men was Hong Kong martial arts; this was true also in popular novels, where the dominant works, first serialized in the newspapers and later sold in paperback, were the historical, kung fu adventure tales of Chinese author Louis Cha.[7]

The permissive society also made an appearance in the cinemas and novels of South Vietnam around 1970. This followed legal challenges early in the 1960s in Europe and the United States toward continuing censorship of cultural products dealing with adult topics, including use of language, depictions of violence, and discussions of sex. The most revolutionary changes, in what is now regarded as a golden age of liberalism, were in sexual frankness. Thus along with others in the world, some South Vietnamese writers began to comment more openly on sex and desire. In continental Europe the new legal freedoms also led to a spate of films that showed relatively explicit scenes of sex but that were justified, at least by the producers, on the grounds that they were intended to be educational. While such films were shown in the backstreets of Soho in London or Times Square in New York, in Saigon they were proudly exhibited at the Rex and other major cinemas. One example from 1970 is *Ingrid*, advertised as "a superproduction under the patronage of the health ministry of the republic federal of Germany. With the competition [*sic*] of famous specialist doctors. . . ." Its sole aim, it insisted, was to combat ignorance and assist young people to understand love. It is a long-standing view of liberal philosophy that permissiveness and tolerance demonstrate the strength of an open society; communist and conservative regimes tend to favor control and constriction. Clearly among the South Vietnamese government leaders at the height of the war, there was genuine support for some measure of liberalism. It is ironic to think that American soldiers may have been able to see legitimate films in Saigon denied them in some of the states back home.

As for films shown in Vietnam from America, these were often one or two decades old. In the 1960s, these included a flood of American cowboy pictures; Randolph Scott, the great star of the 1950s, was a favorite with some young viewers. Other films that made an impact at this time included *Gone with the Wind* and *Ben Hur.* The image of America, therefore, whether in southern drama, cowboy opera, or sandal epic, might have already been out of date long before the Vietnamese got to see it. This highly conservative, fantasy image of American life was reinforced by those U.S. programs for television (itself an overwhelmingly conservative medium) that were available on the U.S. forces' network. These tended to be middle-class sitcoms and romances. However, Vietnamese audiences did get an occasional chance to catch up on American culture. At the start of the 1970s, the ground-breaking Dennis Hopper film *Easy Rider* was shown in Saigon. Students who saw it at the time, however, were disappointed. Their expectation of American film was action, and so they sat throughout the showing waiting for the gunplay and chases to begin. They were ill-equipped to understand American ideas of space and freedom symbolized by the open road when their own senses of space and freedom were constrained by war to the city street.

For U.S. troops in Saigon, there was a cinema near the Au Baccara tearoom that was reserved solely for their use; no Vietnamese was allowed to enter. This, of course, made it an obvious target for the Vietcong, who managed to plant a bomb inside on at least one occasion. There was also an attempt to blow up Saigon's largest cinema, the Rex, in early 1970. At midnight one Sunday, at the end of the evening's showing, a woman's handbag was discovered containing a kilo of plastic explosives and a timer. This attempt on a place patronized almost entirely by Vietnamese, however, seems to have been a rarity.

In Saigon and around U.S. bases, it was naturally a daily occurrence to see Americans. These were almost entirely young soldiers, and if only because of the language gap, it was normal for Vietnamese other than bar girls or pimps and peddlers of drugs to avoid direct contact. In a provincial town near a major U.S. air base, the routine was that American and South Korean soldiers would arrive en masse between about 4:00 and 7:00 P.M. and take up residence in the restaurants and bars. There was also a regular U.S. Army truck that acted as a bureau de change, changing the greenbacks of the U.S. troops for so-called red dollars. Even after 1970, when the U.S. government under the so-called Nixon Doctrine began reducing its troops in Vietnam (cutting the number from about 500,000 to just 140,000 by the end of 1971), Saigon, at least, was still crowded with Americans.

Young Vietnamese men often envied Americans and what they saw as American culture (this was the same among Japanese youth, especially in the 1950s). They copied the American style in fashion and music, they tried to look cool by smoking American cigarettes (the local product was a rough mix of tobacco and paw paw leaves), they dreamed of driving an American car, and they admired the wealth and technology of the American military and society. The women employed on U.S. military bases who worked as cleaners or who ironed the shirts of American soldiers could earn wages in excess of Vietnamese officials. The Vietnamese black market was also largely dominated by goods seconded from U.S. military supplies.

Yet despite the increasing domination of South Vietnam's economy by American interests in the 1960s, the persistence of French cultural influence is remarkable. Thus even though French colonialism had been defeated in the war of 1950–1954, many Vietnamese intellectuals had grown up with a knowledge of the French language and a respect for French literature, music, and values (not least the ideas of liberty and brotherhood). Consequently, there were many middle-aged and older men who encouraged children and students to learn French. In Saigon, two of the elite high schools—Lycée Jean-Jacques Rousseau and Lycée Marie-Curie—were still administered directly by the French government, which provided most of the teaching staff. A popular saying about success and satisfaction for a man's ambitions at the time was "eat Chinese food, live in a French house, drive an American car, and marry a Japanese woman." There was also an ongoing audience for French cinema, perhaps especially with the New Wave of the 1950s–1960s, and for French music (at a more mundane level, the brand of beer most popular with young men was Bière 33, made in Saigon and exported overseas). What this suggests is that South Vietnamese elites during the 1960s–1970s did not reject French influence as cultural imperialism but actually valued it as an element of their own, indisputable, cosmopolitanism.

One of the changes in daily life soon after the Tet Offensive was the appearance in South Vietnam of the first supermarket. This was the Nguyen Du in Saigon. It was sponsored by a local businessman and the charismatic vice president, and former air vice marshal, Nguyen Cao Ky. The first press attaché for the supermarket was a journalist seconded from Radio Saigon, but as he recalled in 2006, the venture struggled initially because it had so little stock. Also, he was drafted for military service before he could really get to work on selling this new concept to the public. Despite these obstacles, the Nguyen Du remained in business until 1975 and slowly was joined by others. The principal memory of people of Saigon is that the supermarkets introduced the revolutionary idea of frozen food. This was a radical challenge to traditional practices: The morning routine of married women was dominated by daily visits to the market for fresh food. The switch to frozen food, however, was hampered by the fact that refrigerators were still a luxury item; one solution in some homes was to cut a small well in the garden, fill this with cold water, and submerge food in bags to maintain freshness.

It is easy to forget how new and even unsettling was this American style of shopping (see the 1960s British spy film *The Ipcress File* for reactions in England to the rise of the supermarket). The more familiar style across Asia was symbolized by the area of the Old Quarter in Hanoi known popularly as "the 36." There one found streets devoted to a single product, such as Bed Street, Shoe Street, Fan Street, and even a street dealing solely in votive papers for funerals. By contrast, the ideology of the supermarket and the mall was all about convenience, speed, concentration of goods and services, and the minimization of direct human contact.

Along with the supermarket, that other modern form of shopping—the mall—also made its debut in Saigon late in the 1960s. At the time the term that was used was *shopping plaza*. About three of these were constructed before the collapse of South Vietnam (it is said that there was only one concrete plant in the country, so civilian construction was generally restricted by the lack of supplies). One of these was called Eden. The plazas were usually of two stories but were filled with boutiques and facilities such as rest rooms.

With the exception of the Tet Offensive of 1968, the war did not aggressively impact on people's daily lives in the cities. There were moments when war-related violence erupted. Typically, however, this was the bombing or shooting of figures of authority in the South Vietnamese regime or, more disturbingly, the lobbing of mortar bombs into a city area; when this happened, no one, whether at home, the office, or at school, was guaranteed to be safe. However, ordinary people did not expect to die or be injured if they walked out of their houses, went shopping, or saw a movie. Instead, the primary impact of war for most civilians was economic.

Inflation for the middle and working classes in 1968 was already above 20 percent. Moreover, the rise of the black market, fuelled by American goods from the army camps, such as tinned foods and toiletries, brought about a new class of wealthy traders working outside of government control. At the same time, accelerating prices undermined the incomes of everyone in previously respected jobs, such as officials and teachers. For them, there was no access to the so-called American sector of trade and service industries for the U.S. military. With the pullback of U.S. forces from 1970 and the increased burden on South Vietnam of carrying the war, the pressure on taxes and wages only increased, while the black marketers continued, albeit on a reduced scale, their businesses; when the military police attempted to round them up, they simply folded their stalls, went into hiding, and returned a short time later. The rapid decline in status of the middle class was a major problem for the government in maintaining public support. The middle class was also the natural home of the student population. However, the law restricted any kind of employment for those who were granted draft exemption while studying. Consequently, it became increasingly difficult for students to remain in class while their parents were struggling. Thus students, at the start of the 1970s, increasingly began to drop out and look for work.

The situation in late 1973 to early 1974, only about a year before South Vietnam disappeared as an independent state, reveals a mix of hopes and fears. The hopes were that the 1973 Paris Peace Accords agreed to by the United States and North Vietnam would help to reduce, though clearly not to end, the violence. This might allow the south to rebuild. In September 1973, a new Faculty of City Planning was announced at Thu Duc Polytechnic University in Saigon; this was to be operational by 1975 and was to introduce the best of modern ideas to the national reconstruction of

Commercial optimism: Air Vietnam new services, 1973. (*The Saigon Post*, September 1973.)

the country. As part of this, Tan Son Nhut airport in Saigon was to be modernized. The national carrier, Air Vietnam, also was optimistic about the commercial future, announcing in mid-1974 that it had purchased three additional jets from the U.S. airline Pan Am and was expanding its services to Hong Kong and across southeast Asia. As a sign that it was entering a new era, it also introduced an in-flight magazine, *Ao Dai*, with all of the stories and photos of beauty, history, and culture necessary to attract domestic and foreign tourists. It even began incorporating some of the sites of war into its tourist schedule; as the advertising for its package tour to the old city of Hue in September 1973 stated, one could visit the imperial tombs, travel along the Perfume River, and also go to Quang Tri along the infamous "Highway of Horrors."[8]

The signs of a breakdown in society, however, came in at least two areas: youth and the economy. The increasing concern about youth was its alienation. This, in fact, was no different to other societies in which the hippie movement had given way to a sense of hopelessness and, from the mid-1970s, was to spawn the less utopian but equally anarchistic punk subculture. As with the United States or western Europe, this sense of alienation also led to an apparent increase in the use of drugs. Thus, late in 1973, there were civic campaigns in Vietnam to reduce drug addiction. A curious moment in this campaign came in September of that year. The Minister of Youth, Education and Cultural Affairs, Ngo Khac Tinh, gave a public address in which he blamed the war, drugs, and the hippie movement for undermining youth morality; according to *The Saigon Post* of September 17, 1973, however, the place at which he gave this address was the Hippie Club.

The government's response to the apparent crisis in youth morality was to propose a national sports movement. This was in line with calls from university heads in South Vietnam (although they added that more boarding houses and places to eat were essential as a way to improve the lives and hopes of students). This use of sport was not an original solution; it had been the received wisdom in the public schools of Britain and among groups such as the YMCA since the nineteenth century that a healthy body promoted a healthy mind (the idea of moral redemption through sport is also, of course, a staple of American popular cinema). However, Minister Ngo instructed high schools across South Vietnam to enhance the teaching and practice of sports for pupils. Interestingly, he added baseball to the usual list of approved and popular sports, such as soccer, volleyball, and table tennis. This undoubtedly was the cultural influence of America. Yet before the movement could take effect, South Vietnam was to be defeated.

At the same time the central government was increasing its crackdown on student protests. This led to more arrests and harassment of politically active students. The level to which the situation was deteriorating is suggested by the fact that the Catholic Students Association chose January

1975 as the time for its first antigovernment demonstration since 1971. Clearly a Catholic association had nothing to gain from supporting any communist ideology, and Catholic students naturally had kept away from the radical Buddhist movements of the early 1970s. By 1975, however, even they felt that they could no longer support a failed government.

Other young Vietnamese had long been signing up for language instruction at the French Cultural Center. In late 1973, it was said that hundreds of young people every day were enrolling for the fee-paying course. This was in response to the departure of U.S. forces and the declining support for Vietnam in Washington. It also implied that young people were looking to France as a possible escape route for the future.

The war was not the sole cause of economic distress in South Vietnam, and South Vietnamese were not alone in suffering spiraling inflation. In fact, it was said that U.S. inflation was at a record level around 1973–1974 due in large part to the oil shock and the massive increase in the cost of energy. Reading the newspapers from Saigon for 1973 to early 1975, however, one cannot escape the impression that South Vietnamese society was imploding even before the North Vietnamese tanks finally arrived. One of the major problems was the continuing dual economy of legal and black market goods, the latter costing the authorities millions of dollars in lost taxes. In May 1974, the government warned businesses in Saigon that they would be shut down if they did not rid themselves of all their smuggled goods.

The breaking point for civilian morale was probably in 1973. At that time, so little rice was delivered to the major cities that in Saigon, an army general was put in charge of organizing emergency supplies from the western provinces. Yet even the army was ineffective in dealing with the crisis; having promised to bring in 120,000 tons of rice between August and September 1973, the actual figure proved to be only 40,000 tons. At Nha Trang the wholesale price of standard rice, not the premium brand known as "Miss Fragrance," leaped by over 40 percent. Some people conceded that part of the blame lay with the disruption of war, although they also noted that hostilities had been low level for several months. They also accepted that the decline in U.S. aid and, with it, the reduction in imported U.S. rice was a factor. However, the dominant and widespread belief was that no matter how many denials they might issue, the culprits were government officials and the monopoly rice traders of Cholon, colluding to exploit the market by hoarding supplies in order to drive up the price.[9]

The knock-on effect of rising food prices was inflation in other areas of daily life. For example, the cost of a ream of paper in late 1973 increased by 50 percent so that it became more expensive to publish books or newspapers. Readership of newspapers was already falling as radio and television became more accessible. One of the advantages of television was the now standard practice of choosing the most attractive male and female duo as newsreaders. The fear of Vietnamese liberals, however, was that the printed media, the principal forum for discussion and the basis of the so-called public sphere of informed and politically engaged civilians, would collapse in the face of inflation and technological change.

By January 1975, the newspaper *Song Than* was insisting that this was to be a year of decision. It was not referring primarily to the war. Instead, its concern was the economy, which it described as in a state of "strangulation." It warned that the people were heading toward bankruptcy and that "the only way to salvage the national economy is peace and an economy which gives direct dealing with rich people. Otherwise it will be hopeless."[10] What it meant was the need for a free and open market, in which any South Vietnamese trader could deal with the wealthy nations of the world and increase his income. In a sign of the central government's loss of control over the economy, however, it was trying to avoid any repeat of the 1973 crisis by offering to guarantee credits only to qualified grain traders; this was intended to help farmers sell their crops and so boost food production. This was only four months before the fall of Saigon.

It may be that nations can rise and fall but individuals persevere. Amid the collapse of the economy, the rising government repression, and the approach of North Vietnamese forces, ordinary civilians attempted to maintain their routines. In January 1975, the cinemas of Saigon were showing the usual mix of Western and Chinese fare—John Wayne playing another cowboy in *Big Jake* (dubbed in French) and the Hong Kong action film *War Lord*—but also, a rare event, a Vietnamese film, *The Beauty and the Clown*. Among the private notices in *The Saigon Post*, one could still see the regular advertisement from Nguyen Trong, in which he described himself as "the best dancing instructor in VN," ready to teach "ballroom dance— international style . . . at studio or home." Despite the war, young men and women in Saigon in and around April 1975 also still chose to marry. The wedding day for one business graduate of Van Hanh University was in March 1975. She was dressed in a lucky red *ao dai*, a Western wedding veil, and was surrounded by her family and friends. The ceremony had the requisite three symbols of love and loyalty: a betel leaf, areca nut, and some lime.[11] The war impacted on the marriage day in three ways. First, the amount of food and the number of gifts was reduced by inflation. Second, the bride's bouquet was of inferior flowers because nothing better was available. Finally, there was anxiety over the quality of the candles; it was crucial to have two large candles, adorned with symbols of good luck, burning throughout the ceremony. If these were of poor quality, perhaps made with too much fat, they would flicker and die before the ceremony was concluded, and this would be the worst of omens.

Thirty years after the wedding, the same bride, who, as a student, had risen each morning with enthusiasm for the day ahead, was living among the Vietnamese diaspora in the West. In a reinterpretation of the symbols of success, she lived in a home certainly grand enough to rival a French house of 1960s Vietnam, she drove a Japanese car (but then so did many

March 1975: Saigon wedding one month before the fall of South Vietnam. (Courtesy of Ms. P. H. Lam.)

Americans), and she was perfectly happy with her Vietnamese (as opposed to Japanese) husband. The one thing that she and so many others had lost, of course, was her home in South Vietnam. However, it was possible to go back for visits, to see relatives and friends and collect possessions left behind years earlier. By contrast, the communist fighters in Vietnam had won the war in 1975 but now had to watch the economy and society increasingly compromise with capitalism. Moreover, during the years of insurgency and war, they had lived solely to one end and, in so doing, had denied themselves much that defined and gave value to human life. It was therefore a moot point as to whether anyone had really benefited from the war of Vietnamese against Vietnamese.

NOTES

1. Figures for car registrations in 1967 and 1968, *The Saigon Post*, 15 September 1968. These show that there was a significant increase for the equivalent months in 1968 to 2,613, although the absolute figure remained small.

2. Qui Duc Nguyen, *Where the Ashes Are: The Odyssey of a Vietnamese Family* (Reading, MA: Addison-Wesley, 1994), 2.

3. "Teenagers Go to War," report in *The Saigon Post*, 13 September 1968.

4. Buddhist conflict and student protests, *The Saigon Post*, 5–7 and 10 May 1970.

5. Nguyen 1994: 35.

6. Election of Mrs. Tran Kim Thoa, *The Saigon Post*, 10 September 1968.

7. A recent example of Cha's fiction is *The Deer and the Cauldron: A Martial Arts Novel* (New York: Oxford University Press, 1997).

8. Air Vietnam package tour to Hue, *The Saigon Post*, 22 September 1973.

9. Rice scarcity and inflation 1973, reports in *The Saigon Post*, 6, 10, 13, and 20 September 1973.

10. Song Than editorial quoted in *The Saigon Post*, 2 January 1975.

11. The popular legend is that a bride was married to the elder of two brothers. By mistake one day, she addressed the younger brother as "husband." To avoid shame and distress to the elder brother, the younger one left the village but fell ill and died by a river, where he turned into lime. The elder brother went in search of him, but coming to the same river, he sat on the lime, also died, and was turned into an areca tree. The young wife also went in search of them and came to the river. There she sat on the lime in the shade of the areca palm and died, turning into a betel vine, which wrapped itself lovingly around the areca tree.

SELECTED BIBLIOGRAPHY

This chapter is based almost entirely on extensive interviews with Vietnamese civilians, supplemented by articles from the Vietnamese newspaper *The Saigon Post*, published by Bui Phuong Thé from 1963. The references below are intended less as sources for the chapter and more as additions to fill in various gaps.

Karnow, Stanley. *Vietnam: A History.* New York: Viking Press, 1983.
    A comprehensive account of the Vietnam war from one of America's most respected Asia correspondents of the 1950s–1960s. See also the excellent WGBH series *Vietnam: A Television History* (1983), for which Karnow was chief consultant.

Logan, William S. *Hanoi: Biography of a City.* Sydney: University of New South Wales Press, 2000.
    The author is a scholar, advisor to UNESCO, and former member of an aid team to assist in the modernization of Hanoi. This is a wide-ranging social and cultural history of the city from precolonial times to the present, extensively illustrated with photographs and maps. Chapter 5, "Under American Bombs," explains life in Hanoi during the Vietnam war.

Nguyen, Qui Duc. *Where the Ashes Are: The Odyssey of a Vietnamese Family.* Reading, MA: Addison-Wesley, 1994.
    One of the few civilian memoirs in English of a Vietnamese youth from the late 1960s. Nguyen's father was a senior government official based at Da Nang. The first few chapters cover the author's youth from 1968 to 1975 and include a description of life in the city of Hue during and after the Tet Offensive.

"Trịnh Công Sơn." http://www.trinh-cong-son.com.
    Information generated by the Vietnamese community in the United States about one of the leading singer-songwriters of wartime South Vietnam.

Trullinger, James Walker. *Village at War: An Account of Revolution in Vietnam.* New York: Longman, 1980.

The author was a refugee relief worker in Da Nang at the height of the Vietnam War. In 1974–1975, he lived in and researched a village near the city of Hue. In this exceptional book he explains the disruption of war in the lives of diverse villagers, from farmers to warehousemen, rice merchants to village officials.

Young, Marilyn B., ed. *The Vietnam War: A History in Documents.* New York: Oxford University Press, 2002.

A useful collection of records on diverse subjects throughout the Vietnam War, carefully selected, carefully set out, and well illustrated.

Index

Aguinaldo, Emilio, Filipino national-
  ist leader, 37, 49, 51–53, 57
Airlines, South Vietnam, 240–41
Austerity campaigns, 70, 84, 121,
  130–31, 133–34
Automobiles, 60, 139, 196, 221–22

Bombing, of civilian targets, 98, 106,
  129, 139, 142, 147, 161, 198, 213–15,
  219, 224
Buddhism, 9, 18, 68, 81–82, 132; and
  militant Buddhist groups, 229

Charity, 72, 74, 205, 226
Chiang, Kai-shek, Chinese nationalist
  leader, 95, 102, 108, 117
Children, 43, 45, 58, 75–78, 136, 142,
  146–48, 150–51, 167–73, 176–77, 207,
  224–27; military role of, 45, 47, 77,
  148; murder of, 11, 14, 58
Christianity, 4–6, 9–10, 29–31, 36, 47,
  68, 167, 184, 202, 205, 212, 241–42
Cinema, 45, 79–80, 84, 118–20, 140,
  143–44, 181–82, 198, 215, 236–37, 243

Clothing, 41, 76, 104, 108, 112, 133,
  138, 149, 173, 178, 180, 185–86, 225,
  230–31
Commerce, wartime conditions of, 5,
  14, 45, 49, 52, 57, 69–70, 98, 102, 106,
  115, 149, 163, 185–86, 197, 205, 221,
  238–43
Consumerism, 34–35, 45, 69–70, 134,
  137, 147, 239
Corruption, in government, 2, 6, 87,
  101, 120, 194, 205, 242
Crime, 2, 14, 17, 87–88, 113–14, 178,
  197, 205, 222–23

Dancing, 35, 232, 243
Disease, 33, 36, 49, 50, 81, 102, 104,
  155–56, 165–66, 216

Education, 32–33, 43, 52, 59–60, 74–78,
  103–5, 145–47, 167–73, 198, 207,
  214–15, 224–27, 238
Elites, 4–5, 13, 18, 25, 31–32, 44, 66, 72,
  87–88, 98, 100, 103, 116, 135, 174,
  181, 196, 211

Emigration, overseas, 155
Ethnic minorities, 2–4, 8, 10, 24,
    175, 186

Food and food supplies, 5, 11, 14,
    19–22, 49–50, 54, 57, 68, 104, 136–
    39, 154, 163, 173–80, 185, 200–201,
    215, 238, 242
Forced labor, of Indonesians, 162,
    165–67, 179
Funerals, 10, 76, 81–82, 149

Guomindang, Chinese Nationalist
    party, 95, 100–101, 107, 113, 117–22

Hippie movement, 230, 241
Hong, Xiuquan, Taiping leader, 4, 11
Housing, temporary for refugees, 204,
    214
Humor, 85–87, 90, 98, 104, 139, 183, 234

Inflation, 101, 105, 110–11, 120, 174,
    180, 186, 239, 242

Katipunan, Filipino revolutionary
    society, 39–46, 49
Khanh, Ly, Vietnamese singer, 232,
    235
Kim, Il-sung, Korean leader, 191–92,
    197, 202
Kim, Song-ch'il, Korean diarist, 193,
    199
Korean Workers Party (KWP), 212

Lotteries, 234–35

Marriage, 8–9, 47, 231, 243–44
Massacres, 7, 11, 42, 49, 58–59,
    78, 209
Militia, 7, 18–19, 23–24, 44, 55, 100,
    209, 212–13
Millenarianism, 5–6, 36, 59
Music, 35, 48, 73, 75, 132, 142–43, 170,
    177, 182–83, 232–35
Muslim communities, 3, 24, 31, 35, 59,
    167, 170, 184

Neighborhood associations, 135–37,
    150

Newspapers, and journals, 37–38, 40,
    45, 55, 75, 78, 86–87, 116, 118, 138,
    140–41, 147, 182, 198, 226, 242

Patriotic associations, 39–46, 74, 134,
    148–49, 207, 213
Police, and policing, 35, 40–42, 68,
    83–84, 88, 113, 116, 120–21, 151–52,
    178, 209, 211, 239
Postal services, 198

Radio, 108, 118, 136, 140, 142–43, 168,
    170, 182, 193–94, 200, 234–35
Rationing, 137–39, 185
Refugees, 6, 12, 43–44, 48–49, 52, 54,
    56, 95, 101–2, 129, 147, 196,
    201–208, 216
Religion, 4, 9–10, 18, 37, 82, 132–33,
    184, 202. *See also* Buddhism;
    Christianity; *Shintō*
Rhee, Syngman, Korean leader, 191–
    94, 199, 204, 212
Rizal, José, Filipino nationalist, 37–39,
    46
Rural conditions, wartime decline of,
    18–24, 46, 50, 71–72, 135, 138, 142,
    147–48, 153–56, 165, 173–80, 186,
    208, 210–11, 215, 224

Sex, and sexual regulation, 6, 8, 74,
    82–83, 150–51, 165, 206, 236
Shintō, 81–82, 132–33
Smuggling, 14–17, 21, 106, 178, 186
Sports, and pastimes, 35, 47, 76–77,
    84, 98–101, 107–8, 141–43, 147, 170,
    225–26, 234, 241
Supermarkets, 238–39

Television, 226, 235, 237, 242
Theatre, 35, 45, 84, 98, 119–20, 144,
    180, 183, 215
Tran, Van Trach, Vietnamese enter-
    tainer, 234–35
Transport, 15–17, 33, 40, 69, 71, 96,
    186, 196, 198, 221–22
Triads, 3, 5, 16
Trinh, Cong Son, Vietnamese musi-
    cian, 235
Tourism, 241

Unemployment, 14, 70, 102, 112, 140, 163–65, 175, 205
Unions, 114–15
Universities, 32–33, 35, 52, 60, 95, 103, 113, 207, 214, 227–28, 240–41; and student lives, 35, 99, 104–5, 120–21, 148, 207, 224, 227–32, 236, 239–42

Wages, 69, 77, 112, 154, 156, 179, 239
War bonds, 71–72, 131–32
Water, wartime supply of, 204

Witchhunts, 201, 208–10
Women, abuse of, 7, 11, 18, 22, 44–45, 49, 55, 58, 112–14, 186, 223, 226; equality of, 6, 8–9, 33, 40, 72–74, 76, 78, 98–99, 109–15, 130, 134, 207, 222, 224, 229, 230, 231; labor in wartime, 35, 47, 69, 82–83, 105, 110–11, 134, 139, 144, 148–54, 156, 172, 175, 180, 206, 213, 221, 238; military role of, 8, 46; as widows, 206–207

Yasukuni shrine, Tokyo, 82, 133

About the Editor and Contributors

Andrei Lankov was a graduate student in Pyŏngyang in the 1980s and is presently associate professor, Kookmin University, Seoul. He has written extensively on North Korean politics, including *From Stalin to Kim Il Sung: The Formation of North Korea 1945–1960* (2002) and *Crisis in North Korea: The Failure of De-Stalinization* (2004).

Stewart Lone is professor of east Asian social history at University College, University of New South Wales, Australia. His major works include *Japan's First Modern War: Army and Society in the Conflict with China 1894–95* (1994) and *Army, Empire and Politics in Meiji Japan* (2000).

Simon Partner is associate professor of Japanese history, Duke University. He is the author of *Assembled in Japan: Electrical Goods and the Making of the Japanese Consumer* (1999) and *Toshie: A Story of Rural Life in Twentieth-Century Japan* (2004).

Bernardita Reyes Churchill is professor (retired), University of the Philippines, and president of the Philippine National Historical Society. Among the many books she has authored and edited are *Centennial Papers on the Katipunan and the Revolution* (1999) and *Resistance and Revolution: Philippine Archipelago in Arms* (2002).

Shigeru Satō is assistant professor, University of Newcastle, Australia. His many writings include *War, Nationalism and Peasants: Java under the Japanese Occupation 1942–1945* (1994), he has been a contributor to Lloyd E. Lee's

World War II in Asia and the Pacific and the War's Aftermath: A Handbook of Literature and Research (1998), and he is presently working on an encyclopedia of Indonesia in the Pacific War.

R. G. Tiedemann is a senior research fellow at the Centre for the Study of Christianity in China, Oxford, England.

Di Wang is associate professor, Department of History, Texas A&M University. In addition to many writings in Chinese, his major work in English is *Street Culture in Chengdu: Public Space, Urban Commoners, and Local Politics 1870–1930* (2003).

Recent Titles in the
Greenwood Press "Daily Lives of Civilians during Wartime" Series

Daily Lives of Civilians in Wartime Africa: From Slavery Days to the Rwandan Genocide
John Laband, editor

Daily Lives of Civilians in Wartime Early America: From the Colonial Era to the Civil War
David S. Heidler and Jeanne T. Heidler, editors

Daily Lives of Civilians in Wartime Modern America: From the Indian Wars to the Vietnam War
David S. Heidler and Jeanne T. Heidler, editors